Holy Brothers

Holy Brothers

Geography, Kinship, and Priesthood in Ancient Israel

Matthew R. Rasure

LEXINGTON BOOKS/FORTRESS ACADEMIC
Lanham • Boulder • New York • London

Published by Lexington Books/Fortress Academic
Lexington Books is an imprint of The Rowman & Littlefield Publishing Group, Inc.
4501 Forbes Boulevard, Suite 200, Lanham, Maryland 20706
www.rowman.com

86-90 Paul Street, London EC2A 4NE, United Kingdom

British Library Cataloguing in Publication Information Available

Library of Congress Cataloging-in-Publication Data Available

ISBN 9781978711280 (cloth : alk. paper) | ISBN 9781978711297 (ebook)

♾️™ The paper used in this publication meets the minimum requirements of American
National Standard for Information Sciences—Permanence of Paper for Printed Library
Materials, ANSI/NISO Z39.48-1992.

To Rachael and Bill,
priests who call(ed) on the name
Psalm 99:6

Contents

Acknowledgments

This project rests on the shoulders of the giant of biblical studies, Frank Moore Cross, now of blessed memory. Though he had ceased teaching well before my graduate work began, his enormous oeuvre has been a constant presence in my academic life—goading, challenging, vexing, and provoking my thoughts at every turn. I am deeply grateful for the guidance, kindness, and long-suffering patience of Jon Levenson, who taught me the joy of creative inquiry and how to think clearly and authentically about the questions I ask. I must also offer effusive thanks to Reed Carlson, whose careful and insightful comments have bettered my scholarly life, both as it is expressed here, and in every other facet. His broad-reaching wisdom and generous spirit constantly help me to nurture what is best and to jettison the worst.

This volume on priesthood exists because of two priests whose lives have made my own indescribably better. The Rev. Canon Dr. Bill Broughton brought me under his wing in our Jerusalem years together. At his table, I sat in the presence of giants in the fields of Biblical Studies, History, Archaeology, and Linguistics, and he made the introductions that opened the doors for me to enroll in a doctoral program. Beyond Jerusalem, Bill was my mentor, my cheerleader, and my truest friend. His death has left a hollow place in my heart that will forever be a hallowed precinct. The Rev. Rachael Pettengill-Rasure is my joy, my light, and my partner, without whose love, support, and patience this project would never have seen the light of day.

The editors and staff at Lexington/Fortress Academic have been enormously helpful in the production of this volume. The errors and inchoate ideas in what follows are many, but the whole is offered to you in the sincerest hope that a greater understanding of ancient Israel's holy brothers might be found as you work to set aright the mistakes I have made.

Introduction

Moses is arguably the central literary figure of the Hebrew Bible, shaping in some way or another every story unfolding in its pages. In his various roles as leader, lawgiver, and prophet *par excellence* his stories dominate four-fifths of the Pentateuch. He alone spoke to God face to face, and he alone received the *Torah*, which came to mark Israel and its heirs as the people of God. Astonishingly, the Hebrew Bible itself contains relatively few references to Moses outside of those passages describing his life and the events immediately after his death, the block from Exodus to Joshua.[1]

His unsurpassed literary importance notwithstanding, the character of Moses poses a vexing problem for the modern historian. There is no direct evidence pointing to the historicity of the character. There are no contemporary[2] references to him, and, indeed, all non-biblical attestations to him (beginning in the Hellenistic Period) are refractions of the biblical account. This figure so central to the Israelite story is barely a shadow to the historian.

The biblical account of Moses describes his legacy not only as a leader, lawgiver and prophet, but also as a priest. This tradition undergirds Psalm 99:6–7.

משה ואהרן בכהניו ושמואל בקראי שמו
קראים אל יהוה והוא יענם בעמוד ענן ידבר אליהם
שמרו עדתיו וחק נתן למו

Moses and Aaron are among his priests, and Samuel among those who call on his name.
They call to the LORD, and he answers them, in the pillar of cloud he speaks to them.
They observed his commandments and he gave them the statue(s).

Here Moses, Aaron, and Samuel are all grouped together here as ideal and archetypal priests, and as ideal and archetypal recipients of the divine instruction. The semantic difference between, on the one hand, Moses and Aaron who are "among his priests" (בכהניו) and, on the other hand, Samuel who is "among those who call on his name" (בקראי שמו) is leveled by the synonymous parallelism.[3] That is, both phrases describe the same functions

1

without any obvious differentiation or distinction between them. All three figures—Moses, Aaron, and Samuel—are the implied subject of "calling to the LORD" (קראים אל יהוה) and they are all three the recipients of Yahweh's responses (יענם and וידבר אליהם). They are all priests and they are all recipients of revelation.[4] Moses' role as a cultic functionary, both alongside and in distinction to his brother Aaron, connects him to the mythological and legal realms of Israelite literature, as well as to discussions of cult, temple, and state in the Israelite world.

While images of priests, prayer, sacrifice, and, eventually, the Temple play a significant role in all biblical periods, reconstructing the practices and organization of the institution is beset by a host of historical, chronological, and methodological problems. In the eighth chapter of his *magnum opus*, *Canaanite Myth and Hebrew Epic*, Frank Moore Cross offered an influential reconstruction of the development of the institution of the priesthood in ancient Israel.[5] In a chapter titled "The Priestly Houses of Early Israel," he presented a programmatic essay that laid the foundation for what I will hereafter call "the Mushite Hypothesis," tying the characters of Moses and Aaron to the cult. Following Wellhausen and others before him, Cross argued that a sub-tribe known in various Levitical genealogies as the Mushites (בני מושי) is connected to (descended from or coalesced around) the character of Moses, and that the priestly identity of the Mushites appropriated the priestly identity of Moses. This claim stands in tension with the plain sense of the biblical text, which presents the individual Mushi in a removed cousinly relationship with Moses, Aaron, and Miriam (Num 26:58–59). Cross argues the connection of the Mushites to Moses has been obfuscated by later priestly traditions, whose efforts gave rise to the final forms of the Levitical genealogies and, indeed, the biblical text.

In this "hypothesis," Cross posited that the institution of the priesthood in ancient Israel was bipartite from its earliest days. This priesthood was hereditary, and one group of priests traced its lineage to Aaron, whereas a second group understood Moses to be its forebear: the Aaronites and Mushites, respectively. Traces of this ancient division may be found in the stories of conflict between these eponymous ancestors in the Pentateuch and in other stories about events at various cultic sites. The potency of this "Mushite Hypothesis" is seen most clearly in the elegant solution it offers to another interpretive difficulty in the history of ancient Israel, the inauguration of a co-high-priesthood in Jerusalem at the time of the United Monarchy. Cross understood this bold move to be a shrewd political maneuver on the part of David, who enfranchised both of the ancient priestly families, the Mushites through Abiathar and the Aaronites through Zadok.[6] Further, the theological, ideological, and political orientations of these rival priestly groups shaped the history of unification and division in the Israelite and Judahite monarchies.

In the work that follows, I will explore the priestly roles of Moses and Aaron in the Hebrew Bible as an avenue of inquiry into the early history of divisions in the Israelite priesthood. The conversation will explore Cross's theory at the intersections of geography, kinship, and priestly roles, or put another way: holy lands, holy families, and holy priesthoods.

In chapters 1 and 2, I position this discussion in, on the one hand, the history of scholarly engagement with the institution of the *early* Israelite priesthood, on the other hand, the Mushite Hypothesis of Cross. Accordingly, in chapter 1, I review the most significant critical accounts of the history of the Israelite priesthood in the early first millennium, giving particular attention to recent work on the social and geographical functions of the priesthood. In chapter 2, I describe the background and history of ideas undergirding Cross's "Mushite Hypothesis," and survey its enduring legacy in modern biblical scholarship.

The central accomplishments of this project are in chapters 3 and 4. In chapter 3, I expand Cross's survey of narrative and topographical descriptions of significant cultic sites in ancient Israel, and I reconsider the character and affiliations of the clergy operative at these sites. The discussion identifies affinities between site lying within a geographical "center" in distinction to a geographical "periphery." This "center" extends from the rise of Mount Hebron in the south, continuing along the crest of the Judean mountain range, and ends at the emergence of the punctuated Ephraimite hills. Most significantly, this center encompasses Jerusalem. The "center" operates in distinction to a "periphery," which would seem to involve sites in the geographical North and perhaps even sites to the south of the "center." In chapter 4, I explore the web of genealogical relationships the Bible describes between various priestly groups, with particular emphasis on the fluidity of these relationships. This fluidity of genealogical affiliation enabled P to innovate one of the most striking and central features of biblical visions of the priesthood, namely the fraternity of Moses and Aaron. Finally, in chapter 5, I briefly describe the competing visions of Moses, Aaron, and their priesthoods in the Pentateuchal sources, giving careful attention to how the visions of Moses and Aaron in P differ in essential and strategic ways from J and E.

Any discussion of the Israelite priesthood is a fraught enterprise. One may not discuss any single feature of it without planting one's feet in at least two or three (or more!) hotly contested topics. As Robert Kugler notes, "every general treatment of [the priesthood] showcases the author's broader views on Israel's and early Judaism's history and literature."[7] That is certainly the case here. I will not in this brief introduction attempt to give an exhaustive account of the methodological commitments of this project, this will unfold in the chapters that follow. However, a few preliminary comments here are warranted.

Peter Altmann has offered a set of four useful categories for North American and European scholars to enter into more meaningful dialogue regarding the Israelite priesthood, and I will use part of his framework for positioning my own discussion.[8] Following a long North American tradition, this project is interested in the institution of the priesthood *prior* to the Exile, and, indeed, it is interested in the memory of the priesthood that gave rise to the descriptions of the Israelite Monarchy. That much of the data and narratives to be analyzed in this study arose or achieved final form in the Second Temple is almost certain. However, the particularly sectionalist and schismatic nature of the unification and division of the Israelite monarchy *as it is remembered*, as well as the role of the cult in this unification and division, all demand that I take seriously the possibility that *some* of the memories are rooted in imperialist concerns and events prior to the Second Temple period. Over the course of this discussion I will attribute political actions and agency to David, Solomon, and Jeroboam. All the while, I gladly concede that historical figures by these names might not actually have made such decisions—or might not have even existed. In the end, I remain convinced that an Israelite political empire did, indeed, exert itself within the Levant early in the first millennium BCE. In service of this feat, the exigences of empire, borders, and cult did fall to *some* manner of chieftain in the vicinity of Jerusalem in the tenth to eighth centuries. In addition, some manner of conflict over the empire, borders, and cult did occur, and the consequences of those actions shaped the stories eventually told, whatever the precise timeline might of have been. That is, I do not need "David" to have been necessarily a "David" extant in the tenth century B.C.E. and actually named "David" for the discussion to proceed. Second, this study attempts to fill in the paucity of evidence in the biblical text with comparative sociological analysis. The visionary work of Jeremy Hutton and Mark Leuchter on the ecological, topographical, and geographical positioning of priest-like groups was hugely formative for this project. Finally, this work seeks to synthesize information across disparate biblical sources and genres as the data relate to visions of priestly authority and to the characters of Moses and Aaron. As a preemptive warning: a reader fully committed to the Second Temple period as the absolute historical reference point for all concerns of the Pentateuchal text will find this study methodologically unsatisfying and historically thin. Further, any reader who rejects, *prima facie*, the possibility of interwoven yet narratologically continuous sources in the Pentateuch, and relying only on a punctiliar redactional-critical analysis will find much of what follows little more than textual alchemy.

At its core, this work seeks to map Cross's vision of a bifurcated priesthood onto the geographical reality of Israelite settlement in the Cis-Jordan in the period associated with monarchic expansion and contraction. I claim that the cult in some form played a significant role in political unification and division, and that this role is not divorced from the memory of a co-high priesthood in Jerusalem and the memory of conflict between Israel and the Jerusalem-to-Hebron corridor—the periphery and the center. My analysis of the Israelite priesthood through the lenses of geography, genealogy, and competing visions of priestly authority—holy lands, holy families, and holy priesthoods—identifies two spectra on which different biblical voices may be positioned with respect to the priesthood: an opposition between a geographical center and periphery, and an opposition between Aaron and Moses. What emerges from these oppositions is a rough shadow of two priesthoods active in contiguous but distinct regions. The priesthoods are not originally hereditary, but essentially *filial*. The interactions between these brotherhoods shape the memory of the history, politics, and cult of the United Monarchy, the Divided Monarchy, and beyond.

NOTES

1. There are 707 occurrences of the name Moses in Exodus–Joshua, and sixty-four in the rest of the Hebrew Bible. Oblique or pronominal references are more difficult to number.

2. Indeed, defining what constitutes "contemporary" is a difficult matter, as one cannot be certain to which precise period Moses belongs.

3. I offer a more detailed analysis of Psalm 99 in ch. 3.

4. Samuel's priestly pedigree is explicitly established 1 Chr 6:7–14 as being that of a Kohathite, and, within the logic of the Chronicler, is tied to the priestly pedigree of his father, Elkanah.

5. Frank Moore Cross, *Canaanite Myth and Hebrew Epic: Essays in the History of the Religion of Israel* (Cambridge, MA: Harvard University Press, 1973), 195–216. Hereafter, *CMHE.*

6. Ibid., 208.

7. Robert Kugler, "Priests and Levites," *NIBD* 4:596–613.

8. Peter Altmann, "What do the 'Levites in your Gates' Have to Do with the 'Levitical Priests'? An Attempt at European-North American Dialogue on the Levites in the Deuteronomic Law Corpus," in *Levites and Priests in Biblical History and Tradition* (ed. Mark A. Leuchter and Jeremy M. Hutton; Atlanta, GA: SBL, 2011).

Chapter 1

Chasing the Priesthood in the Early First Millennium

Much like the character of Moses, the history of the priesthood in ancient Israel is shrouded in mystery. Textual evidence indicates that religious or cultic life found two primary expressions with Israelite society: on the one hand, the individual household level, and, on the other, the communal, regional, or governmental levels. Reconstruction of practices is beset by a host of historical and chronological problems, but the following general observations may be offered from a synchronic perspective. The household level included the veneration of *teraphim* (תְּרָפִים), or idols.[1] That these were maintained in individual houses is seen in details of three narratives: the story of Rachel's stealing the idols of Laban's house (Gen 31:19–35) and hiding them in a camel saddle (בכר הגמל), Micah's installation/ordination (וימלא את יד) of one of his sons as priest to maintain the *teraphim* prior to enlisting the priestly duties of Jonathan (Judg 17:5), and Michal's use of an apparently life-sized *teraphim* as a decoy to hide David's stealthy departure from his house (1 Sam 19:11–16). At this level, the head of the household or some appropriately designated son carried out rituals. Beyond the realm of the individual household, communal sacrifice and veneration took place in shrines (בתי אלהים) and priests assumed these functions. The permeable border between the individual and regional levels is seen in the transition described in the household of Micah at Dan in Judg 17–18. There at Dan, what began as a house shrine served by a member of the family eventually grew into a regional shrine commanding the services of an appropriately trained priest.

MATERIAL EVIDENCE

The material evidence for the Israelite priesthood is very scarce. Remains of shrines or small temples have been excavated at Arad, Dan, and Motza yielding a wealth of archaeological evidence about temple construction and attendant activities, but these sites have yielded nothing about the cultic functionaries that served the sites.

Inscriptions

Two small, inscribed Hebrew seals identify their owners with the title *khn*. The first, CWSS 28,[2] which is unprovenanced and presently located in a private collection reads: *lḥnn b/n hlqyhw / hkhn, belonging to Hanan, son of Hilkiah, the priest.* The second, CWSS 29, was also uncovered outside of the parameters of an official excavation, but has been received into the collection of the Israel Museum, and is thought to have originated in Samaria. It is inscribed on two sides, and reads as follows: (side 1) *lṣdq / bn mkʾ* (side 2) *[lz]kryw / khn dʾr, belonging to Zadok son of Mika // Belonging to Zechariah, the priest of Dor.* Side two also bears a two-winged *uraeus* beneath the inscription. Nahman Avigad has suggested that such a doubly inscribed seal would have been a family heirloom. Because a patronymic is offered only on side 1, he argues that Zadok was the initial owner of the seal and was likely the father of Zechariah.[3] The paleography of this inscription places it in the middle of the eighth century. We might presume that side 1 predates side 2 by roughly a generation based on the content, though the paleography of both sides is indistinguishable. The Bible makes no reference to an Israelite temple at Dor. Further, to date, excavations have uncovered no such temple. Beyond providing confirmation of certain priestly names and raising the possibility of a priesthood associated with Dor, these inscriptions bring little to bear on the understanding of the Israelite priesthood.

Textile Evidence

Ze'ev Meshel has speculated that there is material evidence associated with the cultic garments of the Israelite priesthood. Analyzing over one hundred pieces of finely woven textile fragments discovered at Kuntillet Ajrud—the site of an Israelite outpost containing some textual connections with northern Israel[4]—he has proposed the following:

> We found some fabric made of mixed wool and linen. In one instance the red threads are wool and the blue linen. Garments made of a mixture of linen and wool are expressly forbidden in the Bible (Leviticus 19:19; Deuteronomy 22:11), but it may be that the prohibition was for ordinary people and not priests. The description of the garments of Aaron shows that they were especially splendid. The rich colors could probably be obtained only by dying woolen threads, thus indicating that part of the garments were of wool as they were at Ajrud.[5]

And that is it! Two seals and a maybe a few fancy threads are the full sum of the material evidence concerning the priests in ancient Israel.[6] To understand more fully the history of priesthood scholars must resort to the analysis of biblical text describing the priesthood, giving particular attention to points of discord in the presentations of priesthood from one author to the next and from one period to the next.

TEXTUAL EVIDENCE FOR AND HISTORIOGRAPHY ON THE EARLY ISRAELITE PRIESTHOOD

In what follows, I will survey the most significant attempts to make sense of the varying biblical voices concerning the priesthood, particularly as they provide context for understanding and analyzing Cross's Mushite Hypothesis in chapter 2. For reasons of appropriately contextualizing and interacting explicitly with Cross's theory, this brief survey engages only with those that attempt to describe the Israelite priesthood *within the early first millennium*, that is, prior to and including the First Temple Period. Each major modern reconstruction will be offered in chronological order, with the publication of Cross's theory in 1973 noted. After that, I will articulate those points of Cross's proposal that stand in tension with the most current understanding of the evolution of the Israelite priesthood operative in the early first millennium.[7]

Wellhausen

Julius Wellhausen offered the most influential early vision of the evolution of the Israelite priesthood in the biblical period. He divided this development into three distinct stages, which coincide with the primary divisions he identifies in the political history of biblical Israel: a pre-Monarchy phase in which priesthood was non-hereditary, a monarchic phase with a hereditary priesthood centered in Jerusalem and associated with Levites, and a post-Exile phrase in which the descendants of Aaron gained ascendancy as priests and the previously enfranchised Levites were relegated to secondary functions in the Temple. I will describe each in turn, citing the relevant texts Wellhausen affiliated with each period of demarcation.

The Pre-Monarchical Period

Wellhausen sees within the earliest discernible texts of the Pentateuch—for him, the Yahwistic source—no mention of priests or a hereditary priesthood.[8] In the J account of Moses' descent from Sinai, after writing down the instructions, Moses builds twelve altars, one for each tribe (Exod 24:3–4). He then orders sacrifices to be made: "[Moses] sent the young men of the Israelites, and they offered burnt offerings and sacrificed well-being offerings of oxen to Yahweh" וישלח את נערי בני ישראל ויעלו עלת ויזבחו זבחים שלמים ליהוה פרים (v. 5). J finds no issue with mere youths (נערים) offering sacrifices on this auspicious occasion. Wellhausen argues further that the Levites are afforded no special priestly designation within the early period. Aaron emerges as a leader—indeed, a more eloquent leader than Moses—in Exod 4:14, where he is designated "the levite/Levite" (הלוי) but, Wellhausen argues, not as a priest. Aaron also claims leadership in opposition to Moses in Exod 32, this time as a cultic foil to Moses. Likewise, Moses and, by proximity, Joshua establish themselves as the sole cultic functionaries who can stand in the presence of Yahweh in the tent (33:7–11). In none of these cases is the priestly function tied to Levitic heritage. Wellhausen further notes that the Blessing of Jacob in Genesis 49 betrays no understanding of a priestly function for Levi.

> It is quite impossible to regard this Levi of the Book of Genesis as a mere shadow of the caste which towards the end of the monarchy arose out of the separate priestly families of Judah. The utterance given in Genesis xlix. 5–7 puts the brothers on an exact equality, and assigns to them an extremely secular and blood-thirsty character. There is not the faintest idea of Levi's sacred calling or of his dispersion as being conditioned thereby; the dispersion is a curse and no blessing, an annihilation and no establishment of his special character.[9]

It is only in the subsequent period that priestly associations of the Levites begin to take hold.

The Monarchy and Deuteronomy

Deuteronomy offers the first evidence for the formation of a hereditary class of priests. Priests are endowed by the legal code with a prominent position in Israelite society alongside the other functionaries of Prophets and Judges (Deut 16:18–18:22). It is only in Deuteronomy that Wellhausen sees the standardized equivalence of priests with the term Levites.[10] For Wellhausen the text of the core of Deuteronomy is fixed in the period of Josiah.

The story of Jonathan son of Gershom son of Moses (Judg 17–18) adds another layer of complexity to Wellhausen's understanding of the priesthood at the time of the monarchy. Judges 17:7 raises the essence of the problem: "Now there was a young man of Bethlehem in Judah, of the clan of Judah. He was a levite/Levite residing there." ויהי נער מבית לחם יהודה ממשפחת יהודה והוא לוי והוא גר שם. Jonathan bears the title "the levite/Levite" (הלוי, Judg 17:10ff), but he has Judahite ancestry, and hails from the traditional Judahite territory of Bethlehem. For Wellhausen, the Levite title here was not one of genealogy, but one of priestly function. This Jonathan in his role as Levite established himself as the ancestor of the Danite priesthood and in some way is also considered a descendant of Moses. Wellhausen notes that the other prominent northern priesthood, the Ephraimite priesthood of Eli, is also connected to Moses in 1 Sam 2:27. How then are we to understand a hereditary priesthood operative in the pre-Monarchic, non-hereditary period? It seems that the priesthood of Eli/Moses presents a special case. Wellhausen argues that while Deuteronomy evinces the clearest evidence for a hereditary priesthood arising at the time of Josiah, the Deuteronomistic Historian explicitly antedates its hereditary notions of priesthood onto earlier periods in which it was not yet operative.[11]

The Post-Exile

The emergence of Levites as a distinctive group appears in the monarchical period texts of Deuteronomy and the Deuteronomistic History, but this evolution continues in the Priestly Code. D establishes a distinction between secular and sacred functions, or what in social terms amounts to distinctions between laity and clergy. P extends the thought of D into distinctions among the clergy. Wellhausen posited that "the High Priest is the keystone of the sacred building, which the legislation of the establishes middle Pentateuch establishes."[12] Thus the evolution that began in D, reaches is highest development in P. For Wellhausen, the Priestly Code is divorced from the exigencies and trappings of mundane secular and national life.[13] This insularity was possible, Wellhausen argues, because in the post-Exilic period the Jewish people did not enjoy enough autonomy to necessitate attention to practical matters of administration and governance. The foreign governors placed over Jerusalem and environs attended to these matters, freeing the commune (*Gemeinde*) to devote itself entirely to religious observance and matters of the cult. In this world, the Zadokite priests emerged as the empowered heads of the cult and the Levites as subordinate officials tasked with minor duties in the Temple. For Wellhausen, this social situation necessitates that P was written in the post-exilic period, and that the P stories of Aaronite ascendancy reflect post-exilic social concerns imposed on earlier times. Ezekiel 40–48, who for Wellhausen wrote before P, described the emergence and superiority of the Zadokites as a way of codifying the Josianic reforms in which the Jerusalemite Zadokites participated actively and in which the Levites who served in peripheral sanctuaries were left behind.[14]

Noth

In his comments on the history of the development of the Israelite priesthood, Martin Noth departs somewhat from Wellhausen's schema, though he does not run far afield. Noth admits the possibility that the institution of permanent or hereditary priesthood may have existed at the central shrine as early as the period in which he dates his (much-disputed) Tribal League. At Shiloh, the Elide priests served in the presence of the Ark, and when the Ark was brought into battle it was accompanied by the sons of Eli (1 Sam 4:4 and 11). Noth postulates cautiously: "the office of priesthood before the Ark appears to have been hereditary. But we do not even know whether the priesthood at the amphictyonic central shrine was appointed by the tribes as a whole or whether it was the old local priesthood of Shiloh which undertook the care of the Ark when the central shrine was transferred to Shiloh."[15]

Concerning the later periods, Noth does not shroud his language with such caution. He places the emergence of a centralized priesthood in the time of Josiah (i.e., the centralized priesthood described in Deuteronomy). As Wellhausen, so also Noth understands the beginning of Zadokite ascendancy to be an outgrowth of the Josianic reforms.[16] However, it was in the Persian period that the cult in Jerusalem branded all other manifestations of local cult as "illegal and heterodox."[17] In this context, the Zadokite high priesthood laid hold of their prominence, tying their legitimization not simply to their inclusion in the cult of the Davidic monarchy, but "further back to Moses' brother, Aaron, who was now assigned great prominence in the tradition."[18]

Möhlenbrink

Kurt Möhlenbrink's monumental 1934 article on the levitical traditions of the Old Testament is far different in scope and function from the presentations of the history of the Israelite priesthood discussed above in Wellhausen and Noth.[19] While the latter two attempt to cast a wide view of trends in priesthood synthesizing larges swaths of biblical material, Möhlenbrink presents a very modest—but painstaking—study of the biblical material concerning the Levites. He considers each within the parameters of the genre in which the material occurs. The genres he explores are *Listen* (lists), *Geschichten* (stories), *Satzungen* (legislation), and *poetische Stücken* (poetic fragments). The results of his study situate information about the Levites within particular periods of biblical history. In contrast to Wellhausen, who associates complete biblical corpora with specific time periods, he loosens the moorings somewhat and more freely explores the content of discrete textual units and affiliates them with moments in history. The result is a more dynamic arrangement of ideas in the history of the Israelite priesthood.

Bright

John Bright contended that from at least the time of (what he and others of his time called) the Tribal League the cult of the central shrine was led by a chief priesthood that was "apparently hereditary."[20] Bright expounds on the opening chapters of 1 Samuel as evidence of this position. In this early period, according to Bright, there was no requirement that all cultic personnel be Levites or all priests be descendants of Aaron. However, pedigree and lineage were not irrelevant categories. The pedigree of a priestly line brought a considerable amount of prestige. Defending this position Bright refers to the Danite priesthood and its connection to Moses.[21] On this point of "prestige," one may observe the powerful legacy of Cross's Mushite Hypothesis. In the early editions of *A History of Israel*, on this point Bright observes: "[T]here is evidence that a Levitic pedigree carried considerable prestige. The priests of Shiloh apparently claimed descent from Aaron (note the name 'Phinehas': 1 Sam 1:3; Josh 24:33), as those of Dan did from Moses (Judg 18:30)."[22] However, in the 4th edition, Bright cites Cross's *CMHE* ch. 8 and rearranges his affiliations of the priestly houses: "[T]here is evidence that a Levitic pedigree carried considerable prestige. The priests of Shiloh apparently claimed descent from Moses, as did those of Dan (Judg. 18:30), while the priests of Bethel probably claimed to be of the family of Aaron."[23] This subtle re-affiliation of the Shilonite priesthood from Aaron-descended to Moses-descended betrays the powerful influence of Cross's hand.

The potency of the priesthood was not simply in its cultic function; rather it perpetually played an important role in the political changes and conflicts in ancient Israelite society. In Bright's view, Samuel rose to power by providing direction to the Israelites against the Philistine occupation, and he did so by establishing himself as the defender of Yahwistic tradition and as the rightful heir to the "discredited priesthood of Shiloh."[24] Saul's leadership, too, depended on the support of the political and liturgical support of priesthood as seen in the assistance of the Ahijah in battle with the Philistines (1 Sam 14).[25] In the same way, Bright understands the downfall of Saul as a function of the deterioration of his relationship with the priesthood. Saul's indiscretions in usurping the function of the League priesthood (1 Sam 13:4–15) and violating the stipulations of *ḥerem* (1 Sam 15) ultimately led to his rejection by the priesthood and to the ascendancy of David.[26] David was not so careless.

> It was David's aim to make Jerusalem the religious as well as the political capital of the realm. Through the Ark he sought to link the newly created state to Israel's ancient order as its legitimate successor, and to advertise the state as the patron and protector of the sacral institutions of the past. David showed himself far wiser than Saul. Where Saul had neglected the Ark and driven its priesthood

from him, David established both Ark and priesthood in the official national shrine. It was a masterstroke.[27]

Jeroboam I continued this tradition of incorporating the considerable power of the priesthood into his political aspirations. By rejecting Jerusalem for its strongly pro-Davidic ideology, Jeroboam, a non-Davidic king, needed to enfranchise the ancient priestly centers of Bethel (associated with Aaron) and Dan (associated with Moses).[28] Bright's principal contribution is in his efforts to affiliate the machinations of the Israelite body politic with the concerns of its clergy class.

De Vaux

Roland de Vaux's account of the history of the Israelite priesthood in part 4, chs. 5–8 of his *magnum opus* has held great influence in the study of Israelite religion.[29] He maintains the basic progression of Wellhausen's tripartite model, and describes the distinct periods in the evolution of the office as follows: non-Levitical Priests, Levitical Priests, and Priests and Levites. In the early period of non-Levitical priests, the institution was hereditary for certain families. These families served at a particular sanctuary, but they were not bound to stay. They could move to other places and serve at different locales. That is, the priestly families "formed a group which was bound together not because it lived in one region, but because all its members performed the same functions; they formed a priestly tribe."[30] This migratory aspect of priesthood in the early period would become central to Cross's understanding of the Mushite priesthood and its affiliations across wide geographic domains. For de Vaux, it was not only physical boundaries that were permeable, but also tribal. He asserts that from early times in the period of the Judges, the Israelites "preferred" to have a Levite functioning as a priest, and the only Levitical line traceable to that period is that descended from Moses. However, it is not until the first half of the eighth century that we have clear evidence for the existence of a "priestly tribe of Levi" that "alone exercised the priesthood (Deut 33:8–11). Like the other tribes of Israel, this tribe must have incorporated into itself other stock, but these newcomers were received into an already existing line."[31]

G. E. Wright

In a rather short but influential article entitled "The Levites in Deuteronomy"[32] G. Ernest Wright presented his analysis of the distinction between frequently appearing designations in the book of Deuteronomy: the Levite Priests (הכהנים הלוים), the Levite (הלוי), and the Tribe of Levi (שבט לוי). Wright wrote in a context in which a leveling of these terms was the dominant view, that is, it was assumed that they referred to the selfsame group. This tendency in scholarship is seen most explicitly in the Revised Standard Version. However, Wright points out nine cases in which "the Levite Priests" (הכהנים הלוים) takes on particularly cultic nuances, which do not seem to be borne out by the other Levitical designations. He posits, then, that הכהנים הלוים refers specifically to "altar-priests," and that other designations refer to Levites functioning as "client-priests." The purview of these client priests was not sacrificial but that of religious teaching and exposition for the sake of the people. This function of the priests divorced from traditional cult—or reduced to a secondary role in the cult—is typically associated with P and later texts which observe a stricter division in the roles of the Levites *vis-à-vis* the Aaronites/Zadokites. Contrary to Wellhausen and others, Wright dates this division not to a late P, but to much earlier. "For P the term 'priest' is reserved for the altar clergy of the central sanctuary. For the period of the Tabernacle and for the time after the reform of Josiah in 621 B.C., the term 'the priests the Levites' as used by the Deuteronomists meant exactly the same thing."[33] Deuteronomy does not, however, completely disenfranchise the client priests; rather, it makes special social provision for their welfare in its legal code.

Wright closes his remarks in this small article with an invitation for a colleague to test his assertions about the divisions of the Levites operative in Deuteronomy. John Emerton took up this charge, and, dissenting with Wright, concluded that the client-priest versus altar-priest division did not stand up to scrutiny, and that the only disenfranchisement of any Levitic group in D took place as a result of efforts at cultic centralization.[34]

Rehm

Building largely on the methodology and results of Möhlenbrink, Merlin Rehm conducted a form-critical and text-critical analysis of genealogical and narrative materials pertaining to the Israelite priesthood. Rehm's research was published in its first form in his doctoral dissertation supervised by Cross.[35] The results of his research were condensed and published in the largely influential "Levites and Priests" article in the Anchor Bible Dictionary.[36] In both of these works, Rehm presented a synthesis of the results of his analysis and reconstructed a history of the Israelite priesthood divided into three periods: the Desert Period, the Tribal League (including Saul), and the Monarchical Period. Though Rehm's tripartite version of the history of priesthood resembles in certain aspects that of Wellhausen, the periodization (among other details) is markedly different. The central innovations of Rehm's presentation of the history of the priesthood will be detailed below. Underlying his analysis is his understanding of the flexibility of the term Levite, which he sees as both an ethnic designation and a technical designation of a person pledged to Yahweh. He holds that each of the clans within the Levites "constituted a blood relationship within themselves but not necessarily between them."[37]

The Desert Period

According to Rehm, Levites first emerge as priests in the Desert Period, and Moses is reckoned as among this group (Exod 2:1). There were three main Levitic groups in the Desert Period: the Gershonites, the Kohathites, and the Merarites. They took their names from ancestors in the distance past, but in the Desert "Moses was the chief of the Gershonites, Aaron and Korah of the Kohathites, and Ithamar of the Merarites."[38] Moses had connections with the Midianite priesthood through his marriage to Zipporah, and their sons Gershom and Eliezer/Eleazar (one person, in Rehm's accounting) were also priests. Eliezer/Eleazar took over the chief priesthood after Moses' death.[39] Aaron was also a Levite who engaged in priestly activities (Exod 18). The events of Exod 32 betray a conflict, which subordinated the entire Kohathite line of which Aaron and Korah were the heads. The Gersonites/Mushites and the Merarites/Ithamarites became the dominant priests, and though not annihilated, the Kohathites/Aaronites were isolated, according to Rehm, in Hebron.[40] The Kohathites—related to Korah—were also demoted and punished later (Num 16), though they persisted as a priestly group (Num 26:11). In Rehm's schematic, near the end of the Desert Period, Phinehas son of Eliezer/Eleazar, a Mushite, rose to prominence as a warrior (Num 31:1–12), and his vigor won him perpetual priesthood (Num 25:6–18).

The Tribal League

As Rehm sees the matter, when a central sanctuary emerged to house the Ark during the period of the Tribal League the Levites were tasked with its maintenance. At the sanctuary they expounded Mosaic law and offered sacrifices. Anyone could serve as a priest at peripheral local sanctuaries, but Levites were preferred. At the central sanctuary only Levites could offer sacrifices before the Ark. The "Levitical Priests" who served at the central sanctuary were descendants of Moses (Gershomites) and Ithamar (Merarites). The Aaronite (Kohathite) clan had fallen into obscurity, and there are no references to them in the Tribal League Period.[41]

The Monarchical Period

Rehm understands David's most significant cultic accomplishment to be "the re-establishment of a central sanctuary by bringing the ark of the covenant to

Jerusalem."[42] David surely had political motivations in this move, and Rehm expounds on these as follows:

> At all events we can be quite sure that David wanted to keep all elements of the population happy and that it was therefore his policy to invite as many represen- tatives from local shrines to serve at Jerusalem as possible. Hence, the Mushite/ Libnite Levites no longer had a monopoly on the service at the central sanctuary, as they did during the Tribal League, although they were still represented there by Abiathar.[43]

The other priest David brought to Jerusalem was Zadok, who was descended from the Aaronites/Kohathites who, as Rehm constructs the history, settled in Hebron after their ouster over the golden calf incident in Exod 32. After the Monarchy changed hands from David to Solomon, Zadok rose in prominence and the Aaronite Levites were preeminent in the Jerusalem cult. Henceforth, the term "Levites" referred to Mushites, who were not afforded the same prominence and privileges enjoyed by the Aaronites/Zadokites.[44]

Cross

The views of Cross on the history of the Israelite Priesthood have been sum- marized ever so briefly in the introduction and will be treated in greater detail in ch. 2. The central pillars of the Mushite Hypothesis as articulated by Cross in *CMHE* 1973 are as follows:

1. In the period of the Israelite League and at the time of the early mon- archy there were two competing factions in the priesthood of Israel: a house of Moses and a house of Aaron.
2. David appointed a representative of each house to serve as co-high-priests in the central sanctuary of Jerusalem: Abiathar from the house of Moses, and Zadok from the house of Aaron.
3. Though largely erased by the Aaronite (or Aaronite sympathetic) authors of later times, the Mushites of the Levitical genealogies are identical with the house of Moses.
4. Textual remnants of the struggle between Mushites and Aaronites remain in stories of conflict between Moses and Aaron and in stories of priestly rivalry.

I include reference here for the purpose of noting how his theory fits in this chronological analysis of re-constructions of the priesthood.

Halpern

In one of the first major treatments of issues pertaining to the Israelite priest-hood after the publication of *CMHE* ch. 8, Baruch Halpern published an analysis of the role of Levities in Jeroboam I's religious reforms.[45] Halpern understands the formation of the northern cult under Jeroboam to be a deci-sive event for the unfolding of Israelite history and theology that negotiates power dynamics between the monarch and the institution of the priesthood in multiple forms. The essay outlines what Halpern understands to be the primary compromises and reforms that Jeroboam enacted.

Along with establishing dual capitals at Shechem and Penuel, Jeroboam also established cult centers with bull statues in Dan and Bethel. These highly strategic geographic moves reveal Jeroboam's concerns and interests across the breadth of his new realm. Contrary to the polemical assessment of the Deuteronomistic Historian in 2 Kgs 12:31, Halpern argues Jeroboam did not violate all cultic sensibilities and install laity as priests; rather, he relied on the ancient priestly Aaronite and Mushite families for clergy. However, the indi-vidual priestly families did not act monolithically. Those of the same priestly family that served different sites did not necessarily find political allies in the same personages. This was the case for the Mushites at Shiloh. Though the Mushites originally helped to provide support for Jeroboam's break with Judah, Jeroboam ran afoul of the Shilonite Mushites with his choice to install calf iconography in the other Mushite sanctuaries of Dan and Bethel. Though Cross associates Bethel with Aaronite ties, Halpern asserts that these ties are not ancient, but rather the product of Solomon's aggression into Benjaminite territories through his seizure and allotment of Levitical cities in that territory to the Aaronite priests.[46]

The disenfranchised Shilonite Mushites harbored strong animus against Jeroboam I. Halpern asserts that it was this group that eventually produced the Deuteronomic and Deuteronomic-affiliated texts offering critique of Jeroboam and the bull iconography. Indeed, Halpern contends that Exod 32 "manifests an underlying association with Deuteronomic principles,"[47] and that even the "original story" of conflict over calf iconography is an out-growth of the Shilonite Mushite critique of Jeroboam I. The literary legacy of the Shilonite Mushites continues even in the prophet Jeremiah, who hails from Anathoth, the site to which Abiathar, the scion of the Elide-Mushite line in Shiloh, was exiled by Solomon.

Wilson

In his account[48] of the history of the institution of prophecy in ancient Israel, Robert R. Wilson understands the priesthood to have played an integral part in the formation of prophecy in its earliest days. The larger scope of this book is to provide a socio-historical account of the rise of Israelite prophecy and a clearer understanding of the social and religious principles that guided it. The earliest discernible stage Wilson uncovers in the development of prophecy is associated with Ephraim, and it arises from "the changing social status of the northern Levitical priesthood originally connected with Shiloh."[49] The northern priesthood, much like the prophets, maintained a generally antagonistic relationship with the monarchy. Saul nearly wiped out Ephraimite priests at Nob (1 Sam 22:11–19), when all died except Abiathar. David is the paradigmatic counter-example, who enfranchised the Ephraimite priests in the person of Abiathar alongside the established Zadokites.

In Wilson's reconstruction, the Shilonite/Ephraimite priesthood formed a "support group" for the Ephraimite prophets, particularly throughout most of the divided monarchy when the royal institution was deeply resistant to the Ephraimite perspective. The two notable royal exceptions to this would be the Judean reigns of Hezekiah and Josiah. That these two kings are those praised by Deuteronomistic tradition is no coincidence. While "pre-exilic Ephraimite prophecy played a peripheral role in Israelite society, the Ephraimite view of prophecy now dominates the biblical material"[50] and indeed the perspective of Deuteronomy and DtH is largely that of the Ephraimite prophets (and perhaps, by extension) the priests.

Stager

Lawrence E. Stager described the institution of the Israelite priesthood as a function of population expansion and growing inequality in a sedentary, patrimonial society. The priesthood helped to "absorb a surplus of young males . . . especially those who were not firstborns and, as the frontier was closing, stood little chance of inheriting much of the patrimony or of pioneering new land."[51] That is, Stager imagines the hereditary parameter for priestly function to be, at best, secondary. Young men dispossessed of a family inheritance entered into patron-client relationships with other family units. Even the Semitic root *lwy* (Gen 29:34) implies a relationship of "attachment" to the Levites. Stager, however, does not leave out the possibility of longstanding ethnic lines of priesthood. "It seems more likely that there never was a secular tribe of Levi, just as there was no flesh and blood founder of this line of Levites. Here again, the genealogical idiom is used to map out existing ideal or actual social networks and hierarchies. With such charts, the genealogical trees can be grafted or pruned as the situation requires."[52] The proliferation and flexibility of the Levitical priesthood was a necessity of population growth and provided a way of establishing new kinship connections drawn along lines of social necessity.

Olyan

In his discussion of the role of priestly affiliations and localities in the construction of the Davidic monarchy, Saul Olyan presents three corrections to the Mushite Hypothesis proposed by Cross.[53] First, Olyan rejects Cross's reconstruction[54] of the 2 Sam 8:17 which reads וצדוק בן אחיטוב ואביתר בן אחימלך, that is, giving patronymics to both Abiathar and Zadok (against the MT reading of וצדוק בן אחיטוב ואחימלך בן אביתר). Olyan holds that in the most ancient texts Zadok is without genealogical descriptors or identification. Another significant cultic official deprived of patronymics in the Bible is a third, seldom mentioned, priest installed by David in the Jerusalem cult, Ira the Yairite (*hy'ry*, 2 Sam 20:26; or perhaps *hytry*, 2 Sam 23:38 and 1Chr 11:40).

The second point at which Olyan critiques Cross is his understanding of the geographical origins of Zadok. Cross—following[55] Rehm—affiliated Zadok with Hebron, speculating about the important role Zadok as an Aaronite priest in Hebron would have played in the advancement of their fellow Judahite, David. Olyan, rather, affiliates Zadok with Kabzeel, a Judahite town in the Negeb in the extreme south.[56]

Finally, Olyan presents evidence affiliating Hebron with the Kenites, the group historically connected to Moses through his Midianite marriage.[57] Olyan summarizes the results of his study as follows: "Through Abiathar, the interests of northern Mushites were represented; southern Aaronid interests were personified in Zadok and finally, through, Ira, the interests of the Kenite priesthoods in Caleb and possibly north Judah were represented."[58] Thus Olyan broadened the scope of what David sought to accomplish in the enfranchisement of historical priesthoods into the Jerusalemite cult—incorporating three priestly families and enlisting patronage over a far wider geographical area.[59] Further, Olyan dealt with the personage of Ira, whom Cross's proposal neglected entirely. Granted, it seems that the Deuteronomistic Historian also found this Ira to be inconsequential in the larger scheme of the story of the Monarchy, as he garners little more than a passing reference.

Hutton

In a series of three articles,[60] Jeremy Hutton has presented a compelling case for a cross-cultural comparison between the Levites in ancient Israel and the Ahansal—a Moroccan tribe of holy men situated in the High Atlas Mountains who understand themselves to be in a direct line of descent from Muhammad. By "Levites" Hutton intends generally those engaged in the work of the cult, and not any of the other particular parsings of the term which see the Levites in distinction to other groups of cultic functionaries. Hutton's discussion is characterized throughout by methodological rigor and caution in two areas:

establishing appropriate controls for conducting cross-cultural analysis and nuancing discussion of the text of the Deuteronomistic History with sensitivity to its complicated (and, at times, intractable) redaction history.

The Ahansal group serves an important function mediating at key geographical points where the two primary inhabitant groups who occupy the High Atlas come into close contact. Of the groups, one consists of transhumant pastoralists, and the other consists of sedentarists. The meeting of these groups, as in many places, is fraught with complications and it is prone to conflict. The Ahansal mediate between the groups during the seasonal migrations of the transhumant pastoralists. Echoing the observations of Stager (above), Hutton details the processes of "fusion" and "fission" by which the sacerdotal charism (*baraka*, in the language of the Ahansal) may be used to bring in new members or to retire otiose ones.[61]

In "The Levitical Diaspora (I)," Hutton draws correlation between the arrangement of the Levitical Cities and the role of the Ahansal as arbiters of justice and peace in liminal areas. He argues that "the distribution of the Levitical cities at the extremities of Israel . . . might be correlated to the Levites' function as intertribal arbitrators distributing justice in the gates."[62] He further notes the need for a more in-depth exploration of the topographical and ecological constraints in areas in which the Levites were active.

In "All the King's Men," Hutton, provides a source critical analysis of three passages in the earliest textual strata of 2 Samuel describing David's interactions with priests. Theses are: 2 Sam 15:24–29, David's discussion with Abiathar and Zadok on his escape from Jerusalem; 2 Sam 17:15–21, Abiathar's and Zadok's report to David about Absalom's plot; and 2 Sam 19:12–15, Abiathar and Zadok assisting David to regain control after the revolt.[63] The common denominators in all of these stories at the earliest recoverable level of DtH show Abiathar and Zadok working in close concert with David for the benefit of his reign. Hutton is careful not to attach ideological motives to either Zadok or Abiathar, but rather to see their cooperation with David as the results of a calculation of the best interests for the co-priests of their respective houses. Hutton's methodology of caution with respect to the programmatic details in DtH, and his sensitivity to larger trends and perspectives buried with redactional details, provides a significant methodological corrective for future exploration into the history of the Israelite priesthood.

Leuchter

In his essay "The Fightin' Mushites" and in his monograph, *The Levites and the Boundaries of Israelite Identity*, Mark Leuchter gives the most recent iteration of the *Nachleben* of the Mushite Hypothesis, building intentionally on the work of Hutton, Halpern, and others.[64] In "The Fightin' Mushites" the principal problem addressed is how the Mushites were able to rise to a place of such prominence within a wide geographical area. It is conceivable that a group like the Aaronites would rise to power under the auspices of the monarchy; the rise of the Mushites is more difficult to explain. The texts portray the emergence of the Mushites in the twelfth century, and within the realties of twelfth century Tribal League, no political mechanism like the monarchy existed.

After reviewing evidence pertaining to an independent priestly house of Moses, Leuchter explores stories and textual connections that affiliate the sanctuaries at Bethel, Dan, and Bethlehem/Ephrata with the Mushite line. He asserts that it was Moses' association with warfare and violence that facilitated the Mushite ascendances in the loose tribal associations of the pre-Monarchical frontier. The compelling story of a victorious hero garnered interest and allegiance among the unaffiliated clans. Concerning the incorporation of other priestly clans in the Mushites, Leuchter notes: "Following the rise of a particular Mushite clan to dominance, other priest-saint clans would have sought legitimacy either by assimilating Mushites into their ranks or vice versa."[65] It was this that provided occasion for the great confusion around the Levitical genealogies, as each local group nuanced its own origin story. The original cultural currency of the Mushites as warriors also accounts for the abundant associations of the Levites (in general) and Moses specifically with violence acts.[66] Leuchter's most intriguing assertion about the consequences of Moses/Mushite violence is how he sees the implications of this violence playing out in the legal images of Deuteronomy. "The book of Deuteronomy repeatedly equates the observance of the law with the routing out of threat, evil, and impurity."[67] Deuteronomy has appropriated the violent *ethos* of the ancient Mushites and it establishes the observance of the Torah as the new battlefield on which the faithful *fight the good fight*.

In *The Levites and the Boundaries of Israelite Identity*, Leuchter builds on Hutton's observations about the Levitical parallels with the Ahansal.[68] He develops the idea of the "priest-saint" as a model for understanding the Mushite priesthood.[69] For Leuchter, a group like the Mushites would arise when priest-saints attach themselves to sites with some local memory of a priestly predecessor. In Leuchter's view, in the Israelite world the term Mushite applies to those who do not have a place in the Aaronite central cult. The studies of Hutton and Leuchter provide a significant step forward in the study of the Israelite priesthood by insisting that the priesthood always functions within a matrix of ecological, geographical, and political factors.

NOTES

1. In Biblical Hebrew, the term always appears in the plural, even when it would appear to describe a singular artefact.

2. Nahman Avigad and Benjamin Sass, *Corpus of West Semitic Stamp Seals* (Jerusalem: Israel Academy of Sciences and Humanities, 1997), 59n28.

3. Nahman Avigad, "The Priest of Dor," *IEJ* 25 (1975), 101–105.

4. Namely, reference to *ywhw šmrn* and the presence of contracted internal diphthongs.

5. Ze'ev Meshel, "Did Yahweh have a Consort?: The New Religious Inscriptions from the Sinai," *BAR* 5:2 (Mar/Apr, 1979): 24–34.

6. I have not discussed here the (in)famous ivory pomegranate scepter head bearing the inscription: *lbyt yhwh qdš khnm, belonging to the House of Yahweh, holy (to the?) priests.* This unprovenanced, though putatively Jerusalemite, inscription appeared first on the antiquities market, was originally verified by Lemaire and Avigad, and was purchased by the Israel Museum for over half a million dollars in 1988. Since then its authenticity has been the source of much continued debate with Lemaire defending its authenticity against the team of the Israel Antiquities Authority headed by Goren. See: André Lemaire, "Une inscription paleo-hebraique sur grenade en ivoire" *RB* 88 (1981): 236–239; Idem., "Probable Head of Priestly Scepter from Solomon's Temple Surfaces in Jerusalem," BAR 10:2 (Jan/Feb, 1984): 24–29; Idem., "A Re-examination of the Inscribed Pomegranate: A Rejoinder," *IEJ* 56 (2006): 167–177; Yuval Goren et al., "A Re-Examination of the Inscribed Ivory Pomegranate from the Israel Museum," *IEJ* 55 (2005): 3–34; Idem., "The Inscribed Pomegranate from the Israel Museum Examined Again," IEJ 57 (2007): 87–95; and F.W. Dobbs-Allsopp et al., *Hebrew Inscriptions, texts from the Biblical Period of the Monarchy with Concordance* (New Haven, CT: Yale University Press, 2005).

7. In the interest of establishing a clearer trajectory for the discussion of the Israel priesthood in this project the following review of opinions is precariously selective, engaging actively with those whose work attempts to discern the contours of the priesthood in pre-Exilic times. There are numerous rigorous studies of very fine quality that ought to be included in a comprehensive account of the *status quaestionis*. Among them are Nathan MacDonald, *Priestly Rule: Polemic and Biblical Interpretation in Ezekiel 44.* BZAW 476 (Berlin: de Greyter, 2015), James Watts, *Ritual and Rhetoric in Leviticus: From Sacrifice to Scripture* (New York: Cambridge University Press, 2007), and Antoinus Gunneweg, *Leviten und Priester Hauptlinien der Traditionsbildung und Geschichte des israelitisch-jüdischen Kultpersonals* (Göttingen, Germany: Vandenhoeck and Ruprecht, 1965). Reinhard Aichenbach, "Levi/Leviten," RGG 5:295–295. Ulrich Dahmen, *Leviten und Priester in Deuteronomium: Literarkritische und redaktiongeschichtliche Studium* BBB 110 (Bodenheim, Germany: Philo, 1996).

8. Wellhausen, *Prolegomena zur Geschichte Israels*, 145–146. "In der jehovistischen Gesetzgebung . . . is von Priestern nicht die Rede."

9. Wellhausen, *Prolegomena to the History of Israel*, 149.

10. Wellhausen, *Prolegomena zur Geschichte Israels*, 146. "heir nun tritt zuerst mit Regelmässigkeit der Name Leviten für die Priester auf."

11. Wellhausen, *Prolegomena to the History of Israel*, 143.

12. Wellhausen, *Prolegomena zur Geschichte Israels*, 153. "Der Schlussstein des heiligen Gebäudes, welches die Gesetzgebung des mittleren Pentateuchs aufrichtet, ist der Hohepriester."

13. Ibid., 156. "Vor der Anschauung des Priestercodex steht Israel in der That nicht als Volk, sondern als Gemeinde."

14. Wellhausen, *Prolegomena to the History of Israel*, 147.

15. Martin Noth, *The History of Israel* (trans. P.R. Ackroyd; 2nd ed London: Adam & Charles Black, 1960), 98.

16. Ibid., 339.

17. Ibid., 338.

18. Ibid., 339.

19. Kurt Möhlenbrink, "Die levitische Überlieferungen des Alten Testaments," *ZAW* 52 (1934): 184–231.

20. John Bright, *A History of Israel* (4th ed.; Louisville, KY: Westminster, 2000), 170.

21. Idem., 170.

22. John Bright, *A History of Israel* (Philadelphia: Westminster, 1959), 163.

23. Bright, *A History of Israel* (4th ed), 170.

24. Ibid., 187.

25. Ibid.,190.

26. Ibid.,192.

27. Ibid., 201.

28. Bright (1959), 233 and Bright (2000), 237.

29. Roland de Vaux, *Ancient Israel: Its Life and Institutions* (trans. John McHugh; London: Darton, Longman, and Todd, 1961), 345–404.

30. De Vaux, 360.

31. De Vaux, 362. De Vaux's observation here echoes the earlier assertion of Albright: "In practice we may safely suppose that the Levites were constantly being increased in number by the addition of children vowed by parents to Yahweh, but that the total number was kept down by the defection of the Levites scattered through the country, either through intermarriage or because of inability to make a living as sanctuary attendants" in William F. Albright, *Archaeology and the Religion of Israel* (3rd ed.; Baltimore: Johns Hopkins, 1956), 109.

32. George E. Wright, "The Levites in Deuteronomy," *VT* 4 (1954): 325–330.

33. Ibid., 330.

34. John A. Emerton, "Priests and Levites in Deuteronomy: An Examination of Dr. G. E. Wright's Theory," *VT* 12 (1962): 129–138.

35. Merlin D. Rehm, "Studies in the History of the Pre-Exilic Levites" (Th.D. diss., Harvard Divinity School, 1967).

36. Rehm, "Levites and Priests," *ABD* 4:297–310.

37. Rehm, "Studies," 259.

38. Ibid., 252.

39. Ibid., 253.

40. Ibid., 254n10.

41. Ibid., 284.

42. Ibid., 287.

43. Ibid., 288.

44. Ibid.

45. Baruch Halpern, "Levitic Participation," 31–42.

46. Ibid., 35.

47. Ibid., 41.

48. Robert R. Wilson, *Prophecy and Society in Ancient Israel* (Philadelphia: Fortress, 1980).

49. Ibid., 298.

50. Ibid., 299.

51. Lawrence E. Stager, "The Archaeology of the Family in Ancient Israel," *BASOR* 260 (1985): 1–35.

52. Ibid., 27.

53. Saul Olyan, "Zadok's Origins and the Tribal Politics of David," *JBL* 101:2 (1982): 177–193.

54. See ch. 2, "The Lineages of Abiathar and Zadok."

55. It is likely not correct here to assert that Cross is "following" Rehm on this topic; however, it is the case that Rehm published the idea in his dissertation—directed by Cross!—before Cross himself published the idea, hence "following."

56. Olyan, "Zadok's Origins," 185.

57. Ibid., 192.

58. Ibid., 193.

59. For a different account of the priestly houses vying for power in the Israelite monarchy see J. R. Spencer, "Priestly Families (or Factions) in Samuel and Kings" in *The Pitcher is Broken: Memorial Essays for Gösta W. Ahlström.* (ed. Steven W. Holloway and Lowell K. Handy; Sheffield, UK: Sheffield Academic Press, 1995), 387–400. Spencer argues that the tensions are held between the Aaronites, Levites, and Zadokites.

60. Jeremy M. Hutton, "The Levitical Diaspora (I)"; Idem., "All the King's Men," in *Seitenblicke: Literarische und historische Studien zu Nebenfiguren im zweiten Samuelbuch* (ed. Walter Dietrich; OBO 249; Fribourg, Switzerland: Academic Press and Vandenhoeck & Ruprecht, 2011), 121–145.; and Idem., "The Levitical Diaspora (II): Modern Perspectives on the Levitical Cities Lists (A Review of Opinions)," *Levites and Priests in Biblical History and Tradition* (Atlanta, GA: SBL, 2011), 78–81.

61. Hutton, "The Levitical Diaspora (I)," 227–228.

62. Ibid., 230.

63. Hutton, "King's Men," 136–139.

64. Mark Leuchter, "The Fightin' Mushites," *VT* 62 (2012): 479–500; and Idem., *The Levites and the Boundaries of Israelite Identity* (Oxford: Oxford University Press, 2017).

65. Leuchter, "Fightin,'" 498.

66. Leuchter explores and catalogues these incidents in "Fightin'" on pp. 489–494.

67. Ibid., 499.

68. I offer a more detailed survey of Leuchter's vision of the priesthood in chapter 3.

69. Leuchter, *The Levites*, 65–92, especially.

Chapter 2

The History of the Mushite Hypothesis

The core of Cross's seminal essay "The Priestly Houses of Early Israel," was presented in two lectures given in 1968 and 1969 at Brandeis University and Yale University respectively.[1] The basic premise of the Mushite Hypothesis is that the institution of the priesthood in ancient Israel consisted of factions from at least the period of what he termed "the Tribal League," if not earlier. This priesthood was hereditary; one group of priests traced its lineage to Aaron, and a second group understood Moses to be its forebear—the Aaronites and Mushites. This chapter will survey the development of the Mushite Hypothesis and will situate Cross's work in a larger context of thought about Moses' relationship to the priesthood. The Mushite Hypothesis builds on conceptual foundations laid by others, and then serves as a significant point of departure for subsequent discussions of the priesthood in ancient Israel. This survey will include the following five elements: a discussion of the biblical references to מושי, a review of scholarly understandings of the בני מושי informing the work of Cross, a summary of the details of Cross's hypothesis, a description of the critical issues in Cross's work that will guide the remainder of this study, and a brief synopsis of the legacy of Cross's hypothesis.

מושי AND THE MUSHITES

Before entertaining connections between the Mushites and Moses, it is first necessary to survey how the Mushites appear in the biblical texts and the web of connections in which they exist in the MT and ancient versions of the LXX.[2] The biblical references to מושי appear in the context of Levitical genealogies. The descendants of Levi are divided into three hereditary partitions: the Gershonites (גרשון), the Kohathites (קהת), and the Merarites (מררי)

according to birth order (Gen 46:11 and Exod 6:16). The youngest clan, the Merarites, is divided further into two partitions, Mahli (מחלי) and Mushi (מושי). As the genealogies proceed, Amram עמרם, the father of Moses and Aaron, is the son of the middle clan, the Kohathites (Exod 6:20 and Num 26:58–59).[3] Taken simply at face value, Mushi was born one generation prior to Moses and Aaron, and he was their first-cousin-once-removed.

The character of Mushi and his descendants are referred to by name ten times in the biblical texts, using the locutions: משפחת המושי (Num 3:33 and 26:58), בן מושי (1 Chr 6:32), בני מושי (1 Chr 23:23 and 24:30), and ומושי, which is part of the longer phrase ובני מררי מחלי ומושי, the descendants of Merari, Mahli, and Mushi (Exod 6:19, 1 Chr 6:4, 23:21, and 24:26) and מחלי ומושי אלה הם משפחת הלוי, Mahli and Mushi are of the clan of Levi (Num 3:20).

THE PRE-HISTORY OF THE MUSHITE HYPOTHESIS

By Cross's explicit admission, his development of the Mushite hypothesis builds largely on the work of Wellhausen concerning the history of the priest-hood as articulated in his seminal volume *Geschichte Israels*.[4] Prior to evalu-ating the nuances of how Cross refined and expanded the work of Wellhausen regarding the Mushites, I will first review the status of scholarly understand-ing of the Levite מושי clan up to the point Cross published his ideas in *CMHE* in 1973. To this end, I will review the work of Wellhausen as it pertains to the מושי clan. Then, I will discuss how the views of Wellhausen were developed in the work of Möhlenbrink and further expanded by Rehm in a dissertation he wrote for Cross in 1967. The ideas in that dissertation were instrumental in the final form of Cross's work. Finally, Talmon and Kaufmann also published references to the priestly character and functioning of Moses and his descen-dants prior to Cross's work in *CMHE*. While they interpret the material in a way contrary to Cross, their analysis of the basic data is nearly identical to Cross's own. In this chapter, the work of these scholars will only be described with respect to their views of the מושי clan and/or the connection of this clan with Moses' priestly status.

Wellhausen and Smend

A connection between the מושי clan mentioned in the Levitical genealogies and the character of Moses was first posited by Julius Wellhausen in the first edition of *Geschichte Israels*.[5] The identification is made as part of a larger discussion of Judg 18:30, the description of the priest Jonathan, who served at the altar at Dan. This text, as will become clear in the discussion of Cross's view below and in the discussions of chapter 3, is an important crux in discussions of traditions about Mosaic priesthood. The text describes a local priest at Dan as "Jonathan, son of Gershom, son of Manasseh" (יהונתן בן גרשם בן מ׳שה), where מ׳שה contains the sole occurrence of the superlineal-nun in the MT.[6] The tradition corrects it to read בן משה. Wellhausen draws a direct connection between the priestly roles of the Gershom and Moses mentioned in Judg 18:30 and the mention of גרשם and מוש׳ in consecutive (though reversed) generations of the Levitical gene-alogies. He writes: "In the genealogy of the Priestly Code one of the main branches of Levi, Gershom, is called the oldest son of Moses, and another important branch is called Mushi, the Mosaic."[7]

From there Wellhausen goes on to describe as "*[n]icht unmöglich*" the pos-sibility that the Israelite shrines at Dan and Shiloh, understood to be the oldest in operation, claimed their authority and prestige from their priestly affiliation with the descendants of Moses.[8] However, this suggestion that priesthood in the pre-monarchical period operated hereditarily poses a serious chronologi-cal issue for the understanding of the history and development of the Israelite priesthood that Wellhausen asserts elsewhere in the *Prolegomena* (which was discussed earlier in chapter 1). He ultimately understands this connection to be a product of the monarchic period antedated to the time of the Judges. Similarly, he argues that the connection between the Levites and the events in Moses' life at Massah and Meribah as described in Deut 33:8 establishes Moses as "founder of their rank" for all priests.[9]

Whatever the period of the emergence of the Moses-derived line of priests, it meets its end with the arrival of Zadok on the scene in the early monarchy. Wellhausen argues that the ascendant Zadok is a new priest, unconnected to established priestly lines.

> This Zadok, accordingly, belongs neither to Eli's house nor to that of Eli's father; his priesthood does not go back as far as to the time of the founding of the theocracy . . . rather has he obtained it by the infringement of what in a certain degree might be called a constitutional privilege, to which there were no other heirs besides Eli and his family. Obviously he does not figure as an intermediate link in the line of Aaron, but as the beginning of an entirely new genealogy; the Jerusalem priests, whose ancestor he is, are interlopers dating from the begin-ning of the monarchical period, in whom the old Mosaic *sacerdotium* is not continued, but is broken off.[10]

The immediate reception of Wellhausen's propositions about the connection between the מוש׳ clan and Moses and his larger theorizing about the Mosaic nature of priesthood is difficult to gauge. In Göttingen, where Wellhausen was teaching at the time, his former student and colleague after late in 1889, Smend, seems to have embraced the idea, eventually. The growing currency of Wellhausen's theory can be perceived in the significant revisions made between the first and second editions of Smend's *Lehrbuch der alttestamentlichen Religionsgeschichte*. In the first (1893) edition, Smend discusses the priestly nature that Moses takes on in various texts, usually emphasizing the duality of roles Moses occupies in these texts. For example, he notes that "Moses is priest and seer in one"[11] in his discussion of the Latter Prophets, and likewise he notes that "Moses is, of course, the people's leader and priest at the same time"[12] in his discussion of the beginnings of Israelite religion. However, Smend does not discuss Mosaic authority with respect to other priests or to any hereditary aspect of Moses' priesthood, a topic which he addresses multiple times with Aaron and Levi.[13] In the second edition of Smend's *Lehrbuch* (1899), which incidentally coincided with the fifth edition of Wellhausen's *Prolegomena*, he does include a significant endorsement of Wellhausen's position: "But in ancient times the priests were more likely to derive from Moses, who in the blessing of Moses (Deut. 33:8) appears to be the sole progenitor of the priests."[14] Further, Smend repeats Wellhausen's theory about the connection between Gershon/Gershom, the מושי clan, and Moses: "the other son of Moses, Gershom, also returns to the genealogy of the Tribe of Levi, who even has a Levitic family, Mushi (=Moses)."[15] This subtle change in Smend's perspective from the first to second editions of his work shows the growing currency of Wellhausen's compelling proposal with respect to Moses as a priestly ancestor, at least within his sphere of influence at Göttingen.[16]

Möhlenbrink

The next significant developments attempting to connect the מושי clan with Moses are found in Möhlenbrink's monumental by brief study of stages in the development of the Israelite priesthood, "*Die levitischen Überlieferungen des Alten Testaments.*"[17] This essay is a detailed form-critical analysis of texts pertaining to the Levites dividing the material into: lists, narratives, ordinances, and poetry. Möhlenbrink places the developments he identifies within the texts into a chronological framework, which then provides the basis for his description of the evolution of the institution of the priesthood in ancient Israel. The details of his proposal were discussed earlier in ch. 1, so for now, it suffices to note that he places references to Aaronite and Zadokite lines as secondary additions to more ancient Levitic material, and references to Moses as early. His arguments for a Moses affiliated priesthood arise from his discussion of two key texts: Num 26:58a and Deut 33:8–11.

Möhlenbrink argued that Num 26:58a contains a fragment of a most ancient Levitical list:

אלה משפחת לוי משפחת הלבני משפחת החברני משפחת המחלי משפחת המושי משפחת הקרחי.

These are the clans of Levi: the clan of the Libnites, the clan of the Hebronites, the clan of the Machlites, the clan of the Mushites, and the clan of the Korhites.

Here the Libnites, Hebronites, Mahlites, Mushites, and Korhites are described in parallel, as equal parts of a linear list. Elsewhere, in the Levitical lists these clans are presented as the second generation or second tier of Levites, and in the case of Korah, the third generation. Möhlenbrink argued that the parallel, rather than hierarchical, relationship implied in Num 26:58a is among the oldest Levitical materials attested, coming from the period of Noth's *"altisraelitischen Amphiktyonie"*[18] between the time of Deborah and David. On the inclusion of the מושי clan within this list of original Levitical divisions, Möhlenbrink observes "it remains to be seen whether Mushi is of the 'Mosaic' family," but he goes on further to opine "it is very likely."[19]

Like Wellhausen, above, Möhlenbrink saw within the reference to the Levites in the Blessing of Moses (Deut 33) material establishing Moses as the quintessential priestly ancestor. Indeed, it is through Moses' actions at Massah and Meribah that the Levites gain prestige and authority.[20] Likewise, Möhlenbrink affirms the centrality of the character and actions of Moses for the acceptance of the larger institution of the Levitical priesthood. "Possibly in Deut 33:8–11 we have, in a manner of speaking, the etiological legal foundation of the "Mosaic" branch of the Levites, because here the Levites are uniquely related to Moses—they are "his faithful."[21]

Rehm

The work most anticipating the core ideas of the Mushite Hypothesis as articulated by Cross in *CMHE* ch. 8 is the Th.D. dissertation of Merlin Rehm, supervised by Cross and submitted in 1967.[22] In this dissertation, titled "Studies in the History of the Pre-Exilic Levites," Rehm championed the form-critical analysis begun by Möhlenbrink. With extensive recourse to textual criticism, source criticism, and geographical location, Rehm presented snapshots of history of the Levites in three distinct eras: the Desert Period, the Tribal League, and the Monarchical Period, to use his terminology. A fuller description and critique of Rehm's views of the evolution of the Israelite priesthood were offered in ch. 1, so it suffices here to summarize his understanding of the following aspects of the theory: the role of the מושי clan, and the varied biblical views of the characters of Moses and Aaron.

The מוּשִׁי Clan according to Rehm

As discussed above, Möhlenbrink's understanding of the evolution of the
Israelite priesthood is predicated on his analysis of Num 26:58 as an early
Levitical list preserving a record of clan relationships between the Libnites,
Hebronites, Mahlites, Mushites, and Korhites, which is unadulterated by the
theological agendas of later periods. Rehm conducted a thorough text-critical
evaluation of the verse noting significant variances in the manuscript traditions in the tribes included as well as the order in which the tribes are listed.
In light of the omission of the Mahlites in the manuscript traditions not of the
"Hexaplaric and MSa" variety, he argues that the initial list of the Num 26:58
originally omitted the Mahlites.[23] It could be argued that the omission of the
Mahlites in certain of the manuscripts was a result of haplography occasioned
by *homoiarchton*, due to the proximity of the word Mushites. Rather, Rehm
posits that a scribe added Mahlites to this list because of the close association
of the Mahlites and Mushites elsewhere in the Levitical lists. This claim is
supported by the omission of Mahlites in the Hexaplaric texts, which in the
vast majority of cases reflect intentional correction to the MT. In light of this
text critical evaluation of Mahlites as a secondary insertion in Num 26:58,
Rehm analyzed the stories and genealogies of each of these remaining clans,
arguing that:

> [T]he four main groups of Levites during the Tribal League period were:
>
> Mushites, Hebronites, Korahites, and Libnites. This information is given in
> Numbers 26:58a. As we have contended, the Mushites were the descendants
> of Moses, the Hebronites of Aaron, the Korahites of Korah, and the Libnites
> of Ithamar. We believe that the Mushites and the Libnites were the dominate
> groups, and . . . were the priests in charge of the central sanctuary with its tent
> and ark.[24]

It is important to note that Rehm understands these four clans of Levitical
priesthood to be operative during the Tribal League period. This system
replaced an even more ancient tripartite system of Gershonite, Kohathite, and
Merarite priests who operated in the Desert Period.[25] In the later Monarchical
Period a second tripartite division of the priesthood into Libni-Shimei,
Amram-Izhar-Hebron-Uziel, and Mahli-Mushi clans emerged as an artificial
construction superimposed on the category of Levites. Greater detail about
the consequences of this history will be offered in chapter 2, but for now
it suffices to note that in Rehm's reconstructions the traditions recoverable
from the Tribal League period place the Mushites as peers to the Hebronites,
Korahites, and Libnites.

The Varied Biblical Views of Moses, Aaron, and the Levites

The second aspect of Rehm's work anticipating and contributing to Cross's articulation of the Mushite hypothesis is his evaluation of the vastly different portrayals of Moses and Aaron within biblical literature and his understanding of the relationship between these characters. Rehm's basic contention is that the term Levite is flexible and takes on different meanings in different periods of Israelite history. Moses and Aaron emerge at a moment of transition in the history of the Israelite priesthood, moving from the oldest recoverable traditions of Levites consisting of the tripartite Levites (Gershonite, Kohathite, and Merarite clans) and moving to the later quadripartite Levites (Mushites, Hebronites, Korahites, and Libnites) clans of the Tribal League.[26] The understandings of Moses and Aaron *vis-à-vis* the definition of the Levites at a particular moment in Israelite history are discernible in stories about the Levites and the interactions between Moses and Aaron. Rehm discussed the Moses-Aaron-Levite relationship as recounted in seven biblical corpora: JE, Deuteronomy, Deuteronomistic History, the pre-Exilic prophets, Ezekiel, P, and Chronicles. The most significant points of this analysis are found in his discussions of JE, Deuteronomy, and the Deuteronomistic History.

In Rehm's analysis of JE in Genesis, Exodus, and Numbers, he observes that Aaron emerges as an important leader, but his prestige is always associated with that of Moses. It is only in Exodus 32 that Aaron takes on a significant leadership role, one that is not necessarily priestly, and only in opposition to Moses. Further, in Exodus 32 the Levites make their only appearance in JE, and there they emerge as allies of Moses.[27] Moses is the more important of the two. Also, the established priestly names of Gershom (Exod 2:22 and 18:3) and Eliezer/Eleazar (18:4) are both understood to be sons of Moses, in contrast to the material in the Levitical genealogies (with the exception of 1 Chr 23:15).[28] Synthesizing these details with his analysis of the developmental stages of the Levitical genealogical lists, Rehm posits that in the earliest stages of development in the Desert Period Moses and Aaron emerged as chiefs of separate clans: "Moses was the chief of the Gershonites, Aaron and Korah of the Kohathites, and Ithamar of the Merarites."[29]

Where JE tied the whole of Aaron's prestige to that of Moses, Deuteronomy scrubs Aaron from the narrative almost completely. He is mentioned only in connection with the Golden Calf incident (9:16–21) and in the notice of his death (10:6[30] and 32:50). In contrast, Moses occupies the fore throughout Deuteronomy. Rehm, following the observations of Wright discussed in the last chapter,[31] identifies two locutions of identifying the Levites in Deuteronomy: the Levite (הלוי), who lives in individual towns, and the Levite Priests (הכהנים הלוים) who (will) serve at the central sanctuary. These two groups are given much attention throughout the book; however, Deuteronomy does not identify Moses as a Levite, nor does it mention any role of the Levites in the incident with the Golden Calf.[32]

In Joshua, echoing the division found in Deuteronomy, the Levite Priests (הכהנים הלוים) take on the central cultic function of carrying the Ark, while those designated Levite (הלוי), are allotted no land inheritance but are given special cities in which to live. Rehm understands the migration of Heber the Kenite in Judges 4 to the region around Kedesh (קדש) to have involved the establishment of a sanctuary (מקדש). This places a priestly functionary related to Moses via his father-in-law, Hobab, in the northern reaches of the Levant. Further, Judges 17–18 describe another northern site, the sanctuary at Dan, served by Jonathan, son of Gershom, son of Moses. Rehm postulates that "the whole northern priesthood was Mushite in the early period and at Dan at least until the Captivity of the North."[33] The priesthood of Eli at Shiloh was authorized by his connection to Moses as established in 1 Sam 2:27. Likewise, Abiathar at Anathoth, a descendant of Eli, was also part of the northern Mushites.[34] In contrast, Rehm postulates that Zadok was descended from Aaronites, who served at the sanctuary in Hebron.[35] In the monarchical period the ascendancy of the Mushites came into conflict with the Zadokites as summarized in the previous chapter.

Kaufmann and Talmon

In the three previous sections, I have discussed the primary influences on Cross's articulation of the Mushite hypothesis and the theoretical groundwork on which his theory is built. Before attending to the details to Cross's hypothesis, it is worth mentioning discussions of the character of Moses *vis-à-vis* the priesthood that were put forward prior to Cross's Mushite Hypothesis; namely, those of Talmon and Kaufmann.[36] Cross does not reference these discussions directly; however, they both anticipate certain aspects of his ideas about the role of the Mushites, and, in the case of Kaufmann, problematize his theory.

Kaufmann

In his magnum opus, *The History of Israel Religion from Antiquity to the End of the Second Temple Period*, Y. Kaufmann discussed the changing role of the Levites—and priests more generally—in the period prior to the rise of classical prophecy. He saw within the golden calf incident a monumental battle between factions of the Israelite priesthood with the emergence and vindication of the Levites over and against Aaronites. He assumes the antiquity of the Aaronite priestly line as having its origins in Egypt and justifies this by associating the condemned Elide priest with the Aaronite line. The

Elide priests, Hophni, Phinehas, and Hanamel, all have "Egyptian names" and find themselves in opposition to the adherents of pious Yahwism.[37] He concludes from this that the "Aaronides are the ancient, pagan priesthood of Israel. Presumably, they were swayed by the message of Moses, supported him, and influence the people to follow him."[38] The aftermath of the incident with the golden calf marks the moment of cohesion between the Levites and the "secular" Aaronic priests, bringing them together for sacred service, though with differing roles. Further, making sense of the Jonathan story of Judges 17–18, Kaufmann recognizes that one priestly line, namely at Dan, traces its history to Moses, but he is emphatic that this line is isolated and bears no connection to priestly functionaries elsewhere in ancient Israel. He explains "had [Moses] been considered the father of the priesthood as a whole, there is no accounting for the fact that later he was set aside in favor of the calf-maker Aaron."[39]

Talmon

In his article "Divergences in Calendar Reckoning in Ephraim and Judah,"[40] S. Talmon explores the oft discussed north/south division in Israel in the biblical period. As the title implies, he does this through the lens of the liturgical and social calendar at the time of the religious/political revolt of Jeroboam I. Judges 17 describes the Danite migration northward, which is not confined entirely to the settlement of Dan itself, but to Mount Ephraim (הר אפרים) and even beyond. Talmon argues that Mount Ephraim is "most probably identical with the town of Bethel,"[41] the only central hill country town captured by the Israelites at this point in the narrative of Judges. By extension, he postulates that the family of Jonathan exercised its priestly influence not just in the Dan but throughout Mount Ephraim including Bethel. Thus, when Jeroboam I installed priests and installed the calf-cult in Bethel and Dan, the priests he installed "were but remnants of the family of Moses who had already officiated previously at the central shrines in Ephraim."[42] Members of this class of priests related to Moses are alluded to in the Chronicler's lists of Levitical palace officials in 1 Chr 26:24 (*and Shebuel son of Gershom, son of Moses, was the official over the treasury,* ושבאל בן גרשום בן משה נגיד על האצרות) and perhaps in subsequent references to *Shebuel* in 1 Chr 24:20–22 and 1 Chr 25:20. Talmon argues on the whole that Jeroboam sought to substitute "specific Ephraimite values and traditions for pan-Israelite institutions innovated by David and by Solomon."[43]

As mentioned earlier, Cross does not refer to either of these discussions in ch. 8 of *CMHE*; however, the views expressed by Kaufmann and Talmon with respect to Moses and the Israelite priesthood in the north form integral parts of the hypothesis, which Cross extrapolated to different ends.

THE MUSHITE HYPOTHESIS OF CROSS

Cross's hypothesis weaves together source critical, text critical, genealogical, geographical, and political data into a proposal about two competing priestly houses derived from Moses and Aaron. In what follows, I will survey the details of Cross's proposal, and describe the ways in which it is dependent on the work of others surveyed above. Cross critiqued, expanded on, and departed from this work. I will attend to the following topics: Moses' priestly role, stories of priestly conflict, Levitical genealogies and the heritage of Abiathar and Zadok, and priesthood in the early Israelite monarchy.

The Argument for Moses as a Priest

At the core of the Mushite Hypothesis is the proposal that, in spite of the contexts in which they appear in MT, the enigmatic Mushites[44] traced their ancestry to Moses, and at various times, stood in opposition to a group descended from Aaron. Cross founded his arguments for the priestly legacy of Moses on the work of Wellhausen, best encapsulated in his passing gloss of בני מושי, as "Muschi, der Mosaische."[45] Following leads described above in the works of Wellhausen and to a lesser extent in Smend, Cross began his discussion of his hypothesis adumbrating reasons to support Wellhausen's suggestion of a robust Mushite priesthood operative beneath the veneer of the largely pro-Aaronite biblical texts. In 1 Sam 2:27, the authority of the Elide priesthood at Shiloh derived from an unnamed priestly ancestor active in the events of the Exodus, the clear referent of which is Moses.[46] Likewise, Moses and Joshua act as priests in Exod 33:7–11. Moses is the founder of a priestly order in Deut 31, and, of course, Moses' line continues in the priesthood of Jonathan at Dan in Judg 17–18. However, in Cross's estimation these points did not sufficiently exhaust the extent of all the evidence for an active Mushite priesthood. Cross expands his discussion to the stories of conflict and his analysis of the Levitical genealogies.

Evaluation of the Stories of Conflict

Cross argued that traces of the ancient division between the priestly factions of the Mushites and Aaronites are revealed in the stories of conflict between Moses and Aaron in the Pentateuch and in later stories about events at various cultic sites. Cross presented seven stories of priestly conflict in which the fault lines between the priestly houses may be discerned.

The Golden Calf

That Exod 32:1–24 describes a conflict between Moses and Aaron is beyond all debate. The creation and veneration of the golden calf by Aaron is the central conflict of the wilderness wanderings. Cross divides this passage into its constituent sources, assigning 32:1–6, 15–20, and 35 to the Elohistic source. The Priestly source, as one might anticipate in a story portraying Aaron in such negative light, is not present at all. The combined narrative consisting of J and E assigns blame for the cultic indiscretion to the people, and not to Aaron solely. However, Cross argues that in "the pristine Elohistic form, Aaron was, no doubt, more the central figure."[47] It would be impossible for such a polemic against Aaron to arise in a context dominated by Aaronite priests and scribes. Cross argues that this rules out its potential origins in later period Jerusalem. He also contends that "the polemical form of the tradition of Aaron's bull must have originated in an old northern priesthood, a rival priesthood of non-Aaronite lineage, defenders of an alternate iconographic tradition."[48] Following many of his contemporaries, Cross associates the Elohistic tradition with the northern regions, and, ultimately, he connects this anti-Aaron sentiment with the Mushites serving at the sanctuary of Shiloh. Understanding this polemic to extend to the cultic symbols employed as much as to the priests representing them, Cross proffers that this polemic originating in Shiloh was directed at Aaronites in Bethel. Part of the uncertainty around the affiliation of Bethel arises from 1 Kgs 12:31–33, which describes the religious reforms of Jeroboam I. Among his activities condemned by the Deuteronomistic History there we find: "He also made high-place temples, and appointed priests from among all the people, who were not Levites . . . so he did in Bethel, sacrificing to the calves that he had made. He placed in Bethel the priests of the high places that he had made" (1 Kgs 12:31–32). While it would seem from this passage that Jeroboam first *introduced* veneration of the golden calf at Bethel, Cross argues that this is not the case. The calf was already a part of the native iconography of Bethel. Cross contends that this passage reflects a broad-stroke condemnation of Jeroboam by DtH, not an accurate portrayal of the history of religious iconography venerated there. Further he notes that Judg 20:26–28 reflects "an archaic tradition placing Phinehas the son of Eleazar the son of Aaron at the sanctuary of Bethel in the early era when the Ark was in Bethel."[49] The affiliation of the Bethel priesthood with the Aaronites is a foundational assumption for Cross's hypothesis, and one which will be addressed in depth in ch. 3.[50]

The Ordination of the Levites

The response to the golden calf incident in Exod 32:26–29 forms for Cross
a second story of conflict, establishing Moses as a priestly leader. At Moses'
command the Levites gather at his side and slay three-thousand of their com-
patriots who committed idolatry with Aaron's calf. After the violence Moses
announces to the Levites in v. 29: "Today you have ordained yourselves
(מלאו ידכם) for the service of the LORD, each one at the cost of a son or a
brother, and so have brought a blessing on yourselves this day." Their fidelity
to the Lord against their own sons and brothers won them a special blessing. The nature of this blessing would seem to be spelled out in Moses' final
address to the Levites in Deut 33:8–10, where their vigor is rewarded with
priesthood. Cross remarks about the irony of this harsh critique: "In these
traditions we note that Moses' allies are Levitical priests, confronting the
idolaters, at whose head stands Aaron!"[51] This narrative following the golden
calf episode establishes Moses as the founder and figurehead of the Levite
priests over and against Aaron.

Moses and Midian

Cross argues that Moses' sacerdotal prestige extends beyond the role he
played as the overseer who ordained the zealous Levites described above.
Moses' marital relationship connected him to an even more ancient line of
priests, namely the Midianites/Kenites. In Exod 18, Moses' father-in-law
(חתן), Yethro, is identified as a "priest of Midian" (כהן מדין, v. 1); he offers
burnt offerings and sacrifices to God (v. 12), and he advises Moses in his
administrative duties, providing counsel for him to appoint sub-leaders to
share his work (vv. 13–27). Hobab, identified as a Kenite (Num 10:29) and
as a Midianite (Judg 1:16 and 4:11), offers Moses guidance in the Wilderness.
In Num 10:29 it is unclear precisely how Hobab is related to Moses. There
we find: "and Moses said to Hobab, son of Reuel, the Midianite, father-in-
law of Moses" (ויאמר משה לחבב בן רעואל המדיני חתן משה). The compounding of
the construct phrases muddles precisely to whom the descriptions המדיני and
חתן משה apply—whether to Reuel (so Exod 2:18) or to Hobab (so Judg 4:11).[52]
In either case, the intimate Midianite, and elsewhere Kenite, connections to
Moses stand. Cross remarks that "[t]he survival of such traditions in the face
of rival traditions of utter hostility to the Midianites is remarkable and suggests that Moses' interconnections with the priestly house of Midian were too
old and well established to be suppressed quietly or forgotten."[53] Building on
the work of Aharoni[54] and Mazar,[55] Cross envisions an intertwined Midianite-
Kenite-Mushite priesthood operative in Israel initially in the far south at Arad.
The family of Heber the Kenite, a scion of this Midianite-Kenite-Mushite

priesthood migrated northward, and in Judg 4:11 settled in Kadesh-Naphtali. From this northern position, the Midianite-Kenite-Mushite priests eventually came to serve additional sanctuaries at Shiloh and Dan, while also retaining Kadesh-Naphtali and a stronghold in the far south at Arad.[56]

Baal-Peor

In sharp contrast to the disinterested (if not positive) portrayal of the Midianites found in JE—what Cross terms the Epic tradition—P is unfettered in its condemnation of the Midianite influences on the Israelites. In the JE account of the events at Shittim in Num 25:1–5, Moses commands the Judges of Israel (שפטי ישראל) (v. 5) to carry out executions of the leaders (ראשי העם) who have taken Moabite wives. It would seem Moses responded appropriately to the Moabite miscegenation. However, in vv. 6–15 Cross sees the JE narrative interrupted by P. In this alternate narrative, the corruption of the people persisted as an unnamed Israelite brought into his family (ויקרב אל אחיו) a Midianite woman. To make matters worse, this flagrant indiscretion took place in front of (לעיני) Moses and the assembly of the Israelites. The wrong is ameliorated not by Moses, but by Phinehas—son of Eleazar, son of Aaron, the priest (פנחס בן אלעזר בן אהרן הכהן)—who ran both of them through with a spear as they were entering the tent (הקבה). Yahweh awarded Phinehas' vigorous fidelity by establishing an eternal priestly covenant (ברית כהנת עולם) with Phinehas and his descendants. Cross sees in this text a pro-Aaronite polemic directed against the Midianites (and thus the Mushites)—"the priesthood passed to the Aaronites precisely for their service in cleansing Israel from the taint of Midianite rites!"[57] Cross further draws parallels to the subtle rejection of Moses' priestly authority implied in this text to the rejection of the Mushite sons of Eli in 1 Sam 2:22–25, who are also denounced for their sexual indiscretions in proximity to a holy shrine.[58] Cross further speculates that the "polemical literature reflecting conflicting claims of the great priestly families"[59] was much more abundant than the fragments that remain in the biblical texts.

Aaron and Miriam against Moses

Numbers 12 describes Aaron and Miriam joining forces to critique Moses. They condemn him for marrying a Cushite woman (כי אשה כשית לקח, v. 1), and they question whether it is only Moses who has access to the Yahweh's oracles (הרק אך במשה דבר יהוה, v. 2). For their insubordination they are chastened, and in the story Moses emerges as the peerless mediator of divine knowledge over and against Mariam and Aaron. Expanding on an argument offered by Albright[60] that Cushite is simply a veiled reference to Zipporah as a Midianite, Cross sees within this text an "affirmation of the legitimacy of the Mushite priesthood despite its 'mixed' blood."[61]

Nadab and Abihu, and Dathan and Abiram

The stories of Nadab and Abihu (Lev 10:1–7) and Dathan and Abiram (Numbers 16:1–40) both involve priestly censure. Nadab and Abihu are identified as Aaronite (בני אהרן) in v. 1, they offer strange fire (אש זרה), and are consumed by fire from Yahweh (v. 2). The brief pericope ends with Moses chastising Aaron, and Aaron remaining silent (וידם אהרן). Likewise, the Dathan and Abiram story and the Korah story describe further rebellions by priests. Analyzing these stories, Cross observes:

> In Leviticus 10, two Aaronic clans are repudiated, in Numbers 16, a Levitic clan. The ritual of bringing incense burners to the sanctuary appears in both; in both, fire from Yahweh consumes the sinners. In Leviticus 10, Aaron appears to be rebuked; in Numbers 16 it is the Levites who are rebuked, Aaron who is upheld, and both from the mouth of Moses! In short, a similar theme is used in two contexts, one anti-Aaronite, the other pro-Aaronite in bias.
>
> In Numbers 16–17, however, the tradition of ancient conflicts between Levitic or Mushite priests and the priestly house of Aaron stands far in the background.[62]

In sum, for Cross the stories of conflict reveal three lines of the priesthood functioning at six different sanctuaries geographically dispersed throughout Israel. The Mushites controlled Shiloh and Dan. A line of allied Mushite-Kenite priesthood served sanctuaries at Arad and Kadesh-Naphthali, at the southern and northern extremes of Israel, respectively. The Mushite and Mushite-Kenite lines stood in tension with the Aaronite priesthood of Bethel and Jerusalem.[63]

The Lineages of Abiathar and Zadok

The third portion of Cross's Mushite hypothesis addresses information presented in the lists of Levitical genealogies. The primary question to which Cross attends is how to understand the connection between the clan relationships presented in these Levitical lists and the Mushite/Aaronite opposition. As established earlier, these lists begin with Levi, and the second generation divides the clan into three parts: Gershon, Kohath, and Merari. The clans continue to divide as follows: Kohath, gives rise to Amram, who is the father of Aaron and Moses, while, Merari divides into two clans, one of whom is Mushi. Thus, the relationship between Moses, Aaron, and Mushi is that of first-cousins-once-removed. Cross understands the genealogical relationships imagined here to be the product of a late (and pro-Aaronite) Priestly source located in the Exile. For Cross, the temporal and cultic distance from the origins of these relationships cast doubt on the reliability of their reporting.

Following Wellhausen and Möhlenbrink, Cross identifies Num 26:58 as an earlier and more reliable rendering of the relationships between the Levite clans. As discussed earlier in the work of Rehm, this list is text-critically complicated. Like Rehm, Cross argues that the *lectio brevior* of LXX omitting the Mahlites is the pristine form of this list, which should read: Libnites, Hebronites, Mushites, and Korhites. For Rehm, the division of the Levites presented in Num 26:58 was a second stage in the evolution of the relationships of the Levite clans associated with the period of the Tribal League, and it supplanted the earlier tripartite division of Gershon, Kohath, and Merari, which dominated in the Desert Period. As noted above, Cross associates this rendering of the clan relationships with P, and places it in the Exile. Though Cross deviates from the analysis of Rehm at this point, he is wholly dependent on Rehm's ideas about further evolutions of the priesthood in the Tribal League and how the division of the priesthood presented in the amended form of Num 26:58 relates to the Mushite-Aaronite division. The Mushites boast explicit mention in this rendering of the Levitical clans, attesting to their antiquity and prominence in the Tribal League. The Aaronites receive no such mention. However, Rehm argued,[64] and Cross proffered the same evidence,[65] that the reference to the Hebronites in Num 26:58 encompasses what would eventually become the Aaronites. That the Aaronites are connected with Hebron is made clear in the Levitical Cities lists, which appropriate Hebron (among other locales) to Aaron's descendants as cities of refuge (Josh 21:10–13 and 1 Chr 6:42).

In addition to connecting the Aaronites to Hebron, Rehm offered a second proposal integral to Cross's theory, namely, that Zadok was descended from Aaronites who served at the sanctuary in Hebron.[66] This proposal hardly seems to be novel, since is supported by the evidence in the Chronicler's genealogies.[67] However, as discussed below, Cross understands the Chronicler's and P's late material to be too heavily edited to be useful for reconstructing details of this early period. In any case Cross offers a text critical reappraisal of Wellhausen's argument of Zadok as a *homo novus*, unconnected to established priestly lines. In 2 Sam 8:17 the MT reads: "and Zadok son of Ahituv, and Ahimelek son of Abiathar were priests" וצדוק בן אחיטוב ואחימלך בן אביתר. One expects Zadok and Abiathar to be listed in parallel position in the verse, as opposed to Zadok and Ahimelek. Wellhausen's solution was to argue that the order of names in the verse had simply been reversed, and that the more original read: אביתר בן אחימלך בן אחיטוב וצדוק thus describing Abiathar's ancestry for two generations and giving no genealogical information for Zadok. Against Wellhausen, Cross argues that the corruption apparent in MT resulted from haplography. He proposes that the more original reading was ודצוק בן אחיטוב ואביתר בן אחימלך; however, the name אביתר was lost to haplography [similarity between אב and אח] and was later reincorporated into the verse in the wrong place, likely from a marginal note.[68] Zadok is not an unconnected newcomer; rather, he has ancestry just like his counterpart Abiathar. Cross further argues that the Ahitub referred to as the ancestor of Zadok is not identical with the Ahitub the grandfather of Abiathar.[69]

The connection between Moses and Eli at Shiloh was established in 1 Sam 2:27, and thus, Abiathar, a descendant of Eli, was also part of the Mushite clan.[70] These two connections, Zadok with the Aaronites and Abithar with the Mushites, form the backbone of Cross's theory about the political role of these two priestly houses in the early monarchy.

Priestly Factions in the Political Landscape of the United Monarchy

The final part of Cross's Mushite Hypothesis is its most consequential. Having established the Aaronite lineage of Zadok and the Mushite lineage of Abiathar, Cross posits a novel explanation of David's peculiar choice to inaugurate a co-high-priesthood in Jerusalem at the time of the United Monarchy. Cross understood this bold move by David to be a shrewd political maneuver. David sought not only to unite the Israel and Judah with an administrative center, but also to unite the ancient, competing priestly factions by installing both Abiathar and Zadok in the official cult centered in Jerusalem.[71]

The biblical text does not readily admit to such utilitarian purposes. However, Cross interpolates the political and religious motivations of David by exploring the conditions both immediately prior to David's rise and immediately after. The evidence described above—particularly the stories of priestly conflict in the JE Epic—betray the existence of the competing priestly houses during the Tribal League as well as the cultic centers associated with each house. In the northern rebellion, the activities of Jeroboam I in installing calf-iconography associated with the Aaronites in the northern Mushite sanctuaries of Dan and Shiloh show the endurance of the priestly antagonism two generations after David. Since the conflict between Aaronite and Mushite priests existed at the time of the Tribal League and at the time of the Divided Monarchy, Cross determines that it must have existed at the time of David. Further, David manipulated this historical antagonism and created from it a unified priesthood as an auxiliary to his efforts at statecraft.

Cross dates the origin of the JE Epic and its version of the conflict between the priestly houses to no later than the ninth century. "[A]fter Abiathar was ousted from office by Solomon, Aaronic traditions steadily grew stronger until the Jerusalem priests at the end of the kingdom stood alone with all memory of rival houses and families repressed."[72] The official Priestly gene-alogies and those of the Chronicler are so far removed from the cultic reali-ties of the early monarchy that the ancient relationships and affiliations are redacted entirely through the lens of Aaronite-Zadokite ascendancy.

Questions Posed by Cross's Mushite Hypothesis

The Mushite Hypothesis as articulated in twenty pages of *CMHE* remained largely unrevised throughout Cross's life, and it serves as the primary and often only reference to the idea in the scholarly literature. The theory as it stands raises both methodological and interpretive questions related to the geographical distribution of affiliated cultic centers, the nature of the Levitical genealogies, and the contours of the dependent and independent voices in the Pentateuch.

Geographical Distribution of Cultic Sites

Cross meticulously traced the cultic iconography and priestly affiliations of six cult sites mentioned in the Pentateuch and Deuteronomistic History with the respective priestly houses in the monarchy. His results present a picture of Mushite and Aaronid cultic sites strewn throughout the land in no perceptible pattern. This is contrary to the partitioning of land along distinct geographical areas in the Levitical City list, for example, in the fact that Josh 21:4 allots only southern territories to the Aaronites. Further, the random geographic distribution of the rival-yet-complementary priestly lines stands in tension with the results of recent ethnographic studies about the interac-tions of adjacent sacerdotal groups in pre-modern societies.[73] These studies suggest that priestly groups play an important role in creating and maintain-ing geographical unity.

Genealogies

Intimately related to the consciousness and function of the Aaronite-Mushite opposition is a complex of questions related to the role of genealogy in nego-tiating this opposition. Robert Wilson, in his treatise on genealogies in the ancient Near East and the Bible,[74] has shown there is an intimate connection between the form of a genealogy and its function. There are two primary forms of genealogical material. Linear genealogies trace a single line from generation to generation without regard to branches or "segmentation." That is, linear genealogies are branchless trunks of family trees. These stand in contrast to "segmented genealogies," which may catalogue an array of pater-nal, maternal, fraternal, sororal, and cousinly relationships. Wilson's primary observation concerns the dynamic nature of the relationships described in genealogical texts. He writes: "when genealogies function in the domestic sphere, they relate individuals to other individuals and groups within the society and define social rights and obligations. Genealogies which are used in this way are usually segmented, and their form must change constantly to mirror the changing shape of the domestic social structure."[75] Through various adaptations genealogies may create either cohesion or division within a particular social group as a function of contemporary sentiment. The Aaronite-Mushite opposition proposed by the Mushite Hypothesis thus necessitates a careful reconsideration of the descriptions of, catalyst for, and functions of the division and the way they are described. That is, questions must be asked about which of the divisions/affiliations of the Aaronite and Mushite groups are operative at a particular time, for whom they are operative, and the ultimate origins of the divisions/affiliations.

Source Divisions and Independent/Dependent Voices

For Cross and the scholarly climate in which he wrote, the source divisions of the Pentateuch had been well established in the preceding century. Likewise, the historical and social origins associated with these sources were often (though not always) accepted. Cross's language about the "JE Epic" and its role in the politics of the ninth century, as well as his dating of P in the exile were accepted *de rigueur* at the time, but are now subject to serious challenge and require far greater attention to the integrity of the narratives in which the stories of conflict appear as well as attention to the broad vision of priestly authority within the independent voices of the Pentateuch.

SCHOLARLY LEGACY OF CROSS'S MUSHITE HYPOTHESIS

The Mushite Hypothesis has enjoyed much acclaim since its publication, and was described by Freedman—Cross's frequent co-author and close friend from their graduate school days under Albright—as a "landmark of biblical criticism."[76] It has enjoyed its strongest support among those students trained by Cross's himself and others trained by them—the "Crossite clan," as it were—though it is not limited to them by any means. Scholars outside the "Crossite clan" have exploited the explanatory power of the model of priestly conflict as well as the diplomatic vision of David's religious statecraft.[77] Beyond the realm of critical biblical studies proper, the influence of the Mushite Hypothesis is also seen also in recent renderings of Jewish history and Jewish thought writ-large.[78]

Mark Leuchter's 2012 article "The Fightin' Mushites"[79] and his 2017 monograph *The Levites and the Boundaries of Israelite Identity* are the most recent in the chain of iterations of the Mushite Hypothesis, and we will return to him later. The theory has played roles to varying degrees in biblical commentaries,[80] monographs,[81] articles,[82] and dissertations[83] pertaining to the pre-monarchic and early monarchic periods. Also notably, the memory of the antagonism between the Mushites and Aaronites has been used by Paul Hanson[84] and Jon Levenson[85] as both an analogy to and model for explaining tensions in the Exilic and Post-exilic priestly community. That is the later opposition between Levites and Zadokites is approached through the lens of old tensions between the rival Mushites and Aaronite priesthoods.[86]

CONCLUSION

The biblical text presents the clan of the בני מושי as but one of many other subgroupings of Levites, and the only connection between this group and Moses is that of a somewhat indirect lineage. Wellhausen, Smend, Möhlenbrink, and Rehm posited a connection between the בני מושי and Moses and Aaron. Further, they argued that an array of biblical texts portray Moses as the founder of a priestly line over and against his brother Aaron, whose priestly line features far more prominently. Cross adapted these ideas, and expanded them into a Mushite Hypothesis, in which the Israelite priesthood consisted originally of three ancient branches: Mushite, Mushite-Midianite, and Aaronite, geographically dispersed throughout in Israel. The Mushite and Mushite-Midianite branches at the time of the late Tribal League operated in concert and are indistinguishable. When David sought to unify Israel and Judah, he enfranchised both of the ancient priestly lines by installing Zadok, an Aaronite, and Abiathar, a Mushite, at the royal shrine at Jerusalem. The influence of Cross's theory has waxed and waned as a function of a variety of trends in biblical scholarship. Its immense explanatory power for understanding the faint biblical echoes of a priesthood affiliated with Moses warrants its continued consideration along the lines of the methodical questions raised above. The next three chapters will undertake each of these in turn considering the interrelated topics of lands, families, and priestly authority.

NOTES

1. *CMHE*, 195n1.
2. Echoes of the earliest discernible attempt to understand the מושי of the MT appears in various manuscripts in the Greek tradition, where the anomalous forms

ομουσι/ομουσει appear. See Matthew R. Rasure, "Priests Like Moses: Earliest Divisions in the Priesthood of ancient Israel" Ph.D. diss, Harvard University, 2019) particularly pp. 7–8 for a detailed survey of such variants in the Greek manuscript traditions. The forms with the prefixed o-micron, ομουσι/ομουσει, etc. appear alongside the un-prefixed forms μουσι/μουσει and it would seem that they are used interchangeably. Whatever the motivation, that the Greek tradition developed and utilized two nomenclatures for describing the מושׁי branch of the Levitical line is apparent. The creation of the ομουσι/ομουσει form inevitably results in the distancing of the מושׁי in the MT from any connections with or confusions over the proper name Moses (משׁה), whether or not such a differentiation was intentional.

3. While this reference does understand Amram as the son of Kohath, it describes the relationship between the Libnites, the Hebronites, the Mahlites, the Mushites, and the Korahites in a different way from all other occurrences of the Levitical list: as generational peers, rather than as second or third (Korah) generation Levites. See the discussions of Möhlenbrink, Rehm, and Cross below.

4. Julius Wellhausen, *Geschichte Israels* (Berlin: G. Reimer, 1878), 123–156.

5. Wellhausen repeats the idea from the 1878 edition, unchanged in Idem., *Prolegomena zur Geschichte Israels*, (2nd ed.; Berlin: G. Reimer, 1883) and in subsequent editions.

6. Discussed *inter alia* in section 83 of Israel Yeivin, *Introduction to the Tiberian Masorah* (trans. E.J. Revell; Missoula, MT: Scholars, 1980), 47.

7. Wellhausen, *Prolegomena zur Geschichte Israels*, 148. Noch in den Genealogien des Priestercodex heisst der eine Hauptast des Stammes Levi Gerson wie der älteste Sohn Mose's, und ein anderer wichtiger Zweig heisst geradezu Muschi, der Mosaische.

8. Ibid.

9. Ibid. " . . . Begründer ihres Standes."

10. Julius Wellhausen, *Prolegomena to the History of Israel* (trans. J. Sutherland Black and Allan Menzies; (Edinburgh: Adam and Charles Black, 1885), 126.

11. Rudolf Smend, *Lehrbuch der alttestamentlichen Religionsgeschichte* (Freiberg, Germany: Mohr Siebeck, 1893), 93. "Mose ist Priester und Seher in einer Person."

12. Ibid., 34n2. "Mose ist freilich Volkshaupt und Priester zugleich."

13. See, for instance, the discussions of "Priestvater Levi" (p. 75) and "Priestervater Aharon" (pp. 75 and 93).

14. Rudolf Smend, *Lehrbuch der alttestamentlichen Religionsgeschichte*, (2nd ed., Freiberg, Germany: Mohr Siebeck, 1899), 37n2. "Aber in alter Zeit leiteten die Priester eher von Mose ab, der im Segen Moses (Deut. 33:8) allein als der Priestervater gedacht zu sein scheint."

15. Ibid., 38n2 and following. "Der andere Sohn Moses Gerson kehrt ebenfalls in der Geneologie des Stammes Levi in Priestercodex wieder, der daneben ein levitisches Geschlecht Muschi (=Mose) aufweist."

16. See Leroy Waterman, "Some Determining Factors in the Northward Progress of Levi," *JAOS* 57 (1937): 375–380. Waterman notes there: "Many modern scholars (c.f. ZAW II. 196 [ibid.]) have been convinced that in the Mushites we have the Levitical group which championed the cause of Moses." The reference he intends here is surely

the 1934 Möhlenbrink article cited immediately below, "ZAW LII. 196" rather than "ZAW II. 196," which refers to no related topic.

17. Kurt Möhlenbrink, "Die levitischen Überlieferungen des Alten Testaments," *ZAW* 52 (1934): 184–231.

18. Martin Noth, *Das System der zwölf Stämme Israels*, *BWANT* 4.1 (Stuttgart: W. Kohlmanner, 1930), particularly chapters 3–5.

19. Möhlenbrink, 196. "Ob Musi wirklich das 'mosaische' Geschlecht ist, mag dahingestellt bleiben, sehr wahrscheinlich ist es gewiß."

20. Ibid., 228. "Auf Grund einer Bewährung in einer Zeit kritischer Lage der mosaischen Stiftung habe 'Levi' durch rücksichtsloses Eintreten für Mose die Situation gerettet, und dafür sei ihm das Priesterrecht Eintreten zugesprochen worden."

21. Ibid., Möglicherweise haben wir in Dtn 33:8–11 sozusagen die ätiologische Rechtssatzung speziell des 'mosaischen' Zweiges der Leviten—denn auf Moses werden die Leviten hier besonders bezogen; sie sind 'seine Getreuen.'"

22. Merlin Rehm, "Studies in the History of the Pre-Exilic Levites" (Th.D. diss. Harvard University, 1967).

23. Rehm, 12 and 22.

24. Ibid., 265.

25. Ibid., 228.

26. Ibid., 93.

27. Ibid., 221.

28. Ibid., 101.

29. Ibid., 252.

30. Rehm does not account here for the editorial note provided on Aaron's death in Deut 10:6, ויכהן אלעזר בנו תחתיו, *Eleazar his (Aaron's) son served as priest in his stead.*

31. G. Ernest Wright, "The Levites in Deuteronomy," *VT* 4 (1954): 325–330, and "The Book of Deuteronomy: Introduction and Exegesis," *The Interpreter's Bible* (New York: Abingdon-Cokesbury, 1953) 2:309–329.

32. Rehm, 112.

33. Ibid., 223.

34. Ibid., 224.

35. Rehm, 138. See also Manahem Haran, "Studies in the Account of the Levitical Cities: II. Utopia and Historical Reality" *JBL* 80:2 (1961): 156–165.

36. It is duly worth noting here that this Israeli scholarly tradition of tracing Levitical heritage to Moses seen here in the work of Kauffman and Talmon is still vibrantly alive in the work of Alexander Rofé. For instance his recent article presented in translation on TheTorah.com. Alexander Rofé, "Levites: A Transjordanian Tribe of Priests," TheTorah.com, September 27, 2021, https://www.thetorah.com/article/levites-a-transjordanian-tribe-of-priests. This article is a translation and adaption of an earlier work published as Alexander Rofé, "ברכת משה,מקדש נבו ושאלת מוצא הלויים" in מחקרים במקרא ובמזרח הקדמון מוגשים לשמואל א' ליונשטם במלאת לו שבעים שנה, ed. Yitschak Avishur and Joshua Blau, (Jerusalem: E. Rubinstein's Pub. House, 1978), 409–424.

37. Yehezkel Kaufmann, *The Religion of Israel*, (trans. Moshe Greenberg; Chicago: University of Chicago Press, 1960), 197.

38. Ibid., 198.

39. Ibid., 198n13.

40. Shemaryahu Talmon, "Divergences in Calendar Reckoning in Ephraim and Judah," *VT* 8:1 (1958): 48–74.

41. Ibid., 52.

42. Ibid., 52–53.

43. Ibid., 53.

44. Exod 6:19; Num 3:20, 33; 26:58; 1 Chr 6:4, 32; 23:21, 23; 24:26, 30.

45. Wellhausen, *Prolegomena zur Geschichte Israels*, 148. See also the discussion offered in Charles Hauret, "Moïse était-il prêtre?" *Biblica* 40 (1959): 509–521.

46. *CMHE*, 196.

47. *CMHE*, 198.

48. Ibid., 198–199.

49. *CMHE*, 199.

50. See Talmon, 52.

51. Ibid., 200.

52. Albright has discussed this at length in W.F. Albright, "Jethro, Hobab, and Reuel in Early Hebrew Tradition," CBQ 25 (1963): 1–11. There he posits that Jethro, the father-in-law (*ḥōtēn*) of Moses, and Hobab, the son-in-law (*ḥātān*) of Moses, were both members of the Midianite clan of Reuel. Albright speculates that the Kenite designation is one of profession and refers to metal-working.

53. *CMHE*, 200.

54. Yohanan Aharoni and Ruth Amiran, "Arad: A Biblical City in Southern Palestine," *Archaeology* 17 (1964): 43–53.

55. Benyamin Mazar, "The Sanctuary of Arad and the Family of Hobab the Kenite," *JNES* 24 (1965): 297–303.

56. *CMHE*, 201.

57. Ibid., 202.

58. For a compelling treatment of the Elide material and an argument that the anti-Elide rhetoric in the condemnation of Hophni and Phineas is part of a redactional addition to the 1 Samuel narrative, see: Jaime A. Myers, "The Wicked 'Sons of Eli' and the Composition of 1 Samuel 1–4," *VT* 72 (2022): 237–256.

59. Ibid., 203.

60. William Foxwell Albright, *Archaeology and the Religion of Israel* (3rd ed.; Baltimore: Johns Hopkins, 1956), 205n49.

61. *CMHE*, 204.

62. Ibid., 205.

63. Ibid., 206.

64. Rehm, 265.

65. *CMHE*, 206.

66. See Rehm, 138. It is quite striking that Cross makes no explicit attribution of these ideas to Rehm, who is only mentioned in a single footnote at the beginning of *CMHE*, ch. 8. Rehm's dissertation was submitted December, 1967, prior to December 11, 1968, and April 9, 1969, when Cross presented the core of his hypothesis in lectures at Brandeis and Yale, and well prior to the publication of *CMHE* in 1973. Surely Rehm was developing and expanding Cross's own ideas in his dissertation.

67. 1 Chr 5:27–41.

68. *CMHE*, 213–214.

69. 1 Sam 22:20

70. Rehm, 224.

71. Ibid. 208.

72. *CMHE*, 208.

73. Jeremy Hutton, "The Levitical Diaspora (I): A Sociological Comparison with Morocco's Ahansal," in *Exploring the Long Durée: Essays in Honor of Lawrence E. Stager* (ed. David Schloen et al.; Winona Lake, IN: Eisenbrauns, 2009), 223–34.

74. Robert R. Wilson, *Genealogy and History in the Biblical World* (New Haven, CT: Yale University Press, 1977).

75. Idem., "Old Testament Genealogies in Recent Research," *JBL* 94 (1975), 181.

76. Freedman, "An Appreciation," 6.

77. For instance, see: Robert G. Boling, "Levitical History and the Role of Joshua." In *The Word of the Lord Shall Go Forth: Essays in Honor of David Noel Freedman.* (ed. Carol L. Meyers and Michael P. O'Connor; Philadelphia: *ASOR*, 1983), 241–262; Walter Brueggemann, "Trajectories in Old Testament Literature and the Sociology of Ancient Israel." *JBL* 98:2 (1979): 161–185; A. P. B. Breytenbach, "Who is Behind the Samuel Narrative?" in *Past, Present, Future: The Deuteronomistic History and the Prophets* (ed. Johannes Cornelis de Moor and Harry F. van Rooy; Leiden, Netherlands: Brill, 2000), 50–75; and F.E. Deist, "'By the Way, Hophni and Phinehas Were There': An Investigation into the Literary and Ideological Function of Hophni, Phinehas and Shiloh in 1 Samuel 1–4," *JNWSL* 18 (1992): 25–35.

78. For instance, see: Norbert Max Samuelson, *Jewish Philosophy: An Historical Introduction* (London: Continuum, 2003), 32–34 and Sherwin T. Wine, *A Provocative People: A Secular History of the Jews* (Farmington Hills, MI: International Institute for Secular Humanistic Judaism, 2012), 102–113.

79. Mark Leuchter, "The Fightin' Mushites," *VT* 62:4 (2012): 479–500 and Idem, *The Levites and the Boundaries of Israelite Identity* (Oxford: Oxford University Press, 2017).

80. Such as: William Henry Propp, *Exodus 1–18: A New Translation with Introduction and Commentary* (Anchor Bible 2; New York: Doubleday, 1999), 286ff.

81. Richard Elliott Friedman, *Who Wrote the Bible?* (New York: Summit Books, 1987), and, again, Samuelson, *Jewish Philosophy*.

82. Baruch Halpern, "Sectionalism and the Schism," *JBL* 93 (1974): 519–32; Idem., "Levitic Participation in the Reform Cult of Jeroboam I," *JBL* 95 (1976): 31–42, and Jonathan Rosenbaum, "Hezekiah's Reform and the Deuteronomistic Tradition," *HTR* 72 (1979): 23–43.

83. James R. Callaway, "Aspects of Religion and Culture in the Iron II Period: A Biblical and Archaeological Approach to Cult in Relationship to Kinship, Kingship, and Land" (Ph.D. diss. Southwestern Baptist Theological Seminary, 1996); Alice Wells Hunt, "The Zadokites: Finding Their Place in the Hebrew Bible" (Ph.D. diss., Vanderbilt University, 2003); Alison Lori Joseph, "The Portrait of the Kings and the Historiographical Poetics of the Deuteronomistic Historian" (Ph.D. diss. University of California, Berkeley, 2012); C. Shaun Longstreet, "Native Cultic Leadership in

the empire: Foundations for Achaemenid Hegemony in Persian Judah" (Ph.D. diss., University of Notre Dame, 2003); Thomas David Petter, "Diversity and Uniformity on the Frontier: Ethnic Identity in the Central Highlands of Jordan During the Iron I" (Ph.D. diss., University of Toronto, 2005); Susan Marie Pigott, "'God of Compassion and Mercy': An Analysis of the Background, Use, and Theological Significance of Exodus 34:6–7" (Ph.D. diss., Southwestern Baptist Theological Seminary, 1995); Stephen Christopher Russell, "Images of Egypt in Early Biblical Literature: Cisjordan-Israelite, Transjordan-Israelite, and Judahite Portrayals" (Ph.D. diss., New York University, 2008); David Vincent Santis, "The Land of Transjordan Israel in the Israel Age and Its Religious Traditions" (Ph.D. diss., New York University, 2004); and Samuel Chong Kyoon Shin, "Centralization and Singularization: Official Cult and royal Politics in Ancient Israel" (Ph.D. diss., Union Theological Seminary in Virginia, 1997).

84. Paul D. Hanson, *The Dawn of Apocalyptic* (Philadelphia: Fortress Press, 1975), 95–96, 177, 281 and various places throughout Idem., *The People Called: The Growth of Community in the Bible* (San Francisco: Harper & Row, 1986).

85. Jon D. Levenson, *Theology of the Program of Restoration of Ezekiel 40–48* (Harvard Semitic Monographs 10; Missoula, MT: Scholars Press, 1976), 136–39.

86. The enduring effect of Cross's vision of the priesthood has been criticized recently by James Watts in an unpublished paper presented in 2016 at the "Priests and Levites Section" of the SBL Annual Meeting in San Antonio. James W. Watts, "Priestly Lineages in History and Rhetoric" (unpublished paper, 2016). In this essay Watts raises very important concerns about how data preserved in late genealogical material ought and ought not to be used. He insists that the rhetorical scope and intent of the genealogy is inextricably tied to the interpretation of the data it presents. Watts's rightly calls into question Cross's use of biblical genealogical material as a textual artefact without context. He further notes that Cross employed a similarly myopic methodological move in his discussion of genealogical accounts of Oniad and Hasmonean high priests to specious results (Frank Moore Cross, Jr., "A Reconstruction of the Judean Restoration," *JBL* 94 [1975], 4–18). Watts's methodological corrective regarding the inextricability of genealogy and rhetoric continues the spirit of Robert Wilson's work, and has greatly informed my discussion of genealogical connections in chapter 4 of this study. However, Watts would seem to raise the bar for the admission of genealogical evidence to an impossibly high standard. Watts would have that the only genealogical information that can prove useful with regard to priestly authority is that which explicitly invokes the names of ancestors for the purpose of legitimating priestly authority. Watts claims such explicit invocation only occurs among the Aaronites. If that is the case, the discussion of Jonathan (son of Gershom, son of Moses) leaves one at a loss (Judges 17–18). Watts also raises a somewhat more troubling critique of efforts to search for echoes of priestly division related to the character of Moses. He sees hints of a desire to uncover a "more authentic priesthood," something "less-cultically saturated" than the Aaronites (p. 8). Watts's charge would seem to follow in the spirt of critiques of Wellhausen's rampant anti-Semitism, and perhaps even to echo critiques of the Protestant bias in historical criticism offered by Levenson and Kugel, seen most conspicuously in sympathetic portrayals of the

Northern Kingdom over and against the Jerusalem cultus (see, for example, chapter 4 of Jon D. Levenson, *The Hebrew Bible, the Old Testament, and Historical Criticism: Jews and Christians in Biblical Studies* [Louisville, KY: Westminster, John Knox, 1993]). While the latter concerns are well-documented, it is deeply unfair to cast aspersions on attempts to understand to what extent Moses might have an independent priestly identity by speculation about what biases might have occasioned the inquiry.

Chapter 3

Holy Lands

Geography and the Israelite Priesthood

This chapter will investigate geographical aspects of the memory of the Israelite priesthood set in the early first millennium. I will explore geographic factors related to the evolution of the priesthood by considering two bodies of information: the tribal politics at play in the building and dismantling of the United Monarchy under David, and the descriptions of significant cultic centers as well as and the groups, iconography, and ideologies associated with each. The discussion will take place in five stages. First, I will review the relevant details of Cross's Mushite Hypothesis as it relates to the geographical distribution of sites. Second, I will describe the roles of tribal politics and local clan fealty in David's statecraft, as described in 1 and 2 Samuel. Third, I will briefly summarize relevant details surrounding the priestly activities and affiliations of key cultic sites operative before, during, and after David's reign. Fourth, I will consider the issue of the Levitical Cities lists (Josh 21:1–42 and 1 Chr 6:39–66) and the nature of the evidence presented by these lists as it bears on the question of the geographical distribution of cultic centers. Fifth, I will sketch a picture of what this study has revealed about the geographical distribution of cultic centers in ancient Israel, proposing that the designations of "northern" and "southern"—a commonplace within biblical scholarship—would be more accurately understood as "central" and "peripheral" as it relates to the priesthood.

REVIEW OF CROSS'S POSITION

In his articulation of the Mushite Hypothesis, Cross argued that evidence for the bifurcation of the Israelite priesthood into Mushite and Aaronite houses could be found in the descriptions of various cultic sites and events happening at these locales, particularly as they are mentioned in the Deuteronomistic

History. Cross meticulously traced and affiliated the cultic iconography, personalities, and conflicts associated with various cult sites with the respective priestly houses. It is neither expedient nor necessary to review all facets of his argument at this point. His four most salient points, and, indeed, those most relevant to this study involve the following topics or narratives: Kenite and Midianite migration from the far south; the rejection of the House of Eli at Shiloh; Jeroboam's archaizing cultic revolutions and political motivations; and the affiliation of Zadok with Hebron. I will treat each of these in turn.

Kenite and Midianite Migration

As discussed elsewhere, Cross saw a strong connection between the character of Moses and the Kenites/Midianites. These connections are embedded in the narrative of Moses' marriage and his father-in-law, Jethro, and his kinsman, Hobab. Cross argued that "Moses' interconnections with the priestly house of Midian were too old and well established to be suppressed quietly or forgotten" by those voices in the Pentateuchal traditions frequently hostile to the Midianites.[1]

Cross understood the Midianites/Kenites to have very specific geographical ties to locales in Palestine. Beyond the eponymous affiliation with Midian in the trans-Jordan, Cross followed the work of Mazar theorizing an early Midianite migration to Arad in southern Judah and a group of Midianite priests serving at a sanctuary at Arad excavated by Aharoni in 1962.[2] This migration of Midianites is described in Judg 1:16, and it is resumed in 4:11, with the migration of a certain Heber the Kenite to the region of Naphtali, and specifically to Elon-bezaanannim. At this sanctuary, the judge Jael served alongside Shamgar (Judg 5). Thus, for Cross, kinsmen of Moses through the Midianite/Kenite line served in priestly capacities in the far southern parts of Judah and in the upper Galilee.

Rejection of the House of Eli at Shiloh

The textual lynchpin between the priesthood of Eli at Shiloh and Moses/The Mushites is found in 1 Sam 2:27–28.

> A man of God came to Eli and said to him, "Thus the LORD has said, 'I revealed myself to the family of your ancestor in Egypt (הנגלה נגליתי אל בית אביך בהיותם במצרים) when they were slaves to the house of Pharaoh.
>
> I chose him out of all the tribes of Israel to be my priest, to go up to my altar, to offer incense, to wear an ephod before me; and I gave to the family of your ancestor all my offerings by fire from the people of Israel (ובחר אתו מכל שבטי

ישראל לי לכהן לעלות על מזבחי להקטיר קטרת לשאת אפוד לפני ואתנה לבית אביך את כל אשי
בני ישראל)." "

The text places Eli's priestly progenitor in the Exodus and ties the priestly actions of altar service, incense burning, wearing the ephod, and fire offerings to Eli's ancestor. Cross argues that the unnamed referent is Moses, thus placing priests of the Elide house at Shiloh within the Mushite line.[3] The rejection of the Elide house because of the actions of his sons Hophni and Phinehas takes place in vv. 29–36. These verses also predict the eventual rise of a faithful priest (כהן נאמן) for whom Yahweh will build a faithful line (בית נאמן) and who will serve before the anointed king (משיחי) into perpetuity. For Cross, this promised faithful priest is Zadok, and Cross sees within this text the elevation of Zadok and the Aaronite line to the favored position in the kingdom and the subordination of the Mushites to an inferior position at some point in the future.[4] After the rise of David, the Shilonite priest Abiathar is vested with the high priesthood in the national cult in Jerusalem. Cross elaborates on this choice: "[i]n the era of the Empire, David . . . wisely chose a scion of the Shilonite house, establishing for his national cult place the nimbus of the old Mushite sanctuary, its ark and its priesthood. . . . "[5] The Deuteronomistic Historian makes clear that Zadok is the faithful priest who will take power after the fall of the Elide line.[6] The curse against the Mushite/Shilonite priesthood is repeated in 1 Kings 2:27 at the expulsion of Abiathar from Jerusalem by Solomon. "So Solomon banished Abiathar from being priest (מהיות כהן) to the LORD, thus fulfilling the word of the LORD that he had spoken concerning the house of Eli in Shiloh." With Abiathar the Mushite/Elide out of the high priesthood, Zadok of the Aaronite line reigned preeminent.

Jeroboam's Archaizing Cultic Reforms

Attendant to Cross's understanding of the Mushite character of Shiloh is his assertion that the priesthood at Bethel must have been Aaronite. Indeed, Cross understands the story condemning Aaron for the Golden Calf to have arisen in a Mushite priestly circle at Shiloh as a polemic against the Aaronites serving in Bethel, roughly ten miles to the south.[7] Cross assumes that the Bethel priesthood must be Aaronite because of the choice of Jeroboam I to embrace worship of golden calves at the Bethel sanctuary. Cross did not understand Jeroboam to be introducing a new cultic symbol at Bethel, but rather attempting to appease a long tradition of calf worship in this locale, which might have been censured by David. From this view, Jeroboam sought to "out-archaize" David by re-enfranchising ancient practices made taboo in the emerging centralized cult.[8] For Cross, the calf iconography is the primary piece of evidence linking Bethel to Aaron and the Aaronites. He also cites a passing note in Judg 20:26–28 mentioning that "Phinehas son of Eleazar, son of Aaron," performed priestly duties at Bethel while the Ark of the Covenant was located there.

Cross sees precisely the reverse taking place at Dan with Jeroboam I's installation of a calf at the sanctuary there. Whereas at Bethel Jeroboam was an archaizer, reinstating subordinated iconography, at Dan the Golden Calf was a foreign symbol imported by Jeroboam. In contrast to Bethel, Dan was an old Mushite sanctuary, tracing its origins to the Danite migration and the first Israelite priest to serve there, Jonathan, son of Gershom, son of Moses (Judg 18:30). While the Golden Calf iconography was not native to the Danites, Cross saw within Jeroboam's choice of the Mushite sanctuary the same political savvy which drove David. David installed a Mushite and an Aaronite as high priests in his central sanctuary and Jeroboam I established two national shrines at the northern and southern extremes of his realm, one of Mushite pedigree and the other of Aaronite. Cross does not account, however, for the subordination of Mushite cultic iconography implied by the preference for the calf.

The Affiliation of Zadok with Hebron

The final significant geographical affiliation of the priestly houses Cross makes is the claim that Hebron is an Aaronite city. The primary datum from which he makes this argument made is the apportioning of Hebron to the "sons of Aaron" in the Levitical Cities lists. Secondarily, Cross's association of Hebron with the Aaronites arises from his assertion that Zadok is an Aaronite affiliated with Hebron. Cross argues:

> There is much to commend the attachment of Zadok to the house of Aaron in Hebron and to the well-known shrine there where both David and Absalom were anointed king. In 1 Chronicles 12:27–29 in a notice purporting to list the members of the house of Aaron who rallied to David in Hebron, a certain Jehoiada (bearing a name later popular among the Zadokites) is listed as commander *(nagid)* of the Aaronid forces and with him an aide named Zadok. Such a connection between David and Zadok is precisely what we should expect, tying Zadok to David before the transfer of the capital to Jerusalem.[9]

In sum, Cross argues in the Mushite Hypothesis that Elon-bezaanannim in Kadesh-Naphtali in Upper Galilee is Mushite, as is Dan. Shiloh in the central hill country is Mushite, but Bethel just ten miles to the south is Aaronite. Hebron, nineteen miles south of Jerusalem, is Aaronite, as well, but Arad at the southern tip of the Dead Sea is Mushite. His results present a picture of Mushite and Aaronite cultic sites scattered throughout Palestine. In Cross's model, there is no perceptible pattern or arrangement of cultic sites nor of the affiliations of the priests who served them.

TRIBAL POLITICS IN THE UNITED MONARCHY

As it is described in the Deuteronomistic History, unifying the tribes of Israel and Judah required judicious navigation of an array of issues besetting the tribes. First and foremost was the ever-present Philistine threat, of particular concern to the Judahite, Benjaminite, and Ephraimite territories. For these tribes boarding Philistine territory, their survival and livelihoods depended on maintaining strength enough to hold their powerful neighbor in check. Of course, each tribe had its own set of localized practices with respect to economy, security, and cult, as well as concerns related to each of these. David's effort at statecraft succeeded in so far as he navigated and appeased this collection of concerns. That the United Monarchy soon began to hemorrhage and eventually to disintegrate shows that all of these localized concerns were not mitigated effectively for long. Though the narrative is not forthcoming about the specific religious and cultic aspects of the divisions, the stories of unification and disintegration nonetheless expose traces of some of the divisions David's effort at statecraft sought to mollify.

Tribal and Geographical Factors in the Formation of the United Monarchy

The capture of Jerusalem is of unparalleled importance in the unification of Israel and Judah. This central position provided certain strategic advantage, but even more, as the Deuteronomistic Historian tells the story, it removed a significant and previously impenetrable Jebusite stronghold at the border between southern Benjamin and northern Judah (2 Sam 5:6–9). For the purposes of the present discussion, two locations of cultic and administrative significance just prior to the establishment of Jerusalem shed important light on the cultic and administrative currents David had to navigate on the path to unification in Jerusalem.

Kiryat Yearim

The settlement of Kiryat Yearim sat on the border between Judah and Benjamin (Josh 15:9) and was claimed as Judahite territory (18:14–15). This town rose to prominence as the home of the Ark of the Covenant after its capture from Shiloh (1 Sam 4:1–11), sojourn with the Philistines (5:1–12), its divinely initiated recovery (6:1–18), and its twenty-year settlement in Judah

(6:19–7:2). Its prominence as a significant locale within Judah is remembered in Psalm 132:6, which describes excitement about Yahweh's enthronement in Zion spilling out both just to the north of Jerusalem in Kiryat Yearim (there called שׂדי יער)[10] and in Ephrath, between Bethlehem and Hebron.

Three times when mentioning the locale of Kiryat Yearim, the book of Joshua offers clarification about the name.

Joshua 15:9

The boundary extends from the top of the mountain to the spring of the Waters of Nephtoah, and from there to the towns of Mount Ephron; then the boundary bends around to Baalah—that is, Kiryat Yearim (ותאר הגבול בעלה היא קרית יערים).

Joshua 15:60

Kiryat Baal—that is, Kiryat Yearim (קרית בעל היא קרית יערים)

Joshua 18:14

And it ends at Kiryat Baal (that is, Kiryat Yearim), a town belonging to the tribe of Judah (והיו תצאתיו אל קרית בעל היא קרית יערים עיר בני יהודה)

This association of Kiryat Yearim with Baal and Israelite appropriations of Baalistic tradition into the conception of Yahweh have been explored and discussed widely. This has been treated quite definitively in the work of C. L. Seow. Seow has argued that the veneration of Yahweh at Kiryat Yearim would have demonstrated an affinity for a feisty warrior God who was on the rise against enemies, rather than an established or otiose divine king. Thus, David's procession of the Ark from its twenty-year sojourn at Kiryat Yearim was a brilliantly calculated and orchestrated appropriation of the divine warrior myth. "Yahweh was more like Ba'l—a god for whom kingship was a status to be gained through the eventual defeat of the enemies."[11] This same is true of David. The Divine Warrior now established as king of the Cosmos has chosen David as his anointed leader in the newly captured capital, Jerusalem, to rule over the newly established kingdom extending from Dan to Beersheba.

By and large, the Deuteronomistic Historian downplays the importance of Kiryat Yearim for the central cult David established.[12] The Baalistic elements Seow describes at length are all buried beneath a veneer of the establishment Yahwism of the Deuteronomistic History in its various iterations. However, one list of officials in David's court survives, offering tantalizing details about the continued importance of Kiryat Yearim and its particular cult. Second Samuel 20:25b–26 offers an account of the names of officials in the

Jerusalem court. "Zadok and Abiathar were priests; and Ira the Yairite was also David's priest (עירא היארי היה כהן לדוד)."

Who was this "Ira the Yairite," and why would he be listed alongside the high priests Zadok and Abiathar?[13] A comparable listing of a third priestly official may also be found among the court officials of Solomon in 1 Kings 4:4b–5. "Zadok and Abiathar were priests; Azariah son of Nathan was over the officials (על הנצבים); Zabud son of Nathan was priest and king's friend (וזבוד בן נתן כהן רעה המלך)." In both cases, the high priests are named followed by a third priest—Ira or Zabud—who is described in special relationship to the king. The particular details offered, merely לדוד and רעה המלך, are too scant and too ambiguous to parse at length. Yet, it would seem to imply that Ira and Zabud held some manner of special role in the court, and that this role was different in its character from the office of the high priest. In the case of Zabud, his patronymic establishes his relationship to a certain Nathan. While specific identification of this Nathan is not beyond all doubt, the most likely candidate is the prophet Nathan, who informed David of the scheming of Adonijah and who presided at the coronation of Solomon.[14] This same Nathan's son, Azariah was chief of the deputies (על הנצבים) and it would follow that Zabud also had a high-ranking advisory position encompassed by the designation רעה המלך. The similarity in syntax between the descriptions of Zabud and Ira compels one to conclude that Ira, too, was a high-ranking priestly official in David's court, who by his own actions or those of his kindred had proven himself useful in the king's rise to power.

The description of Ira as היארי is a *hapax legomenon*. The root *y'r* yields no compelling cognates, as any relationship to the Nile (יאר) makes little sense. There are, however, two further intriguing possibilities. 2 Samuel 23:24–39 (|| 1 Chr 11:26–47) contains the list of David's "Thirty" (actually thirty-seven) valiant heroes, and named among them is a certain Ira the Ithrite (עירא היתרי) (v. 38). The Ithrite (היתרי) clan is mentioned in 1 Chr 2:53 as one of the clans from Kiryat Yearim. Though there is no substantial text critical evidence to suggest an emendation to היתרי[15] in 2 Sam 20:26, the fact remains that it seems quite unlikely that there is both an *Ira the Yairite* (היארי) and an *Ira the Ithrite* (היתרי) in David's retinue.

Alternatively, the possibility exists that the singularly occurring היארי is a misspelling not of the Ithrite clan, but evidence of a quiesced or misheard *ayin*, and that the intended form was actually היערי. Though a gentilic form from יער is also not attested elsewhere, it would follow that היערי would be a logical and grammatically cogent form for a person hailing from Kiryat Yearim (קרית יערים).

Either way, this Ira, priest and vizier to David, is likely connected to the cult of Kiryat Yearim in the northern reaches of Judah. It seems quite reasonable that a cultic official so positioned would have played an instrumental role in the development of the mythological and liturgical framework of David's emerging cult. The Baalistic theme of an emerging warrior king making a triumphal procession into the new seat of kingship is the sort of liturgical display one might expect from a priest from Kiryat Yearim/Kiryat Ba'al. Though Ira never realizes a place as high priest in the newly established Jerusalem cult, he was positioned to be a key transitional figure in the emergence of the new cultic and administrative realities of the United Monarchy. As such, the priestly triad of Abiathar, Zadok, and Ira mentioned in 2 Sam 20:25b–26 mirrors the priestly triad of Moses, Aaron, and Samuel in Ps 99:6 discussed later in this chapter.

Hebron

Above, I reviewed the evidence presented by Cross for the association of Zadok with Hebron and the Aaronite tradition. The evidence is not all one would desire for establishing this connection so central to the Mushite Hypothesis. The identification of Hebron as an Aaronite site hangs on the appropriation of Judahite and Benjaminite cities to the Aaronites in the Levitical Cities lists. I will discuss these list in further detail later in this chapter. The nature of the evidence presented in these lists must be weighed judiciously because as a whole these lists present a utopian vision of the geography of Palestine and the priestly holdings within it. However utopian the vision of the Levitical Cities lists might be, it is a utopianism filtered through a lens with a distinctly Judahite hue. While the extent to which the information maps to a historical reality at any given point is still largely up for debate, the broad contours of the information presented with respect to Judah and Benjamin might be taken with somewhat more confidence. These lists envision and attend a cult marked by Aaronite hegemony, a hegemony actualized in the post-Solomonic Judahite monarchy and enshrined as the ideal in later texts. The utopian flights of fancy described in the north and in the far periphery are not attained in the Judahite territory in closer proximity to the immediate concerns of the list. Cross is not alone in his optimism about the reliability of the Levitic Cities lists concerning the Aaronite nature of Hebron. Haran, whose understanding of the priestly associations of various shrines differs widely from the view of Cross, also sees Hebron as an ancient and prestigious Aaronite sanctuary from which Zadok hailed.[16]

The second facet of Cross's affiliation of Zadok with an Aaronite Hebron is based on a pattern of the name Jehoiada appearing in relationship with Zadok. A person named Jehoiada rallied to David's aid in Hebron in 1 Chronicles 12:27–29, and as contemporaries, the possibility exists that this Jehoiada and Zadok were related to one other. Elsewhere, the name Jehoiada appears as a kindred of Zadok in 1 Kgs 1:8, 26, 32, 38, 44; 2:35; and 4:4.

That Hebron and its environs play an important role in the foundation of the monarchy is beyond refute. It is at Hebron that David ascends to the throne; it is at Bethlehem just to the north that Samuel anoints David as king; and it is to Hebron that Absalom goes to proclaim himself king after fulfilling vows to Yahweh (2 Sam 15). The cultic officials at Hebron and environs would matter to the fledgling monarchy. However, it should be noted that it is Samuel (whose priestly pedigree springs from his association with the Mushite sanctuary at Shiloh) who anoints David in Bethlehem. Further, there is no explicit mention of the direct involvement of priests or other cultic officials with the coronation of Absalom in Hebron.

Saul Olyan has challenged Cross's assertion of Zadokite and Aaronite associations with Hebron and has suggested that it was a native Hebronite priestly faction there that played a significant role in the politics of David's accession and Absalom's revolt, namely, the Calebites. The Calebites were a Judahite tribe (Num 34:19) whom Moses and Joshua granted a special possession of land identified as Hebron (Judges 1:20 and Josh 14:13–14). The nature of this land grant is clarified in Josh 21:12 as involving not the city of Hebron itself nor the pasture lands around it, but rather "the fields of the city and its villages (ואת שדה העיר ואת חצריה נתנו לכלב בן יפנה באחזתו)." That is, the Calebites appear to have been a prominent land-holding group in Judahite affairs. Olyan connects the character of Ira the Jairite (discussed above in 3.2.1.1), a priest in David's court, with Hebron and the Calebites there. He offers three pieces of evidence for this connection. First, Olyan assumes that the gentilic adjective היתרי applied to Ira in 2 Sam 23:38 and 1 Chr 11:40 is indeed the preferred description of Ira and that this associates Ira with the "South Calebite Levitical city" Jattir mentioned in proximity to Hebron in Josh 21:14.[17] Olyan speculates that Jattir is "Calebite," though this speculations runs contrary to the plain sense of v. 14, which designates Jattir as an Aaronite priestly possession and, it would seem, not part of the Calebite possessions. Second, Olyan draws a connection between the adjective היתרי and the character of Jethro, the Midianite priest and father-in-law of Moses. This would imply that the priesthood as it exists at Jattir is related to the Midian priesthood. Finally, Olyan draws a connection between the character of Heber the Kenite and the city name Hebron. From these three points, he argues that the sanctuary of Hebron is served by an order of Calebite priests tracing their lineage to the Kenite/Midianite priesthood and maintaining some tradition/memory of Jethro as a priestly progenitor. Olyan further speculates that the Calebite priesthood at Hebron took a special role in the coronation of Absalom in defiance of David, Abiathar, and Zadok. He writes:

The success of Absalom's attempted coup depended on the support of a major priestly clan and neither the Zadokite Aaronids nor the Shilonites patronized this

cause. One or more of the Kenite clans were probably involved. The appointment of Ira the Ithrite could well have been an attempt on the part of David to
conciliate the Calebites and at the same time serve to lessen regional and clan
rivalries among the priesthoods of the United Monarchy. Through Abiathar, the
interest of northern Mushites were presented; southern Aaronid interests were
personified in Zadok and final, through Ira, the interest of the Kenite priesthoods
in Caleb and possible north Judah were represented.[18]

Olyan's proposal poses several problems. The linguistic connection between
the proper name Heber the Kenite and the toponym Hebron raises interesting
possibilities; however, it does seem quite strained. There is a Heber mentioned
in 1 Chr 8:17 who is not a Calebite or even a Judahite, but a Benjaminite, and
there is another Heber mentioned in Gen 46:17 who is an Asherite. The fact
that the Heber in question is described as הקיני also poses a serious problem
for the proposed association with Jethro through the toponym Jattir. As will
be discussed in 5.3.1–5.3.2 in E, the person identified as "father-in-law of
Moses" (חתן משה) is named Jethro and he is a Midianite; likewise, in J, חתן משה,
whether he is named Hobab or Reuel, is also a Midianite.[19] In contrast, in
Judg 1:16 and 4:11 there are Kenite descendants of Hobab (חבב חתן משה) who
migrate throughout the Cis-Jordan. It is only in the Judges text (not in J or E)
that these characters who are elsewhere Midianites become Kenites, and the
name of the Midianite-*cum*-Kenite ancestor in Judges is Hobab not Jethro. It
is not clear that there was ever a tradition in which a character named Jethro
was a Kenite. Finally, the association of the typonym Jattir (yattîr or yattir)
with the gentilic *hayyitrî* poses a modest problem. One might expect in place
of *yitrî* the form *yattirî* to describe one hailing from a locality called Jattir.[20]

Without imagining the machinations of a class of Calebite priests and their
vacillating support for David's rise to power, it is far more straightforward to
account for Calebite support from the United Monarchy arising from David's
strategic marriage to the widow of the Calebite chieftain, Nabal.[21] There is no
mention of priestly involvement with or support for Absalom's revolt against
David. Absalom himself indicates to David that his intention is to travel to
Hebron to worship Yahweh (עבדתי את יהוה, 2 Sam 15:9), but no other characters are named as involved with this worship. Calebite involvement in the
uprising is not mentioned explicitly either. Finally, it is not at all clear that
a politically strategic response to the Absalom revolt would be for David to
bring into his inner circle a new priest of a faction that recently facilitated
a coup against him. The Calebite population of Hebron certainly plays an
important role in the ascendancy of David, but this role is not through a
Kenite/Calebite Ira. The sacerdotal interests of Hebron and environs are
embodied in the character of Zadok.

Tribal and Geographical Factors in the Fall of the United Monarchy

The Deuteronomistic Historian does not describe Absalom's southern-focused revolt as having had religious motivations or cultic consequences. In Jerusalem, David enlists Abiathar and Zadok as well as their sons to inquire of Yahweh on his behalf as the revolt developed and to act as informants for him (2 Sam 15:24–29, 17:15–20).[22] Beyond passing mention of Absalom's intent to pay vows and to worship Yahweh in Hebron (15:7–9), the cult and its leaders in Hebron show no signs of involvement with the revolt. The passivity of the local Aaronite clergy in Hebron and environs is not surprising, given that Zadok, one of their own, had recently risen to the high priesthood in David's Jerusalem. The first revolt against the United Monarchy did not damage the delicate religious garment David so masterfully wove, but it would not take long for the fabric to unravel under the stress and heat of tribal politics. For present purposes, I will describe three aspects of cultic and administrative significance which expose the seams in David's unified polity and provide important details about the constituent parts of the unified kingdom and cult.

The Expulsion of Abiathar

As David lay on his deathbed in the company of Abishag, Adonijah conspired to take control of the kingdom. Joab, the commander of David's army, and Abiathar cast their lot with Adonijah's plan to succeed his father[23] while Zadok, Nathan, and David's other advisors withheld their support. When Solomon secured the throne for himself he ordered the executions of Adonijah (1 Kings 2:25) and Joab (2:34) by the hand of Benaiah son of Jehoiada. However, Solomon spared the life of Abiathar. Rather than dispatching Benaiah to deliver a message, Solomon himself spoke with Abiathar.

1 Kings 2:26–27

The king said to the priest Abiathar, "Go to Anathoth, to your own field; for you are doomed to die. But I will not put you to death this day, because you carried the ark of the Lord GOD before my father David, and because you shared in all the hardships my father endured."

Of the two reasons offered for sparing his Abiathar's life, the first is the more puzzling. Solomon refused to execute Abiathar because of his priestly service rendered before the Ark of the Covenant. In other biblical narratives, improper priestly service in proximity to the Ark warranted immediate death executed by God (Lev 10:1–7 and 2 Sam 6:7). However, here it appears that for Abiathar proper service before the Ark is salvific in so far as it restrains Solomon's judgement and helps him to avoid the fate of the co-conspirators.

Solomon's words to Abiathar raise further questions about why Abiathar would have a field at Anathoth. The Deuteronomistic History makes clear that Abiathar is connected with the house of Eli at Shiloh in 1 Kings 2:27, where the banishment of Abiathar is understood to fulfill the prophecy about the downfall of the Elide line. Abiathar is further connected to the town of Nob through his father Ahimelek (1 Sam 21:1; 22:9, 11, 19). Nob is located in the vicinity of Anathoth just a few miles north of Jerusalem.[24] In the Levitical Cities lists Anathoth—as are all Benjaminite sites—is assigned to the Aaronites in Josh 21:18 and 1 Chr 6:45. As addressed below in 4.4 the antiquity of this association is dubious, and it would appear that the Benjaminite region was quite thoroughly Mushite, extending to the area immediately adjacent to Jerusalem and up to the Aaronite settlement of Kiryat Yearim in the west.

Martin Cohen has argued that Solomon dispatched Joab, Adonijah, and Abiathar as he did to eliminate the threats in ways appropriate to the nature of the particular threats posed.

> They were simply not to be trusted, not only because of their support of Adonijah, but because of their institutional associations. They were part of the old guard leadership. Solomon killed the powerful Joab; the Bible indicates that it was done on David's advice. He banished Abiathar and the rest of the Shilonites to Anathoth. He did not kill them, he explained, because they had borne the ark of Yahweh. Most likely this lame argument concealed the political reality that because of their connection with the ideology of Yahwism, the Shilonites could still command vast loyalty and sympathy among the populace of Israel. Destroying them was certain to arouse even greater disaffection than their deposition.[25]

For Solomon, and to an extent for the Deuteronomistic Historian, Abiathar represented a dangerous problem that had to be solved. There is even a hint of Deuteronomistic condemnation of Abiathar in an appearance of the list of officers in David's service. 2 Samuel 20:25b–26 lists the significant priestly confidants of David as Abiathar, Zadok, and Ira. In 2 Sam 8:17–18 this same accounting takes on a different tone. "Zadok son of Ahitub and Ahimelech son of Abiathar were priests . . . and David's sons were priests (וצדוק בן אחיטוב ואחימלך בן אביתר כהנים . . . ובני דוד כהנים היו)." The switch of the names Abiathar and Ahimelek here is most frequently treated as a simple text critical problem.[26] However, the tone of the passage warrants additional consideration of this simple error. Whereas 2 Sam 20:26 and 1 Kings 4:4b–5 list the secondary priests Ira and Zabud as priests in the royal retinue, here David's sons are identified as priests.[27] The Deuteronomistic Historian's disapproval of the appointment of laity to the priesthood is palpable in its description of Jeroboam I performing the same action in 1 Kings 12:31. That here David is accused of some part of the sin of Jeroboam and that David's chosen (Mushite) priest, Abiathar, is misidentified could well be understood as a subtle slight to the memory of Abiathar's role in the Davidic co-high-priesthood. Here David and key aspects of the clergy serving in his cult are parodied by a voice in the pro-Solomonic (and hence, pro-Aaronite) camp.

The expulsion of Abiathar from Jerusalem fits into a pattern of antagonism between Solomon and priests in the north. In 1 Kgs 11:29–39, Ahijah from Shiloh delivers his prophecy to Jeroboam I condemning Solomon and the Jerusalem priesthood for a long list of cultic offences. Ahijah's message portends the rise of Jeroboam and the end of unified kingdom and cult.

The Sale of the Asherite Cabul

Another significant affront of the Solomonic regime to Northern Israel—and particularly to the priests serving there—is the sale of the Cabul region to King Hiram of Tyre in 1 Kgs 9:10–14.[28] Joshua 9:24–27 identifies a locality called Cabul within the domain of the northwestern coastal Tribe of Asher. The Joshua text implies that Cabul is a city. However, in 1 Kings 9:11 and 13 the ironic name the Land of Cabul (ארץ כבול) is applied to twenty cities in the Land of Galilee. This moniker would seem to derive from Hiram of Tyre's denigrating comment about the quality of the city offered in return for his generosity in supplying materials for Solomon's building projects.[29] Solomon sold this territory and in so doing dispatched a significant portion of the Asherite territory adjacent to the Tyrian border. Baruch Halpern has observed that the sale of the Cabul region would have included three or four cities appropriated to the Gershonites (Mushites) in the Levitical Cities lists: Abdon, Rehob, Mishal, and perhaps, Hekath. "Their loss meant the loss of one third of the Gershonite cities, a blow of no small proportions to the clan prestige."[30] Halpern's observation rests on the historical reliability of the information in the Levitical Cities lists as it pertains to the northern territories. Whether such a large portion of northern levitical cities were lost in this transaction, the sale of any such cities by the central Jerusalem administration would be an affront to the geographical integrity of the Northern polities and to any priesthoods serving in that region. Such an affront betrays Solomon's distinctly Judahite- and Jerusalem-focused priorities.

Samuel, Zadok, and Abiathar

Psalm 99 is among a set of texts often designated as "Enthronement Psalms."[31] Like others in this category, this psalm offers praise of Yahweh as king enthroned on the cherubim (v. 1), seated in Zion (v. 2) which is also his footstool (v. 4), and establishing justice in the world (v. 4). In the closing part of the psalm, vv. 6–9, there is a shift from the prescription of praise to remembering the actions of Yahweh in Israelite history. In vv. 6–7a key cultic officials are named and their interactions with Yahweh are described.

משה ואהרן בכהניו ושמואל בקראי שמו
קראים אל יהוה והוא יענם בעמוד ענן ידבר אליהם
שמרו עדתיו וחק נתן למו

Moses and Aaron are among his priests, and Samuel among those who call on his name.
They call to the LORD, and he answers them, in the pillar of cloud he speaks to them.
They observed his commandments and he gave them the statue(s).

Moses, Aaron, and Samuel are all grouped together here as the ideal and archetypal priests. The semantic difference between, on the one hand, Moses and Aaron who are "among his priests" (בכהניו) and, on the other hand, Samuel who is "among those who call on his name" (בקראי שמו) is leveled by the synonymous parallelism of the two lines. That is, both phrases describe the same functions without any obvious differentiation or distinction between them. There is no implied contrast in the categories. They are all priests.[32] All three figures—Moses, Aaron, and Samuel—are the implied subject of קראים אל יהוה, and they are all three the recipients of Yahweh's response (יענם and ידבר אליהם). While elsewhere in the Hebrew Bible one need not be a priest to "call" (קרא) on Yahweh's name, the specific action in view here in this psalm so focused on the temple is that of "priestly mediation."[33] Peter Mommer argues that the Deuteronomistic Historian appropriates a memory of Moses's intercessory role into its understanding of Samuel.[34] Echoes of this tradition may also be found in Jer 15:1, where Moses and Samuel both intercede before Yahweh on behalf of the people.

For the Deuteronomistic Historian, Samuel is a transitional figure whose priesthood began in Shiloh, but who took on a role theretofore unknown in Israelite history. Samuel exercised authority as a pan-Israelite/Judahite leader holding authority from "Dan to Beer-Sheba" (1 Samuel 3:20). Indeed, Samuel dispatched his children to administer in Beer-Sheba in the south of Judah (1 Sam 8:2). DtH portrays Samuel as laying the foundation for the rise of the monarchy generally, and for David's cultic organization of the United

Monarchy. The Shilonite priest Samuel exercised authority to anoint David king at Hebron far away from his original sphere of influence. The syncretism of David's priesthood was such that that historical boundaries of priestly activity were redefined. David himself took on priestly activities, wearing the ephod (2 Sam 6:14) and installing his own progeny as priests (2 Sam 8:18). The redactor of the Deuteronomistic History was quite uncomfortable with this fluidity in the early monarchy and parodies it in its comments about David's promiscuous ordinations describing these activities in the same terms reserved for the activity of Jeroboam I (1 Kings 12:31). Samuel embodies the same manner of charismatic flexibility exercised by David as architect of the United Monarchy. Indeed, it was Samuel who laid the foundation for the monarchy politically, ideologically, and cultically.[35]

As such, it is significant that in Psalm 99:6 Samuel is placed on the level of Moses and Aaron as the foundational priests of the Jerusalem cult. The status of Samuel *vis-à-vis* Moses and Aaron in Psalm 99:6 mirrors the status of Ira *vis-à-vis* Abiathar and Zadok in 2 Sam 20:25b–26. As such, the perspective of Psalm 99 differs significantly from the voice of the redaction of the Deuteronomistic History critical of Abiathar and of his key place within the Jerusalem cult of David's United Monarchy (2 Sam 8:17–18).

OTHER LOCI OF PRIESTLY ACTIVITY AND CONFLICT IN ANCIENT ISRAEL

In this section, I will discuss two additional cultic sites in ancient Israel not addressed in the prior section: Shechem and Bethel. Of particular interest is the overlap between the political/geographical bifurcation of Israel and the key cultic personnel and the iconography associated with priests at these locations. Observations about the origin, antiquity, and memory of the earliest priestly and geographical divisions of the Israelite tribes shed new light on their broader affiliations with the Israelite priesthood.

Shechem

Shechem stands out among all other Cis-Jordanian cultic sites as being the only locale where Moses himself describes ritual/priestly activities taking place (Deut 11:30 and 27:9–15). Moses commands the construction of an altar of unhewn stones and plaster on Mt. Ebal (Deut 27:4–8), and Joshua fulfills Moses command, building this altar in Josh 8:30–32. At the covenant ceremony to take place on Mounts Ebal and Gerizim, the Levites are to announce prescribed blessings and curses marking entry into the Promised Land. Its role in the Patriarchal narratives and its significant place in the scope of Deuteronomy notwithstanding, Shechem does not figure largely in the stories of the cultic and political sagas of the Deuteronomistic History. However, its importance in the stability of the United Monarchy is betrayed by two references in the division narrative in 1 Kings 12. Rehoboam visits Shechem in v. 1, where he is crowned king of the northern territories. In v. 25 Jeroboam I does not simply visit Shechem, but (re)builds the city and resides there for a time. That these kings attempting to garner northern Israelite support would devote time and resources in Shechem speaks to the strategic significance and regional sway the site holds.[36]

The importance of Shechem was not solely cultic. Archaeological evidence from Tell Balâṭa shows an active center in the Middle and Late Bronze Ages and its persistence with gradual decline as a city of modest significance into the time of the monarchy. J. David Schloen has described the role of Shechem in Iron I positioned along caravan routes into the central hill country. In particular, he notes the movement and presence of Midianites in the region.[37] Mark Leuchter sees within this economic relationship at an interreligious site a prime occasion for the emergence of a group of priest-saints to mediate potential conflicts. He writes: "If trade at Shechem invited the need for sacral license and covenant-making among different groups, Mushite priest-saints would be suitable agents to carry this out among Midianite-Kenite caravaners who traversed the site."[38] The connection of Mushites to other Midianites at Arad plays a significant role in Cross's Mushite Hypothesis and I surveyed that evidence in chapter 2. We find in Shechem a place where both the memory of Moses and the social conditions that give way to a group like the Levites/Mushites converge.

Bethel

Bethel necessarily plays a significant role in the discussion of divisions in the ancient Israelite priesthood because Jeroboam I chose this locale along with Dan as the sites for his northern national shrines. Cross understood Bethel to be an Aaronite sanctuary, and, as such, he understood the iconography of the Golden Calf to be at home in Bethel. By endorsing the veneration of Yahweh with the iconography of the Golden Calf as a feature of the nascent national cult, Jeroboam was merely affirming iconography with an established history at Bethel. This differs from what Cross understood Jeroboam to be doing at Dan. As a Mushite sanctuary with ties to the stories of Jonathan son of Gershom son of Moses (Judg 18:30), Jeroboam imported iconography previously unknown there. From this perspective, Jeroboam's actions accomplish two things. Like David, he sought to build a coalition of Mushites and Aaronites in his reformed cult by elevating a site affiliated with each clan to the position of state-cult. Second, Jeroboam sought to appeal to currents desiring the veneration of Yahweh through the symbol of the calf which the E tradition affiliates with Aaron. Indeed, Cross sees within the narratives critical of Aaron a polemic against the Aaronite priesthood at Bethel.[39]

The picture Cross and Halpern paint of the reform cult of Jeroboam raises certain questions about its political coherence. If the Aaronite bull were installed at Mushite Dan and presumably clergy with it, how would one appease the established priesthood there? If Aaronite Bethel was allowed to keep its established iconography, was Dan allow to co-venerate its native iconography alongside the calf? There emerges in this picture a marked inequality and favoritism for the Aaronites and their symbols. Was Jeroboam so foolish as to succumb immediately to the southern myopia that afflicted Solomon and brought down Rehoboam?

These problems are largely resolved if one assumes that Bethel was originally a Mushite sanctuary, not Aaronite. I argue that Jeroboam did not try to create a shadow of David's Mushite/Aaronite cult in Jerusalem with a Mushite Dan and an Aaronite Bethel. Rather, Jeroboam sought to re-create David's synthesized Jerusalem cult at two historically Mushite sanctuaries. Jeroboam mimicked the cultic innovation of David in the melding of Aaronite and Mushite traditions, and presumably in installing Aaronite and Mushite priests at both Dan and Bethel. Like David, Jeroboam sought to create a unified pan-Israelite cult. Unlike David, he envisioned this cult with sanctuaries located at the northern and southern ends of his realm and more accessible to the general populace.

This is how Jeroboam came to be reviled by traditions both in the north (Ahijah, 1 Kings 14:1–18) and in the south (1 Kings 13:1–32). For the Aaronites in the central Jerusalem establishment, Jeroboam tore asunder the magnificent monarchy of David. In the same step he humiliated the Mushites in the North by forcing on them the veneration of the iconography of their more powerful rivals.

Is there evidence, then, of the Mushite character of Bethel? In Judges 20:25–28 there is an account of Phinehas, son of Eleazar, son of Aaron ministering before the Ark (עמד לפניו) while it resided in Bethel. The explicit association here of Phinehas as "Son of Aaron" would seem to intimate that Bethel possesses an ancient tradition of Aaronite priestly service. However, Phinehas here is not merely identified here as בן אהרן but also בן אלעזר. This locution is not the standard way of identifying Phinehas,[40] but the affiliation here with Eleazar is intriguing. In the E account of the genealogy of Moses, the names of Moses' sons are Gershom and Eliezer (אליעזר, Exod 18:3–4). That both Moses and Aaron would have sons of such similar names (indeed, graphically identical) betrays the equivalence of the traditions surrounding them, and it evinces the genealogical fluidity described in greater detail in ch. 4.[41]

To the ambiguity of Eliezer/Eleazar's paternity, we may also add that the name Phinehas (פינחס) itself has two significant connections to Moses and the Mushites. Phinehas is the name of one of Eli's sons who served as priests in the Mushite sanctuary at Shiloh. The name Phinehas is also conspicuously non-Semitic. Like Moses' own name, it is Egyptian in origin.[42] The term *Pa-nehesi* means "Nubian" or someone of dark skin.[43] This detail recalls the E account of Num 12 in which Aaron and Miriam speak against Moses on account of his Cushite wife, אשה כשית (v. 1).[44] That Phinehas is attested as the name of a Mushite priest active at Shiloh, that Phinehas' name is of Egyptian origin with a meaning that bears similarity to details in the E account of Moses' history, and that the father of this priestly Phinehas bears a name so similar to Moses' son all point to associating the name Phinehas with the Mushite priestly tradition.

Furthermore, if we affiliate Bethel and its priesthood with the Mushite tradition, a picture emerges of solidly Mushite territories in the north with Aaronite sites located only in north-central Judah. The only sites associated with Aaronite tradition are Hebron and environs (likely including Bethlehem) and extending up to Kiryat Yearim. The Mushite sites are Arad and Elon-Bezaanannim, Dan, Shechem, Shiloh, and Bethel.

THE LEVITICAL CITIES LISTS

The Levitical Cities lists found in Josh 21:1–42 and 1 Chr 6:39–66[45] record the systematic allocation of cities throughout Canaan to four groups of priests: the Aaronites, the Kohathites, the Gershonites/Gershomites, and the Merarites. These cities are to be given to the Levites from the territorial inheritances of the other tribes. In the Joshua account, the apportioning is conducted by the priest Eleazar and Joshua, and it takes place at the famous priestly city of Shiloh.[46] The list in Chronicles presents no such narrative framework. The lists differ from one another both in their organization and in a handful of details.

Efforts to understand the nature of the lists have been motivated by two desires. First, to know how the information preserved in the lists may be situated in the history of ancient Israel. That is, from what places and times in biblical history do the lists speak. Second, to understand how the information preserved in the lists relates to historical and geographical realities in ancient Palestine as may be known from other avenues of inquiry.

The scholarly commentary on and analysis of these lists is abundant. A full review of the history of scholarship on the Levitical Cities lists does not warrant space in this discussion, and indeed, such a review has been done quite comprehensively by Jeremy Hutton in 2011.[47] It will suffice here briefly to summarize Hutton's two principal findings in his detailed survey, and to expand briefly on his analysis.

The first point in Hutton's study relates to the aura of historical verisimilitude created by the lists, or as Hutton phrases it: "we occasionally catch glimpses of an apparently authentic historical reality."[48] This authenticity is found in the orientation of the cities found in the lists along the boundaries between the regional inheritance allocations to the Israelite tribes. That is, these priestly cities are located precisely in places where one would expect to find priestly enclaves, whose duties involve the mediation of tribal and intertribal disputes. The second result of Hutton's survey is his claim that the lists in their present forms are "fabrications designed in part to legitimize the Aaronid Priests of the Persian period."[49]

These carefully measured and politic statements are certainly borne out by all of the evidence available, and yet one is beset by the incongruity and irony of having ancient kernels of historical reality fixed within an impenetrable Persian period matrix. Are these texts really no more forthcoming than a Persian casemate wall backfilled with Iron I pottery shards? If so, is it still possible that one might find a potsherd of appreciable size and contour to fix within a known typological sequence?

Such a fragment of information exists in the allocation of cities in Judah to the Aaronite priests. These lists apportion the cities in the regions of Judah, Simeon, and Benjamin to the Aaronites, and cities in the northern regions to remaining levitical subgroups. Mark Leuchter sees the Levitical Cities list, and particularly the iteration of the list in Joshua 21 as a "site of memory."[50] Memory[51] operates in this text on three different levels: that of the Persian Period priests seeking to justify the Aaronite/Zadokite control of their present context; that of the priestly division operative in the period of the Monarchy; and that of a tribal pre-monarchy when the cultic lives of Israelites focused around local sanctuaries.[52]

The period of greatest interest for this study is the transition between the pre-monarchy and the monarchy. Investigation of this period is fraught, as even the most forthcoming of our literary sources originate, at best, in the monarchy itself, if not later. The period of exile notwithstanding, Jerusalem and southerly environs were served by some manner of Aaronite or Zadokite priesthood based there from the Monarchy onwards. The association of at least part of the Judahite region with the Aaronites in these lists should be understood as an authentic historical reflection of the continuity of Aaronite control of the northern Judahite hills and as far south as Mount Hebron.[53] Likewise, that the apportioning the cities in the Joshua account takes place at the hands of Eleazar and Joshua in the northern site of Shiloh (which is not historically Aaronite) betrays a lingering memory of regions outside of the historical Aaronite control. In other words, the "Persian period Eleazar" exercises authority at a location that an "Iron I period Eleazar" never could have. A similar "grab" for territory is found in the apportioning of cites in the areas of Benjamin and Ephraim to the Aaronites, pushing the boundaries of their historical domain just as at Shiloh.

The most significant point of critique of the historical value of the materials preserved in the Levitical Cities lists is the idealized visions they offer of the Levitical cities and their attendant grazing lands.[54] Identical allotments are made in every locality without regard for local topography and environmental factors. Such idealism is not necessarily late, but surely arose from a grandiose centralized vision of the greater Israel rather than from a position acquainted with the topographical and environmental realities present in each situation.

The region from the southern slopes of Mount Hebron through Ephrath and Bethlehem and continuing just to the north of Jerusalem forms a topologically unified region.[55] This elevated region sits along the central "spine" of the Judahite mountain range and is bounded by the decent from Mt. Hebron to the Negev in the south, and in the north by the more starkly punctuated hills of the Benjaminite and Southern Ephraimite region. In the period of the Divided Monarchy, the transition from the broad slopes of the central Judahite range into the punctuated hills of south Benjamin became the definition of the northern and southern polities. The Aaronites held authority in the Judahite center area over the long term of Israelite history—in their historical origins, in the consolidated Jerusalem cult, and even after the return from Exile.

To the extent that the Levitical Cities lists describe the Aaronite control of the Jerusalem-to-Hebron corridor, they are bound by realistic concerns and first-hand knowledge of the areas controlled. In those portions which the Levitical Cities lists describe territory beyond the borders of the Jerusalem-to-Hebron corridor, their idealism overtakes their accuracy.

PRIESTLY FUNCTIONARIES AND THEIR DOMAINS

In an important series of studies already surveyed, Jeremy Hutton has presented a sociological comparison of the social position and function of the Levites in Israel to cultic functionaries in the High Atlas Mountains.[56] Analyzing ethnographic work on the Ahansal, a group of *marabouts* active in Morocco, Hutton, it will be recalled, has proposed a collection of parallels between the groups. These parallels are found both in the political function of these holy men and related to this in the geographical distribution of the sites at which they operate. Appropriating the observations of Gellner's work on the Ahansal, Hutton postulates that the Israelite cultic sites are situated at ecological and topographical boundaries. He writes: "[t]his suggests that the distribution of the Levitical cities at the extremities of Israel, already noted by several scholars . . . might be correlated to the Levites' function as inter-tribal arbitrators distributing justice in the gates."[57] Sites of cultic significance emerge at frontiers where priests have settled to carry out certain mediating/priestly functions. The success or prestige of particular priestly houses depends on the success and power of the patron leaders whom the priestly houses serve.

Mark Leuchter has developed Hutton's idea into the notion of the "priest-saint," and explored it as a model for understanding the nature of the priesthood of Moses. In opposition to the idea that Moses was a priestly chieftain, whose authority was carried on by appointed heirs typically passed down to sons, Leuchter sees within Moses a different typology of authority and priestly charism.[58] The locations associated with these priest-saints—their sanctuaries, their sepulchers, and objects affiliated with them—emerge as centers to which other aspiring priest-saints may attach themselves. For Leuchter this is the genesis of the Mushite priesthood—priest-saints who attach themselves to sites with some localized memory of the activity of Moses and a legacy of this priestly functioning. The Levites, too, hail from the same stock, but in reaction to Mushites. In private correspondence, Leutcher clarified that the "Mushites were part of a clan that claimed lineage descent from Moses, while the Levites subsequently formed around them as a check against their power, recruiting Moses as a patron-saint rather than as a lineage founder."[59] The studies of Hutton and Leutcher suggest that priestly groups play an important role in mapping geographical unity, a unity which is defined by a collection of ecological and topographical factors in the long term, and political factors in the short term.

In her penetrating analysis of descriptions of the cult at Shiloh, Susan Ackerman attends to questions of the nature of cultic performance in that sanctuary and who has authority to conduct sacrifices.[60] Ackerman postulates that the cultic centers of ancient Israel fall into two categories: regional sanctuaries and state-sponsored temples. She asserts: "through the course of pre-exilic history, priests at ancient Israel's regional or provincial sanctuaries . . . were significantly divorced from the execution of these sanctuaries' sacrificial rituals, and this in contradistinction to the priests' engagement in these same sacrificial rituals at the large, state-sponsored temples."[61] Ackerman understands Shiloh as an example of one of these provincial sanctuaries. She argues that the collections of materials praising the virtue and importance of the Shiloh sanctuary[62] have their origins in the late seventh century and simply appropriate to Shiloh the sentiment and language Deuteronomy itself reserves for Jerusalem.[63]

While I would concede with Ackerman that the actual practice of sacrifice at Shiloh might well have been conducted according to the logic of a provincial sanctuary rather than a state-sponsored temple, it is difficult to maintain that the significance of Shiloh as a cultic site was merely that of a provincial sanctuary in the imagination of the Deuteronomistic History or of other voices in the Bible. That is, Shiloh might have been a minor provincial cultic site, but it is *remembered* by voices outside of those localized to the late seventh century as place of pan-Israelite significance. Beyond the central role of Shiloh in the narratives of 1–2 Samuel, Shiloh is the location from which Joshua assigns the Levitical Cities to the Israelite tribes. Though these cities lists are likely located in the Persian period, which undoubtedly saw Jerusalem as the center of the Israelite cult, Shiloh still retained such a memory of priestly importance and prestige that it serves as the setting for the priestly allotment so integral to the self-conception of the Persian period cult.[64]

Disagreement on the pan-Israelite importance of Shiloh aside, Ackerman's emphasis on the difference between regional and state-sponsored temples is of great importance. The dichotomy of central and peripheral is a constructive matrix in which to consider the institution of the Israelite priesthood and its evolution through time. David's choice of a central shrine in the center of the loosely federated polities of Israel and Judah was an effort to migrate the cultic foci of Israel and Judah into a single site. Sites once central within their independent domains we relegated to peripheral positions. This likely includes both Shiloh and Hebron. As the Deuteronomistic History presents the story, this migration to the central sanctuary was better tolerated in Judah where greater efforts were made on the part of the administration to appease the population and to enfranchise the priestly groups historically associated with the Judahite regions, namely the Aaronites.

Cross's account of the Mushite Hypothesis envisions the random geographic distribution of the rival priestly lines. In it, Mushite and Aaronite towns sit side by side, without regard for the larger environment in which the priests function, and with no accounting for how the priests maintain authority and significance beyond their cultic service at shrines. The analysis above has more carefully delineated the limits of Aaronite influence as historically seated in the mountainous region of Judah from the rise of Mount Hebron in the south to the northern environs of Jerusalem at Kiryat Yearim. This region comes to define "the center."[65] For David and Solomon, for the Deuteronomistic Historian, for the Persian period writers and beyond, it is the center for the cult and the chosen cultic officials. It is the center for political administration in the United Monarchy, the Southern Kingdom, and the Persian period. The other regions, from the block in the north and even to displaced sites like Arad, are relegated to the periphery. The Aaronites hold the center, and the Mushites the periphery.

CONCLUSION

In the discussion above, I have presented detailed evaluation of the priestly narratives and affiliations of the sites of Kiryat Yearim, Hebron, Anathoth, Bethel, and Shechem. The analysis has shown that Kiryat Yearim and Hebron display a collection of affinities and connections to the politics and religious policies of the establishment cult of the Davidic and Solomonic periods, that is, to the policies favorable to a centralize Aaronite priesthood. On the other hand, Bethel, Anathoth, and Shechem display connections to the Mushites. Building on Cross's earlier work correlating the concerns of Elon-bezaanannim, Shiloh, Dan, and Arad with the Mushites, a picture emerges of a solidly Aaronite north-central Judah and a completely Mushite north, with at least one Mushite locale in the southern periphery. This picture is also borne out with the analysis of the Levitical Cities lists when read with attention to the "memory" of the texts. Finally, in light of the geographical distribution of cultic centers, I have suggested that the designations of "northern" and "southern"—while still appropriate for describing political realities, with respect to the cult are better understood as "central" and "peripheral."

NOTES

1. *CMHE*, 200.

2. Aharoni and Amiran, "Arad: A Biblical City," 43–53; Idem., "Excavations at Tel Arad: Preliminary Report of the First Season," *IEJ* 14 (1964): 131–147; Y. Aharoni, "Excavations at Tel Arad: Preliminary Report of the Second Season." *IEJ* 17 (1967). 233–249: "'Arad: Its Inscriptions and Temple," *BA* 31 (1968): 2–32.

3. The identification of this unnamed priestly ancestor is a matter of contention. Others contend that Moses is not the referent here, but rather Levi. The text of Deut 18:5 is striking similar to 1 Sam 2:28. "It is Levi [the clear referent of בו] Yahweh chose from all of your tribes to serve and to administer in the name of Yahweh, he and his sons . . . (כי בו בחר יהוה אלהיך מכל שבטיך לעמד לשרת בשם יהוה הוא ובניו כל הימי). See, for example, Jürg Hutzli, *Die Erzählung von Hanna und Samuel: textkritische und literarische Analyse von 1. Samuel 1–2 unter Berücksichtigung des Kontextes, ATANT 89* (Zurich: Theologischer Verlag, 2007), 169. Walter Dietrich, *1 Samuel 1–12,* BKAT 8.1 (Neukirchen–Vluyn, Germany: Neukirchener, 2011), 148. The similarity of the description of the priestly ancestors notwithstanding, it should be noted that there is no known story where Levi is the recipient of divine revelation while in Egypt.

4. *CMHE*, 202.

5. Ibid., 207.

6. Richard Nelson sees the dynastic succession of Zadok over Eli to be a redactional trope, emphasizing what is truly important to the Deuteronomist, namely "dynastic promise and royal obedience and disobedience" (p. 188). In this way, the

transfer of *priestly* role is not in focus so much as merely the transfer of power. This reading follows Nelson's broader program which understands the Deuteronomist to be uninterested in matters of priest and cult. Richard D. Nelson, "The Role of the Priesthood in the Deuteronomistic History," in *Reconsidering Israel and Judah: Recent Studies on the Deuteronomistic History*, ed. Gary N. Knoppers and J. Gordon McConville (Winona Lake, IN: Eisenbrauns, 2000): 179–193.

7. Ibid., 199.

8. Ibid.

9. *CMHE*, 214–215.

10. Here called the "fields of Ya'ar," though perhaps better to understand it as the "hills of Ya'ar" on analogy with "the hills of Moab" (שדי מואב/שדה מואב) in Gen 36:35; Num 21:20; Ruth 1:1–2, 6, 22; 2:6; 4:3; 1 Chr 1:46; 8:8. Hebrew *śadeh* cognate to Akkadian *šadū*, "mountain." Kiryat Yearim is located in the vicinity of where the central Judean mountain ridge begins to give way to the punctuated Ephraimite hills.

11. C.L. Seow, *Myth, Drama, and the Politics of David's Dance* (Atlanta, GA: Scholars Press, 1989), 208.

12. Mark Leuchter explores the the history and significant of the Baal-*cum*-Yahwistic cult at Kiryat Yearim in his insightful essay, Mark Leuchter, "The Cult at Kiriath Yearim: Implications for the Biblical Record," *VT* 58 (2008): 526–43. In this essay he posits that the cult there was Aaronite (533–4, 541).

13. Rodney K. Duke, "Ira" *ABD* 3:446.

14. It is possible, though unlikely, that the Nathan referred to here is David's son by Bathsheba mentioned in 2 Sam 5:14, 1 Chr 3:5 and 14:4, and thus is Solomon's full-blooded brother. If this is the case, the phrase רעה המלך for a member of the king's own family is highly enigmatic.

15. Though the Syriac does, indeed, read *ytyr*, *Ithrite*.

16. Menachem Haran, "Levitical Cities, II," 161. Compare also to the view of Albright that Zadok was an Aaronite, in Albright, *Archaeology and the Religion of Israel*, 110.

17. Olyan, "Zadok's Origins," 191.

18. Ibid., 193.

19. Numbers 10:29.

20. In contrast, if *hayyitrî* is to denote a relationship to Jethro (spelled both and *yitrō* and *yeter*) then the segholated spelling (assuming an original **yitr*) poses no problem.

21. Jon D. Levenson, "1 Samuel 25 as Literature and as History," *CBQ* 40 (1978): 11–28; and Jon D. Levenson and Baruch Halpern, "The Political Import of David's Marriages," *JBL* 99 (1980): 507–18.

22. 2 Sam 15:24 raises questions about precisely which of David's high priests came to his aid when facing the Absalom revolt.

והנה גם צדוק וכל הלוים אתו נשאים את ארון ברית האלהים
ויצקו את ארון האלהים
ויעל אביתר עד תם כל העם לעבור מן העיר

That the sentence begins וְהִנֵּה גַם is problematic as it does not clearly resume the action of a previous statement. הִנֵּה גַם appears only twice elsewhere (Gen 32:18 and Eccl 2:1) and in both of these cases it is logically dependent on a prior phrase. Furthermore, the action וַיַּעַל אֶבְיָתָר does not follow in a logical progression of action from וַיִּצֹקוּ. . . . It would seem that the sentence would better begin with וַיַּעַל אֶבְיָתָר וְהִנֵּה גַם, though this has no ancient manuscript evidence. Also ambiguous here is the nature of the action suggested by וַיַּעַל. Is the stem G or C? Does the text describe Abiathar offering sacrifices while Zadok and the other priests escape from the city (i.e. reading עלה in the C, albeit without the expected direct object for the locution), does Abiathar simply "go up" to some unspecified location while the rest of the priests leave, or does Abiathar join Zadok and the others in the departure to safety? Abiathar's involvement in David's resistance to Absalom's revolt is suppressed or muddled in the account. For another perspective see Mark Leuchter, *The Levites*, 111.

23. The nature of this support is described in 1 Kings 1:7 with the enigmatic phrase אַחֲרֵי אֲדֹנִיָּה וַיַּעְזֹרוּ. This locution עזר (verb) + אחר (preposition) does not appear elsewhere in Biblical Hebrew, and while the general meaning is apparent, the nuance of this phrase over and against the more common עזר + ל or אל + עזר is lost.

24. For the approximate location of Nob see Isa 10:32 and Neh 11:32.

25. Martin Cohen, "The Role of the Shilonite Priesthood in the United Monarchy of Ancient Israel," *HUCA* 36 (1965): 59–98, 90.

26. So Cross in *CHME*, 196.

27. The readings of 2 Sam 8:18 in LXX (και υιοι Δαυιδ αυλαρχαι ησαν) and Targum Jonathan (*wbny dwyd rbrbyn hww*) call into question the reference to כהנים in MT. The Targum's *rbrbyn* is quite common, used to render a variety of Hebrew terms for leaders and officials; however, term αυλαρχαι is quite rare, appearing only here. A related *hapax legomonon* αυλαρχια(ς) appears in 1 Kings 2:46h (3 Kingdoms 2:46h), which is a large expansion found only in the Greek tradition with no known Hebrew *Vorlage*. The terms are not found elsewhere in Greek literature and appear only in these two references. They mean something like *ruler* (αρχων) *of the court-yard* (αυλη), and it is unclear what Hebrew terms would be in view, though certainly not כהנים. Given the use of such an uncharacteristic term in LXX and such a common term in the Targum, it would seem that the renderings are interpretive, attempting to whitewash David's radical action of instituting his own sons as priests. In private correspondence, Jon Levenson has raised the possibility of reading סכנים in place of כהנים. While this suggestion does eliminate the problem raised by David's activity, the Greek and Aramaic versions of Is 22:15 intimate that סֹכֵן would occasion the use of the terms παστοφοριον and *prns*, respectively. The subtle critique of David's action is precisely the point envisioned by this particular voice/redaction of the Deuteronomistic Historian.

28. For a discussion of the unity of this geographical region see Zvi Gal, "Cabul, Jiphthah-El and the Boundary Between Asher and Zebulun in the Light of Archaeological Evidence" *ZDPV* 101:2 (1985): 114–127.

29. In the narrative, the etiology of the name for this land would seem to derive from Hiram's dismissive scoff at Solomon's offer. 1 Kings 9:13 מָה הֶעָרִים הָאֵלֶּה אֲשֶׁר נָתַתָּה לִּי אָחִי וַיִּקְרָא לָהֶם אֶרֶץ כָּבוּל עַד הַיּוֹם הַזֶּה. The epithet אֶרֶץ כָּבוּל (preposition *k* +

negative particle *bl*) may be compared to כבלי Job 35:12, כאין Isa 40:17; 41:11–12; 59:10; Hag 2:3; Ps 39:5; 73:2, and כלא Dan 4:35. This epithet appears to be a secondary, etiological etymology.

30. Baruch Halpern, "Sectionalism and the Schism," 523.

31. Mowinckel identifies Pss 47, 93, 95, 96, 97, 98, 99, and 100 in the category of *Thronbesteigungspsalmen*. Sigmund Mowinckel, *Psalm Studies* vol. 1 (trans. Mark E. Biddle; Atlanta, GA: SBL Press, 2014), 183.

32. Samuel's priestly pedigree is explicitly established in 1 Chr 6:7–14 as being that of a Kohathite, and, within the logic of the Chronicler, is tied to the priestly pedigree of his father, Elkanah.

33. Charles Augustus Briggs and Emilie Grace Briggs, *A Critical and Exegetical Commentary on the Book of Psalms* vol. 2 ICC (New York: Charles Scribner's Sons, 1907), 309.

34. Peter Mommer, "Samuel in Ps 99," *BibNot* 31 (1986): 27–30, specifically pp. 29–30. Mommer also deals with the enigmatic/problematic way in which this Psalm imagines Samuel interacting with Yahweh in the pillar of cloud. On the other hand, Mowinckel sees the priestly/intercessory roles of Moses, Aaron, and Samuel playing out in the leveling of past and present effectuated in cultic performance—as Moses and Aaron once were for Israel, so now Samuel currently is. See also Mowinckel, *Psalm Studies*, 328.

35. Hutton has suggested—quite rightly—that the character of Samuel is a product of the redaction of 1 Samuel and therefore is "historically specious." Hutton, "All the King's Men," 131. That Samuel functions as an archetype of David in his political reach and charisma is certainly borne out by the narratives. This similarity is also seen in the antagonist relationship of these two characters to Saul, who is haunted—literally and metaphorically—by both Samuel and David.

36. Adam Zertal has argued that the cultic significance of Shechem—and particularly the site of *El-Burnat*, on the slope of Ebal—extends far beyond what I have described above. Zertal conducted extensive surface surveys of the area beginning in the 1970s, and led excavations on *El-Burnat* from 1982 to 1989. He claims that the large stone structure on at *El-Burnat* is precisely the stone structure referred to in the command and execution of the altar in Deut 27:4–8 and Josh 8:30–32. See Adam Zertal, "Has Joshua's Altar Been Found on Mt. Ebal?" *BAR* 11:1 (1985): 26–43; Idem. "An Early Iron Age Cultic Site on Mt. Ebal: Excavation Seasons 1982–7: Preliminary Report," *Tel Aviv* 13–14 (1986–87): 105–65. Also, Ziony Zevit, *The Religion of Ancient Israel*, 196–201. Zertal's assertion has met much opposition, particularly from Rainey and Kempinski. See Anson F. Rainey, "Zertal's Altar—A Blatant Phony," *BAR* 12.4 (1986): 66; Idem., "Notes on Two Archaeological Sites," *Eretz-Israel* 29 (2009): 184–187; Aaron Kempinski, "Joshua's Altar—An Iron Age I Watchtower," *BAR* 12.1 (1986): 42. Zvi Koenigsberg has offered a full-throated and enthusiastic defense of Zertal's altar. He further posits that the memory of the altar at Ebal/Shechem as a major cultic center plays out dramatically in the account of Jacob crossing his hands to bless Ephriam and Manasseh (Gen 48:14–18). Zoenigsberg sees in this action the ascendance of Shiloh in Ephraim as the premier

pre-Monarchic cult site over Shechem/Ebal in Manasseh. See Zvi Koenigsberg, *The Lost Temple of Israel* (Boston: Academic Studies Press, 2015), 117–120.

37. J. David Schloen, "Caravans, Kenites and Casus Belli: Enmity and Alliance in the Song of Deborah," *CBQ* 55 (1993): 18–38.

38. Leuchter, *The Levites*, 72.

39. *CMHE*, 198–199. See also Halpern, "Levitic Participation," 34.

40. It is found in Num 25:7, 11 (in the P account of Phinehas' investiture by Moses) and Ezra 7:5.

41. William Propp takes this argument a step further, positing that the divisions in the names Gershom and Gershon, Eleazar and Eliezer are a creation of the Priestly writer attempting to divide a Mosaic/Mushite branch from the Aaronites. See William H. Propp, *Exodus 1–18: A New Translation with Introduction and Commentary*, The Anchor Bible (New York: Doubleday, 1998), 286.

42. Richard E. Friedman has recently argued that Levites are the only characters in the Hebrew Bible that have Egyptian names; these are: Hophni, Hur, Phinehas (2X), Merari, Pashhur, Moses, and Mushi. For Friedman, the association of the Israelite priesthood with a collection of authentically Egyptian names is an important factor in approaching questions of the historicity of the Exodus. See Richard E. Friedman, *The Exodus* (New York: HarperOne, 2017), 32–37. *Contra* Friedman, Donald B. Redford argues that only the names Hophni, Phinehas, and Moses (perhaps, also, Mushi?) are native Egyptian, and it pushes the evidence too far to identify a connection between the entire collection of Levites and Egypt. However, he notes that all three of these characters are associated with Shiloh, which retains an explicit memory of the connection between the Shilonite priesthood and Moses role in the Exodus (1 Sam 3:27–28). See Donald B. Redford, *Egypt, Canaan, and Israel in Ancient Times* (Princeton, NJ: Princeton University Press, 1992), 418–19.

43. Raymond O. Faulkner, *A Concise Dictionary of Middle Egyptian* (Oxford: Griffith Institute, 1991), 137.

44. See earlier discussion in ch. 1 of the term "Cushite" with relevant bibliography.

45. Compare these to Num 35:1–8.

46. Though Shiloh is not one of the cities appropriated for Levitical use in either of the lists.

47. Hutton, "The Levitical Diaspora (II)," 45–81.

48. Ibid., 80.

49. Ibid.

50. Leuchter, *The Levites*, 19.

51. For more on the theoretical conception and function of "memory" in the analysis biblical texts see Daniel D. Pioske, *David's Jerusalem: Between Memory and History* (New York: Routledge, 2015); and Idem. *Memory in a Time of Prose: Studies in Epistemology, Hebrew Scribalism, and the Biblical Past* (New York: Oxford University Press, 2018).

52. Leuchter, *The Levites*, 19.

53. Leuchter makes a similar argument for the Gershonide control of the northern region described in the Levitical Cities lists as reflecting the memory of monarchical period traditions. The Zadokite/Aaronite priests of the Persian period would have no

ideological incentive for allocating territory to their priestly rivals. See Leuchter, *The Levites*, 120.

54. Benjamin Mazar, "The Cities of the Priests and Levites," in *Biblical Israel: State and People*. (ed. Benjamin Mazar and Shmuel Ahituv; Jerusalem: Magnes Press, 1992); Tryggve N. D. Mettinger, *Solomonic State Officials. A Study of the Civil Government Officials of the Israelite Monarchy* (Coniectanea Biblica 5; Lund, Sweden: Gleerup, 1971); Robert G. Boling, "Levitical Cities: Archaeology and Texts," in *Biblical and Related Studies Presented to Samuel Iwry* (ed. Ann Cort and Scott Morschauser; Winona Lake, IN: Eisenbrauns, 1985), 23–32; and Menaḥem Haran, "Studies in the Account of the Levitical Cities: I. Preliminary Considerations," *JBL* 80:1 (1961): 45–54.

55. See the appendix in Rasure, "Priests Like Moses," pp. 180–188 for a set of eighteen satellite composite images showing the geographical and topological unity of the triangular region defined by Jerusalem, Kiryat Yearim/Abu Ghosh, and Hebron.

56. Hutton, "The Levitical Diaspora (I)," "The Levitical Diaspora (II)," and "All The King's Men."

57. Hutton, "The Levitical Diaspora (I)," 230.

58. Mark Leuchter, *The Levites*, 70.

59. Mark Leuchter, personal communication, May 26, 2020.

60. Susan Ackerman, "Who is Sacrificing at Shiloh?" in *Levites and Priests in Biblical History and Tradition* (ed. Mark A. Leuchter and Jeremy M. Hutton; Atlanta, GA: SBL, 2011), 25–43.

61. Ibid, 29.

62. For example Ps 78:60, Jer 7:12, and Jer 26:6–9.

63. Ackerman, "Who is Sacrificing," 40.

64. The importance of Shiloh as a rival to Judah is further hinted at by the enigmatic and textually problematic reference found in Gen 49:10, which reads:

לא יסור שבט מיהודה ומחקק מבין רגליו עד כי יבא שילו ולו יקהת עמים

The scepter shall not depart from Judah, nor the staff from between his feet. Until he comes to Shiloh, the homage of the peoples is his.

Frequently in contemporary scholarship, the contextually problematic reference to Shiloh (עד כי יבא שילו) is amended to read עד כי יבא שי לו, translated something like "until tribute comes to him," with Judah as the implied antecedent of the pronoun לו. In the middle of the twentieth century, this problem was deemed by Moran as "the most famous *crux interpretum* in the entire Old Testament. William L. Moran, "Genesis 49.10 and its use in Ezekiel 21.32," *Biblica* 39 (1958): 405–25. A more recent survey of opinions is found in Serge Frolov, "Judah Comes to Shiloh: Genesis 49:10ab, One More Time," *JBL* 131 (2012): 417–22. Marco Treves has proposed that the ambiguity in the line reflects an intentional scribal intervention in the reception of the verse. He argues that the phrase עד כי יבא שי לו is the more ancient form, arising sometime in the Davidic or Solomonic periods. However, after the revolt of Jeroboam I instigated by Ahijah the Shilonite, a "sarcastic" editor added a marginal comment on the verse: עד כי יבא איש שילו "until the Man of Shiloh comes." The word איש was subsequently lost to haplography, situated between the *alef* of יבא and *shin* of שילו. We have then preserved in the traditions of this verse, both the more ancient form of the poem and a commentary on it arising sometime after the division of the monarchy. Marco Treves, "Shiloh (Genesis 49:10)," *JBL* 85 (1966): 353–56.

65. Defining the Judahite center in this way brings clarity to the enigmatic description of Jerusalem in Psalm 48:3 with the terms: הר ציון ירכתי צפון קרית מלך רב, "Mount Zion, at the recesses of Zaphon, city of the Great King." It is quite widespread in modern scholarship to understand this reference to Zaphon as the mythic elevation of Jerusalem—the abode of Yahweh—above Mt. Zaphon—the abode of Baal—far to the north in Syria. However, with the topographical integrity of the region from Hebron to Kiryat Yearim in view, the description of Jerusalem as ירכתי צפון envisions not its mythological status but its physical location at the northern reaches of the Judahite center.

Chapter 4

Holy Families

Genealogy of the Levites, Moses, and Aaron

The next issue in the awareness of an Aaronite-Mushite opposition concerns genealogy. Read as a comprehensive whole, Moses and Aaron are brothers in the Pentateuchal narrative,[1] and they are of pure Levite parentage. The assertion of the Mushite Hypothesis that the בני מושי consists of a group descended from (or coalesced around) Moses stands in tension with the plain sense of the biblical text, which presents Mushi in a removed cousinly relationship with Moses, Aaron, and Miriam (Num 26:58–59).[2]

The Aaronite-Mushite opposition proposed by the Mushite Hypothesis thus necessitates a careful reconsideration of the descriptions of, catalyst for, and functions of the Levitical family divisions and the ways they are described. That is, questions must be asked about which of the divisions/affiliations of the Aaronite and Mushite groups are operative at a particular time, for whom they are operative, and the ultimate origins of the divisions/affiliations. In this chapter, I will analyze the genealogical complexes which describe the relationships between Moses, Aaron, Miriam, and Mushi. First, I will consider the methodological issues at stake in approaching genealogical material in the Hebrew Bible. I will then discuss textual and text-critical matters related to the P account of Levitical genealogies. Finally, I will explore two test cases related to the fluidity of genealogical texts: Num 26:58a and the fraternity of Moses and Aaron.

METHODOLOGICAL ISSUES IN THE
USE OF BIBLICAL GENEALOGIES

Genealogical information plays an important role within biblical literature. Characters are specified and differentiated with the use of patronymics, which is the simplest manifestation of genealogical data. The most robust expression of the importance of genealogical information is found the so-called *Toledotformel* of the Priestly source,[3] which organize the entire Priestly document around the theme of genealogical reflection.[4] Literary interest in genealogical affiliation is not merely a feature of the Hebrew Bible, but occupies a significant place in the New Testament[5] and Jewish Pseudepigrapha,[6] and rabbinic literature as well. At various points in the history of biblical interpretation, the perceived reliability of the genealogical information presented in the Bible has evolved.

Summary of Positions

Robert Wilson[7] and James Sparks[8] have each traced the evolution in scholarly understanding of the historical character and reliability of biblical genealogical information. The development may be described as taking place in roughly four stages: antiquity, early critical scholarship, twentieth-century skepticism, and twentieth-century positivism. Wilson articulates the methodological foundation for a fifth option, understanding genealogical information presented in the biblical material to reveal a network of social, tribal, and political relationships. A brief review of the stages of development in the scholarly understanding of biblical genealogies is in order at this point.

Antiquity to Ewald

In the New Testament, the Rabbinic writings, and through the majority of Western history the genealogies of the Hebrew Bible were understood to be accurate sources for the reconstruction of the history and familial relationships in ancient Israel. Through the Rabbinic period and in enduring in traditional *halakhah*, the genealogical lists are vital for establishing pure and noble ancestry in the present. The idiom משפחות מיוחסות appears frequently in Rabbinic literature to denote those families of traceable and well-connected lineage.[9] Flavius Josephus derives his own authority from the integrity of the priestly line from which he is descended.[10] Further, in *Against Apion* he describes the purity of priestly lines maintained in the first century of the common era by means of appeals to ancient genealogical tables.

For our forefathers did not only appoint the best of these priests, and those that attended upon the divine worship, for that design, from the beginning; but made provision that the stock of the priests should continue unmixed, and pure. For he who is partaker of the priesthood, must propagate of a wife of the same nation; without having any regard to money, or any other dignities: but he is to make a scrutiny, and take his wife's genealogy from the ancient tables; and procure many witnesses to it. And this is our practice, not only in Judea; but wheresoever any body of men of our nation do live: and even there an exact catalogue of our priests' marriages is kept.[11]

Even in the early wave of historical-critical scholarship and far removed from the personal and communal concerns of genealogical pedigree which drove Josephus and the Rabbis, Heinrich Ewald understood the genealogical material in Genesis to be largely reliable. Particularly impressed with the attempts in Genesis to describe "very accurate time distinctions" he felt that the work as a whole displays "a genuine historical spirit."[12]

Wellhausen

Wellhausen was not the first to cast doubt on the historical reliability of the genealogical materials in the Hebrew Bible,[13] but he was the first to articulate a detailed literary argument for dismissing the historical claims of the genealogical materials. His suspicion of the biblical genealogies arose entirely from their position within the Priestly source of the Pentateuch and his understanding of the lateness of this source. Whether contained in P sections of the Pentateuch or in Chronicles, Wellhausen understood any historical information appearing in these later texts to be hopelessly corrupted by the biases of the later authors. He quipped of the genealogical material in Chronicles: "If you are looking for historical knowledge about ancient Israelite conditions here, you have to lay down to hear the grass grow."[14] Wellhausen granted that the genealogical information preserved in P might have some historical antecedent but that it has been thoroughly adapted to the post-Exilic concerns of the author of P. For Wellhausen, even the genealogies found in the Yahwist are more firmly rooted in the concerns of the age in which they were written than in the age in which they purport to occur. He writes: "The historic-political relations of Israel are reflected with more life in the relations borne by the patriarchs to their brothers, cousins, and other relatives. The background is never long concealed here, the temper of the period of the kings is everywhere discernible."[15]

Noth

Whereas Wellhausen understood the genealogies of P, J, and Chronicles to have some basis in prior history—albeit a basis thoroughly manipulated and augmented in their present forms and contexts—Martin Noth viewed the biblical genealogical material as even more thoroughly a literary construction. He writes: "In the Pentateuchal narrative, the combination of the themes and individual traditions is often accomplished through the fabrication of a variety of kinship ties between the acting persons."[16] Noth divides the genealogical material into the categories of "authentic genealogy"[17] and "secondary genealogy." For Noth, the authentic genealogy is a list that had some independent significance and existence prior to its incorporation into the biblical narrative. This does not mean that the list has any great historical value or veracity, only that it had some existence prior to its incorporation into the biblical narrative. For Noth, the lists of six tribes or twelve tribes as well as the census of Num 26:4bβ–51 fall into this category. In other words, these lists were of primary significance to the contours of the narrative being told. In contrast to this, Noth describes as "secondary genealogies" those lists in which "certain figures have been connected with each other who were independent subjects of tradition and concerning whom various things were narrated."[18] Secondary genealogies serve to bind together elements in the Pentateuchal narratives which originally were independent or unrelated. Of particular significance for the project at hand, Noth identifies that the biblical account of Moses' familial relationship to be a leading example of secondary genealogy at work. Noth observes at length:

> In the sphere of the adjoining Pentateuchal themes Moses, who was developing into the central figure, gathered about himself a family by means of all sorts of narrative combinations, although this family remained essentially smaller in extent. In it the emphasis was almost always on the relationships of individuals to Moses, without concern for the relationships of the rest of the family members to one another. Here the primary factor apparently was the narrative element of Moses' foreign wife. The combination of this element with the old tradition of the meeting with the Midianites at the "mountain of God" led to the Midianite father-in-law of Moses who at the first was unnamed but subsequently, through the inclusion of an element of Kenite tradition, was initially designated as "Hobab, son of Reuel." And then to this combination also belonged the Midianite wife of Moses. Later on Moses received a brother in the formerly independent figure of Aaron who, in turn, brought along with him Miriam as a sister. Everything else was added by virtue of the fact that various priestly orders claimed the great Moses, and in the end claimed even more the original priest Aaron, as their ancestors. Thus the Levitical priesthood made Moses—at first in a general way—into a "Levite" (Ex. 2:1 [J]). In addition

Moses received two ancestors of priestly orders as sons, whose mother, curiously enough, then had to become the Midianite wife. The family of Moses finally received its greatest increase, however, through Aaron, who for his own part probably had been designated at a rather early time in the Levitical priestly order as "Aaron the Levite" (Ex. 4:14 [J[s]]). To him the postexilic high priesthood traced its lineage. This high priesthood, together with the entirety of the remaining cultic personnel, constituted the basis of the great Levitical genealogy of P in which Aaron, and with him Moses as well, found a definite place and also received parents with definite names.[19]

For Noth, the principal function of genealogical material, be it "authentic" or "secondary," was in service to the larger narrative unfolding; ether as a basis for the narrative itself in the case of the "authentic" or as a device used to allow otherwise independent narratives to cohere. As relates to the character of Moses, Noth understands the affiliation of Moses with Aaron as "secondary genealogy" in action; that is the fraternal connection is created for the purpose of melding the narratives of originally independent characters. The same is true of Miriam, and of Moses' priestly "sons" Gershom and Eliezer.

Albright and Cross

Wellhausen and, to a lesser extent, Noth placed little confidence in biblical genealogical material as a reliable historiographic source. William Foxwell Albright answered this skepticism with a bold and outspoken positivist reading of the genealogies. Albright expanded on the work of ethnographers showing the prodigious memories of people in tribal societies to recall genealogical information, particularly when those societies had access to writing. Since the Israelites had access to writing from at least the ninth century—and in Albright's estimation, well before that—he was confident that the genealogies of Genesis presented a historically reliable account of the patriarchal period and even earlier.[20] The Mushite Hypothesis of Cross is largely formed by these assumptions with a few measured caveats.

ROBERT WILSON ON GENEALOGIES

Robert Wilson, in his work on genealogies in the ancient Near East and the Bible, has shown there is an intimate connection between the form of a genealogy and its function, and any assessment or discussion of the historicity of genealogical material must always have the form and function of the particularly genealogical list in view.[21]

Methodology and Interpretive Principles in Wilson's Work

Wilson investigates the topic of genealogy in the Bible with the aid of socio-logical and anthropological comparison of the biblical material with other bodies of genealogical evidence: contemporary accounts and practices of the tribal cultures of the Tib (sub-Saharan African) and Humr (Baggara Arab) peoples and inscriptional evidence from the ancient Near East, principally Mesopotamian, but with reference to Ugaritic, Phoenician, Punic, Moabite, Aramaic, Egyptian, and pre-Islamic Arabian evidence. The work is driven by three questions: Did the writers (or producers) of genealogical lists consider genealogy a historiographical genre? Do oral and written genealogies have the same forms and functions? What is the relationship of genealogies to narrative, and what is the direction of this relationship?[22] For Wilson, this last question arises in reaction to Noth's work on biblical genealogy, and particularly Noth's designation of "secondary genealogy" and its function as a literary tool for binding otherwise disparate narratives.

Wilson's analysis of the historiographic character of genealogical material moderates the skeptical positions of Wellhausen, on the one hand, and the historical positivism of Albright, on the other. Genealogies can preserve material of historiographic significance, provided that the questions modern historians wish to ask of the genealogies align with the kind of information the genealogy was composed to communicate. History is not the primary function of genealogical texts, but historical information can be a gleaned as a byproduct. Genealogies, Wilson writes, "seem to have been created and preserved for domestic, politico-jural, and religious purposes, and historical information is preserved in the genealogies incidentally."[23]

The inseparability of form and function for genealogical material is of utmost importance for Wilson's work, and it is this inseparability that leads him to his most tantalizing results for the present study. Summarizing his comparative analysis of oral genealogies, he writes:

> Even when the genealogy serves as a charter for a lineage, the lineage itself may function in several different spheres, and in each sphere its form may be different. This means that a lineage functioning in a domestic sphere may have a different structure from the same lineage functioning in the political or religious sphere. As a result, the lineage genealogy must also alter its form in order to continue to reflect the lineage structure in various contexts. This fact may cause several conflict genealogies to exist at the same time, but each one can be considered accurate in its own context.[24]

That is, contradictions in genealogical information can co-exist by virtue of the differing contexts in which the system of genealogical relationships is operative.

Genealogical Terminologies

There are two primary forms of genealogical material. Linear genealogies trace a single line from generation to generation without regard to branches or "segmentation." That is, linear genealogies are branchless trunks of family trees. These stand in contrast to "segmented genealogies," which may catalogue an array of paternal, maternal, fraternal, sororal, and cousinly relationships. Wilson's primary observation concerns the dynamic nature of the relationships described in genealogical texts. He writes: "when genealogies function in the domestic sphere, they relate individuals to other individuals and groups within the society and define social rights and obligations. Genealogies which are used in this way are usually segmented, and their form must change constantly to mirror the changing shape of the domestic social structure."[25] Segmented genealogies are about establishing and enforcing social order, division of labor, and rank within the family or social system. In contrast, linear genealogies function to make specific claims to power and authority.

Fluidity

In his analysis of both the oral genealogies of the Tib and Humr peoples and the various written genealogies preserved in inscriptions from Mesopotamia, Wilson has noted that all genealogies are marked by fluidity. The genealogical genre is not merely occupied with record-keeping as such might be defined by modern historians; rather, its aims are more immediately tied to the context which warrants the articulation of genealogical information. Wilson surmises:

> Where two or more versions of the same genealogy exist, it is usually possible to detect changes in the relationship of names within the genealogy or to note the deletion or addition of names. This sort of fluidity may occur because the names involved are unimportant and thus liability to be forgotten or at least to be poorly remember. On the other hand, fluidity may be crucial for understanding the genealogies and may indicate significant shifts in social relationships.[26]

This fluidity does not simply exist in the oral genealogies of modern tribal peoples or in the inscriptional genealogies of Mesopotamia. Genealogical fluidity and the apparent discrepancies this fluidity can create are also present in biblical material.

Genesis 4 and 5

To illustrate this genealogical fluidity in practice, Wilson offers a test case from Genesis 4 and 5.[27] This test case described by Wilson forms the pattern for my own analysis of the Levitical genealogies and of the fraternity of Moses and Aaron in this chapter, so his treatment of it will be explored thoroughly. Genesis 4:1–2 and 17–26 and Genesis 5 present two versions of the antediluvian descent of humankind from Adam, the first found within Yahwistic material and the later in Priestly. The lists do not stop at the same place, but generally move from Adam to Lamech. The overlap of names between the two list is significant; however, the discrepancies in order are many. Adam stands at the beginning of both lists, referred to as האדם and J (4:1) and simply as אדם in P (5:1). In J the first generation of Adam's progeny includes Cain (קין), Abel (הבל), and Seth (שת). P refers only to Seth. In both J and in P, Seth sires Enosh (אנוש) (4:26, 5:6). The J account traces in detail the progeny of Cain, reciting the so-called Cainite/Kenite genealogy. This includes the following:

First Generation: Cain (קין)
Second Generation: Enoch (חנוך)
Third Generation: Irad (עירד)
Fourth Generation: Mehujael (מחויאל)
Fifth Generation: Methushael (מתושאל)
Sixth Generation: Lamech (למך)

The Priestly account traces the lineage of Seth; however, it includes many of the same names as the J account, albeit with alternate spellings. In P we find:

First Generation: Seth (שת)
Second Generation: Enosh (אנוש)
Third Generation: Kenan (קינן)
Fourth: Mahalalel (מהללאל)
Fifth: Jered (ירד)
Sixth: Enoch (חנוך)
Seventh: Methuselah (מתושלח)
Eighth: Lamech (למך)

The most obvious tension between these lists is the rendering of Lamech as a descendant in the direct line of Cain in the case of the Yahwist and of Seth the case of the Priestly writer. The number of generations it requires to arrive to Lamech differs: six in the case of J, and eight in the case of P. Though there are differences in spelling between certain names of the two lists, the sonic (if not etymological) similarity leaves little doubt that comparable names are in view: קין (J) and קינן (P), עירד (J) and ירד (P), מחויאל *l* (J) and מהללאל (P), מתושאל (J) and מתושלח (P). Moreover, the order in which the similar names are rendered differs between the lists. *Qayin* in J is the first generation from Adam, and *Qênān* is the third in P. In J, the third, fourth, and fifth generations are *ḥānôk, 'îrād,* and *mᵉḥûyā'ēl*. In P, this order is reversed in the fifth, sixth, and seventh generations: *mahălal'ēl, yered,* and *ḥānôk*.

Wilson proffers a list of potential theological and ideological rationales for the discrepancies described above. These involved situating both the Yahwist and the Priestly writer at very particular moments in history and presume both the greater antiquity of the J material as well as the Priestly writer's access to the pre-existent J material. These rationales have little bearing on the present study. However, in his analysis of the anthropological evidence for the internal logic of genealogical material Wilson has quite correctly noted the malleability of the form and function. He explains: "in a society at a given time there may be several apparently contradictory versions of the same genealogy. These versions are not viewed as contradictory by the people who use them, however, for the people know that each version is correct in the particular context in which it is cited."[28] That is, these contradictory versions are not necessarily reacting to one another. One is not intended to subvert or to replace the other because the internal logic of genealogical accounting is able to tolerate such discrepancies and does not understand these tensions to be problematic. The points of discrepancy which produce such angst in a modern reader attempting to evaluate the historicity of the claims were outside the concerns driving J and P. The Yahwist offered an account of the genealogy of Cain from Adam to Yabal, Yubal, and Tubal-Cain, by way of Lamech. The Priestly writer also wrote an account of the generations from Adam to Noah also by way of Lamech, and many of the same people in the genealogy of J. Each of these linear genealogies sought to focus attention on the characters named at the end of their lists. For J, this provided opportunity to introduce the etiologies of transhumant pastoralists, musicians, and metalworkers (Gen 4:20–22),[29] and for P, this occasioned the introduction of the great hero Noah. To these ends, J and P used at their disposal a collection of names of renown—or names that sounded similar to names of renown—associated with the antediluvian period. In so doing each has attempted to inculcate within their readers a sense of historical verisimilitude for this earliest time. Another example of this sonic and etymological fluidity is found in the priestly genealogies in the character of Eleazar son of Aaron (אלעזר) and Eliezer son of Moses (אליעזר).

Principal Results of Wilson's Work

Wilson's comparison of anthropological and ancient Near Eastern genealogies with biblical materials has yielded three results of immediate relevance to the present study. The first regards the malleability of genealogical material by which otherwise unrelated individuals may be grafted into a lineage. "The degree of filiation involved is frequently implied in the kinship relation by means of which the genealogical relation is made. For example, the person who is joined as a "brother" has a higher status than one filiated as a "son" or a "sister's son.""[30] Thus, through the process of filiation the genealogy becomes an reflection of a person's position in society and the rights, privileges, and authority afforded that person.[31] As we have seen at length, Jeremy Hutton has described a similar process at work among the Ahansal, a Berber tribe in the Atlas mountains of Morocco.[32] Citing the field studies of Gellner, Hutton refers to a scenario in which legal-cultic functionaries from a defunct line attached themselves to a more influential line of functionaries and were able to participate in the enterprises of their adopted family.[33] By this process of "fusion," as Hutton terms it, an effective filiation to place.

The second finding of significance for the present conversation concerns the fluidity of the genealogical information, and the ability of the internal logic of genealogical accounting to adapt to its immediate context. Genealogy is not intended as "historical record" as modern readers might understand that term. Genealogies may be accurate in the spheres in which they are functioning immediately but not necessarily in contexts beyond that. Wilson writes: "genealogies may be accurate in the spheres in which they are functioning but not in other spheres. The genealogies may therefore provide the modern historian with valuable insights into the domestic, political, and religious perceptions of the people who use the genealogies."[34] "In a given society, segmented genealogies being used for differing purposes may exhibit a great deal of variation" he points out, "for the society's political, economic, and religious configurations may be quite different. In such cases the apparently conflicting genealogies are in fact accurately reflecting the way in which the society sees itself in a particular social sphere."[35] Thus evaluation of genealogical relationships described between particular individuals or biblical personalities must not be regarded as absolute, but as expressions of a finite set of relationships, which may or may not include religious, professional, and political elements. A discrepancy between two or more renderings of genealogical relationships is not necessarily a "mistake" as such but a reflection of some other manner of relationship.

The third accomplishment of Wilson's work relevant to this study is the clarity he brings to Noth's categories of "authentic" (or in Wilson's preferred parlance, "primary") and "secondary" genealogies. As summarized above, those genealogies deemed "authentic" are those that had some existence prior to their incorporation into a narrative context. That is, the details—relational, historiographic, and otherwise—contained in the authentic genealogies inform and shapes the narrative into which they are set. In contrast, the "secondary" genealogies are ones whose details spring from the exigencies of the narrative. Wilson argues that Noth's category of secondary genealogy is "too vague to be useful." In light of his own work, he clarifies that in future analyses what Noth deemed "secondary" would better be clarified into three categories: "[g]enealogies in which both names and kinship links are taken from narrative traditions"; [g]enealogies in which the names are taken from narrative traditions and the kinship links supplied by the compiler of the genealogy"; and "[g]enealogies in which the names are drawn from independent lists and the kinship links supplied by the compiler of the genealogy."[36] We saw the second and third categories operating in the genealogies of Genesis 4 and 5 above.

ISSUES IN THE PRIESTLY GENEALOGIES

Having reviewed the methodological issues at stake in interpreting genealogical relationships, I now turn attention to three complexes of data related to the Mushite Hypothesis. First, I will discuss the segmented genealogy of the Levite tribes, with particular emphasis on the place of Mushi within this structure and the text critical and interpretive issues involved in understanding this material rightly. Second, I will examine the fraternal relationship between Moses and Aaron and the possibility of multiple views of this fraternity in the biblical sources.

Genealogical Ambiguity in the Lists of the Levite Tribes

In Genesis 46:11, the Priestly writer first articulates that the children of Levi are named Gershon (גרשון), Kohath (קהת), and Merari (מררי). This listing is reflected in subsequent lists of the divisions of Levite tribes. The various subtribes (משפחות) are organized according to these primary divisions. Exodus 6:16–25 gives the fullest list of the descendants of Levi as shown below.

Abbreviated versions of this segmented genealogy organized around the trio of Gershon, Kohath, and Merari in the first generation from Levi are found in elsewhere in P in Num 3:17–21, 27 and 33. It is also found in 1 Chr 5:27–41 and 1 Chr 6:1–15, and Num 26:57.

Numbers 26:58a

A significant problem is posed by information presented in Num 26:58a. The whole of Numbers 26 is devoted to a detailed presentation of the tribes and subtribes of Israel. This is accomplished by naming the sons of the tribal ancestor and immediately following the name with the subtribe derived from the name of the son, that is, (*l*) + *PN*, ה משפחת + *gentilic from PN*. After the names of the sons are enumerated, each of the lists then concludes with the statement: ה משפחות אלה + *gentilic from Tribal Ancestor*.

0	1	2	3	4	5
Levi	Gershon	Libni Shimei			
	Kohath	Amram	Aaron	Nadab Abihu Eleazar Ithamar	Phinehas
			Moses		
		Izhar	Korah	Assir Elkanah Abiasaph	
			Nepheg Zichri		
		Hebron			
		Uzziel	Mishael Elzaphan Sithri		
	Merari	Mahli Mushi			

For example, in Num 26:5–7, the listing of the Twelve Tribes begins:

ראובן בכור ישראל בני ראובן
חנוך משפחת החנכי
לפלוא משפחת הפלאי

לחצרן משפחת החצרוני

לכרמי משפחת הכרמי

אלה משפחת הראובני

This pattern continues for Simeon (vv.12–14), Gad (vv. 15–18), Judah (19–22), Issachar (23–25), Zebulun (26–27), Manasseh (29–34), Ephraim (35–37), Benjamin (38–41), Dan (42–43), Asher (44–47), and Naphtali (48–50). In all of these cases the pattern continues and the list of the subtribes ends with the phrase אלה משפחות ה + *gentilic from Tribal Ancestor.* The account of the Levites deviates from this pattern. In Numbers 26:57–58a, we find:

ואלה פקודי הלוי למשפחתם

לגרשון משפחת הגרשני

לקהת משפחת הקהתי

למררי משפחת המררי

אלה משפחת לוי

משפחת הלבני

משפחת החברני

משפחת המחלי

משפחת המושי

משפחת הקרחי

Where elsewhere אלה משפחת functions as the concluding formula for the list, it does not, in this case, end the list. Appended to the list are the names of Libnites, the Hebronites, the Mahlites, the Mushites, and the Korahites. The Libnites, Hebronites, Mahlites and Mushites are all names associated in the lists discussed above in 5.3.1 with the second generation from Levi, while the Korahites are from the third generation from Levi. Thus, this account of the Levite tribes deviates from the accounts of all other tribes in Numbers 26 in the syntax used and in the extent of the generations named. Though the list has expanded beyond the first generation, the list is not inclusive of all the names in the second generation. Amram, Shimei, Uzziel, and Izhar are omitted as well as all names other than Korah from the third generation. Why would the list expand beyond the first generation? Why would the names be included after the closing formula?

The problems posed by Numbers 26:58a have been discussed by Möhlenbrink,[37] Waterman,[38] De Vaux,[39] and treated at length by Rehm.[40] To the extent that consensus exists it is that the information contained in this "expansion" of the list of subtribes dates to a different period from the more conventional list of Gershon, Kohath, and Merari.

Text Critical Issues

Beyond the literary intrusion of the 26:58a, the text as it is preserved in the MT also poses a serious text critical challenge. MT records a list of five names names: מִשְׁפַּחַת הַקָּרְחִי, מִשְׁפַּחַת הַמּוּשִׁי, מִשְׁפַּחַת הַמַּחְלִי, מִשְׁפַּחַת הַחֶבְרֹנִי, מִשְׁפַּחַת הַלִּבְנִי. The Egyptian, Lucianic, Catenae, and Byzantine texts of LXX read: δημος ο Λοβενι δημος ο Χεβρωνι δημος ο Κορε και δημος ο Μουσει, omitting reference to the Mahlites and reversing the order of the Mushites and the Korathites. While the omission of the Mahlites in the other textual traditions of LXX could have resulted from haplography, the overwhelming evidence from the other traditions and the tendency of the Hexaplaric evidence to be corrected to MT weighs against its originality. The frequency[41] with which Mushi and Mahli appear as a pair elsewhere in the MT likely occasioned its addition here.[42] Following Rehm, I conjecture then that the more original reading contains only the names Libnites, Hebronites, Mushites, and Korathites.

Whether with five names or with four, the issue of why and when these additional names have been appended to the seemingly complete list remains. The combination of just these names without the names of the other second and third generation Levites does not appear elsewhere. The insertion is firmly embedded within a large block of Priestly narratives and legislation. There are no narrative reasons for attempting to affiliate the text with another Pentateuchal source. This development then must have taken place within P itself showing an inherent fluidity it is understanding of how genealogical material may be appropriated.

Who Are the Mushites?

Merlin Rehm has argued that the configuration of genealogy recognizing the four subtribes of Libnite, Hebronites, Mushites, and Korathites represents a second stage in the development of the Israelite priesthood. In the earliest stage, which Rehm identifies as the Desert Period, the Levites were divided into the three primary subtribes that dominate all of the lists of Levites except for Num 26:58a; namely, the Gershonites, the Kohathites, and the Merarites. In this earliest period, the characters of Moses and Aaron emerged as priests in these lines: Moses from the Gershonites, and Aaron from the Kohathites. The affiliation of Aaron with the Kohathites is without controversy, as this is how P presents the genealogy of Aaron elsewhere.[43] The affiliation of Moses with the Gershonites stands in tension with the tradition of Moses and Aaron as brothers, and thus of Moses also as a Kohathite.

The evidence for associating Moses with the Gershonites is threefold. First, Moses names his own son Gershom in both the Yahwist source (Exod 2:22) and in the Elohist source (18:3). Though there is no incontrovertible evidence for the practice of papponymy in the Hebrew Bible, Noth has noted the practice among the Jews of Elephantine.[44] That a name can be reused within a dynasty is quite reasonable and was practiced within ancient Israel. Even if Moses is understood to be further removed from Gershon, the son of Levi, his use of the name Gershom for his own son displays his affinity for the line. The narratives in J and E of Moses's association with the priestly Gershonites is not the only text connection between Moses and this line. Judges 18:30 describes the priesthood of the Levite Jonathan serving in the house of a certain Micah at Dan. As discussed above in chs. 1 and 2, this Jonathan is identified as "son of Gershom, son of Moses" (בן גרשום בן משה). Finally, Rehm suggests that the "gradual disappearance" from the biblical stage of both Moses and Gershom as priestly functionaries also attests to their likely connection. "In other words, the fact that both Moses and Gershon were de-emphasized in the later stages of the Old Testament history may indicate that it was known that they represented one and the same Levitic group."[45] For Rehm, the reference to the Mushites in Num 26:58a is merely another way of referring to the Gershonites, one reflecting the political and religious climate of a later date (which for Rehm is the Tribal League). Likewise, the Hebronites (associated with Aaron) are a reference to the Kohathites. In the standard genealogy (Exod 6) the mention of the Libnites would function to represent the Gershon tradition. The mention of the Korathites might speak to their emergence as an antagonist group.[46] In this view, the appending of the list of select second and third generation Levites is a way of contemporizing the list to include those levitical tribes most active at a particular moment in Israelite history. This observation is instructive even if Rehm's situation of this moment in the Tribal League can no longer be accepted. If this is what is happening, it would appear to be an internal development within P.

Genealogical Fluidity in the Levitical Lines

The analysis above of Num 26:58a has demonstrated genealogical fluidity in the biblical presentation of the Levites in two ways. First, the appending of the secondary list of the Libnite, Hebronites, Mushites, and Korathites to the established Levitical subtribes of the Gershonites, the Kohathites, and the Merarites shows dynamic fluidity in the understanding of generational barriers. Second, the choice by the Priestly writer to include certain second- and third-generation names and not others shows the adaptability of the genealogical genre to the needs and concerns of the occasion for which the genealogy is recounted. That the entirety of the second and third generations were not included, only a subsection thereof, shows that the genealogical logic of the Israelites also tolerated the practice described by Wilson and others as "telescoping" or the collapse (or omission) of all or parts of generations in a given articulation of a genealogy.[47] Unfortunately, in this case, the reasons motiving the inclusion of specifically Libnite, Hebronites, Mushites, and Korathites remain largely speculative.

The Fraternity of Moses and Aaron

A yet more striking case of the genealogical fluidity within P is found in the account of Moses and Aaron as brothers. The biblical references to the relationships between Moses, Aaron, and Miriam are as follows:

Exod 6:20a (P)

ויקח עמרם את יוכבד דדתו לו לאשה ותלד לו את אהרן ואת משה

Amram took Jochebed his kinswoman as a wife, and she bore him Aaron and Moses.

Num 26:59b (P)

ותלד לעמרם את אהרן ואת משה ואת מרים אחתם

She bore to Amram Aaron, Moses, and Miriam, their sister.

Exod 7:1, 28:1, 4, and 41, Lev 16:2, Num 20:8 amd 27:13 (P)

אהרן אחיך

[spoken to Moses] Aaron, your brother

Lev 10:4 (P)

ויקרא משה אל מישאל ואל אלצפן בני עזיאל דד אהרן ויאמר אלהם קרבו שאו את אחיכם מאת פני הקדש אל מחוץ למחנה

Moses called to Mishael and Elzaphan, the sons of Uzziel, the uncle of Aaron, and he said, "Come near and carry your brothers away from the front of the sanctuary to a place outside the encampment."

Deut 32:50 (D)

אהרן אחיך

[spoken to Moses] Aaron, your brother

1 Chr 5:29[48]

ובני עמרם אהרן ומשה ומרים

The children of Amram are: Aaron, Moses, and Miriam

Exod 2:1, 2a and 4 (J)

וילך איש מבית לוי ויקח את בת לוי תהר האשה ותלד בן . . . ותתצב אחתו מרחק לדעה מה יעשה לו

A man from the House of Levi married a Daughter of Levi and she conceived
and bore a son . . . *His sister* stationed herself at a distance to know what would
become of him.

Exod 4:14 (J)

ויחר אף יהוה במשה ויאמר הלא אהרן אחיך הלוי ידעתי כי דבר ידבר הוא

The Lord was angry with Moses, and he said, "What about Aaron, *your Levite
brother?* I know that he speaks fluently.

Exod 15:20a (E)

ותקח מרים הנביאה אחות אהרן את התף בידה

Miriam the prophetess, *the sister of Aaron*, took the tambourine in her hand

The Priestly writer records the birth of Moses and Aaron (Exod 6:20). The
birth order recorded there is confirmed in 7:7 (also P), where Aaron is identified as three years older than Moses, and following the listing conventions
elsewhere in P, we may surmise that Aaron is the older of the two. Miriam
appears as the sister of both Aaron and Moses in Num 26:59a, a tradition
echoed in the 1 Chronicles 5:29a. Seven times in P and once in D, God refers
to Aaron in direct speech with Moses and describes him as אהרן אחיך, your
brother Aaron. All of these descriptions conform to the expected genealogical
relationships described in Exod 6:16–25, illustrated above.

Two of the descriptions of the relationships between Moses, Aaron, and
Miriam introduce some ambiguity in these established ties. In Lev 10:4,
material quite firmly and incontrovertibly ensconced in P, Moses describes
Uzziel as דד אהרן, the uncle of Aaron. This relationship conforms to the P
genealogy articulated in Exod 6:16–25. There Uzziel is a Kohathite, the
youngest brother of Amram, the father of Moses and Aaron. However, the
specific naming of Uzziel in relationship to Aaron and not to Moses is striking. The proximity to Aaron is more fully in focus in this text because of the
intense concern for cultic propriety which dominates this section of Leviticus
10. Leviticus envisions the cult as the domain of Aaron, and while proximity

to Aaron does not ensure security in the cult (Lev 10:1–3), one's genealogical relationship to Aaron is an essential part of the roles assigned to the cultic
functionaries. In this case, the description of Uzziel as דד אהרן, does not seem
to preclude the fact that, in the mind of P, Uzziel is also the uncle of Moses.

Such reciprocity of the relationship does not seem to be in view in Exod
15:20a. Miriam appears here for the first time in the Hebrew Bible by that
name.[49] She is introduced as אחות אהרן, *the sister of Aaron.* The brotherhood
of Aaron and Moses is mentioned nowhere in E. However, the antagonism
against Moses by Aaron and Miriam—who are brother and sister—plays out
quite dramatically in the Elohist narrative of Numbers 12. In contrast to the
Priestly writer, it cannot be assumed that for the Elohist the identification of
Miriam as the sister of Aaron would also imply that she is the sister of Moses.

The Yahwist account introduces even great ambiguity into the network of
relationships between Moses, Aaron, and Miriam. Aaron first appears in the
J narrative in Exod 4:27, when God speaks to him and calls him to go into
the wildness to meet Moses. The J story begins in Exodus with the account
of Moses' inauspicious birth (2:1–4). An unnamed Levite man marries and
unnamed Levite woman. An unnamed older sister watches over the unnamed
child, delivers him to the daughter of Pharaoh, where eventually the child
receives the name Moses (2:10). This account stands in tension with the P
presentation of Moses' origins. First, P envisions Aaron as the first child,
and Moses as the second. Given that Miriam is listed third, it would follow
that she would be the youngest, though perhaps she has been moved out of
birth order by reason of her gender. In contrast, the Yahwist presumes that
Moses' sister is older and, indeed, old enough to take care of and to watch
over the infant Moses away from the rest of the family. Further, in P Aaron
is three years older that Moses. The J account makes no mention of an older
son, nor does it reckon with how an older son might have escaped Pharaoh's
infanticidal decree.

The picture of the relationship between Moses and Aaron in J is further
illuminated by Exod 4:14 in which God chastises Moses for his reluctance
to speak and commends the skills of אהרן אחיך הלוי, Aaron, your Levite
brother. At first glance, this would seem to repeat the locutions P and D use
to describe the relationship between Moses and Aaron; however, here we
find an important qualification. While P and D use the phrase אהרן אחיך, J
here qualifies the character of this filial relationship with the adjective הלוי.
Aaron is not the "brother" of Moses in the meaning of a male born of the
same parents, but is a "brother" in the sense of a member of the same tribe:
Aaron is Moses' Levite brother. So important to J is Moses' membership in
the Levite tribe that it is the first detail mentioned in the account of Moses's
life. This meaning of "brotherhood" is expanded further four verses later in
4:18, where Moses asks his father-in-law Jethro: "let me go, that I may return

to my kin in Egypt (אלכה נא ואשובה אל אחי אשר במצרים)." Aaron first appears in
the J narrative in 4:27 when God speaks directly to him and asks him to meet
Moses in the wilderness.[50] No mention is made there of a filial relationship
between them. For these reasons, it would appear that for J the extent of the
connection between Moses and Aaron is their membership in the Levite tribe.

If neither J nor E has any knowledge of the brotherhood of Moses and
Aaron, it would seem that this innovation took place within the mind of P,
or in some otherwise unknown source available to P. In J and E, Moses are
Aaron are two independent Levite leaders call by God to bring redemption
to the Israelites. In P, they become brothers. Aaron's status is endorsed by
Moses, and Aaron functions with Moses's imprimatur. As we have seen
above, P is a hub of genealogical innovation and preservation. P creates the
brotherhood of Aaron and Moses, even as it reimagines the priestly subdivi-
sions of the Levites according to the concerns of its present-day cult.[51] The
effect of making Moses and Aaron brothers is that it allows both Aaron and
Moses to rise to positions of prominence, and it affirms the cultic authority
of Aaron's rightful heirs.

Name Affiliations as Tertiary Genealogy

The Levitical genealogies preserved in the biblical text are far more malleable
than they would appear. The social organization described in the segmented
genealogies of the Levites presents a picture of a priestly hierarchy, but this
is but a momentary snapshot. However, this hierarchical arrangement was
not static. My analysis above has shown the fluidity of these affiliations in
the within the P source itself. There appears to be operative with P process
at play whereby Levitical affiliations are communicated not simply through
patrimony (real or imagined) but also through name affinity groupings. That
is, the priestly name under which one operates can be a more reliable indica-
tion of the priestly tradition of which one is a scion than patrilineality.[52] These
priestly name affiliations are stronger than even the genealogical complexes
in which the individuals bearing those names are placed.

CONCLUSION

The evidence presented in this chapter has illustrated the following points.
First, genealogical material in the Bible follows overarching patterns demonstrated in genealogical material found in tribal societies and in the ancient
Near East. The chief patterns among these are fluidity and contextuality. The
biblical genealogical material is useful as a historiographic source only to the
extent that one may discern echoes of context and account for the fluidity

present in the texts. Second, the genealogical material in P demonstrates significant fluidity of the genealogical genre. The Priestly writer exploits this malleability it at least two ways: the surprising emphasis on second and third generation Levitical subtribes in Num 26:58a, and the invention of the brotherhood of Moses and Aaron.

NOTES

1. With Aaron, three years older, according to Exod 7:7.
2. *CMHE*, 206. Concerning this point Cross follows Exodus 6.
3. Gen 2:4; 5:1; 6:9; 10:1, 32; 11:10, 27; 25:12–13, 19; 36:1, 9; 37:2; Exod 6:16, 19; 28:10; Num 1:20, 22, 24, 26, 28, 30, 32, 34, 36, 38, 40, 42; and 3:1. Similarly, see Ruth 4:18; 1 Chr 1:29; 5:7; 7:2, 4, 9; 8:28; 9:9, 34; and 26:31. For more information, see Sven Tengström, *Die Toledotformel und die literarische Struktur der priestlerlichen Erweiterungsschicht im Pentateuch* (Coniectanea Biblica, Old Testament Series 17.8; Uppsala, Sweden: Seiten, 1981).
4. Tengström, *Die Toledotformel.*
5. Matt 1:1–17 and Luke 3:23–38.
6. Jubilees 4:1–33
7. Robert R. Wilson, *Genealogy and History in the Biblical World* (New Haven, CT: Yale University Press, 1977), 1–8.
8. James T. Sparks, *The Chronicler's Genealogies: Toward an Understanding of 1 Chronicles 1–9* (Atlanta, GA: SBL, 2008), 1–20.
9. For example, *b. Qidd.* 70b:13 and *m. Ketub.* 12b:2.
10. *Life of Josephus* 1:1, cited from *The Life; Against Apion* (trans. Henry St. J. Thackeray; Cambridge, MA: Harvard University Press, 1926).
11. *C. Ap.* 1:7.
12. Heinrich Ewald, *The History of Israel*, vol 1. (London: Longmans, Green & Co., 1869), 81.
13. Among others see: Ignaz Goldziher, *Mythology among the Hebrews and Its Historical Development* (London: Longsman and Greeg, 1877); W. Robertson Smith, *Kingship and Marriage in Early Arabia* (London: A & C Black, 1903); and Hermann Guthe, *Geschichte des Volkes Israel* (Tubingen, Germany: J.C.B. Mohr, 1904).
14. Wellhausen, *Prolegomena zur Geschichte Israels*, 224. "Wer hier geschichtliche Erkenntnis über altisraelitische Verhältnisse sucht, muss sich darauf legen, das Gras wachsen zu hören."
15. Wellhausen, *Prolegomena to the History of Israel*, 321–322.
16. Martin Noth, *A History of Pentateuchal Traditions* (Englewood Cliffs, NJ: Prentice-Hall, 1972), 214.
17. Robert Wilson objects to the terminology "authentic" vs. "secondary" used by Bernhard W. Anderson in his English translation of Noth's work. Wilson argues that *eigentliche Genealogie* is better understood as "primary genealogy" in the sense of "genealogy as such." The terminology of "authentic" conveys a sense of historical

reliability which Noth does not associate with any manifestation of the genre of genealogy. See Wilson, *Genealogy*, 6n13.

18. Noth, *Pentateuchal Traditions*, 215.

19. Ibid., 218.

20. William Foxwell Albright, *From Stone Age to Christianity* (2nd ed; Garden City, NY: Doubleday/Anchor, 1957), 236ff.

21. Wilson's research on biblical genealogy comes from his early scholarly work springing from his 1972 Yale dissertation supervised by S. Dean McBride. The published record of this research is found primarily in the following four works. Robert R. Wilson, "Old Testament Genealogies in Recent Research." *JBL* 94:2 (1975): 169–89; *Genealogy and History in the Biblical World* (New Haven, CT: Yale University Press, 1977); "Between 'Azel' and 'Azel' Interpreting the Biblical Genealogies," *BA* 42 (1979): 11–22; and "Genealogy, Genealogies," *ABD* 2:929–32.

A more recent treatment and reimagining of the use of genealogical material can be found in Andrew Tobolowsky, *The Sons of Jacob and the Sons of Herakles: The History of the Tribal System and the Organization of Biblical Identity*, FAT 2 (Tübingen, Germany: Mohr Siebeck, 2017): 2–11.

22. Though Wilson does not articulate this concerns in quite this way, J.J.M. Roberts summarized these concerns in his review of Wilson's work: J.J.M. Roberts, "Genealogy and History in the Biblical World by Robert R. Wilson," *JBL* 98 (1979): 115–117.

23. Wilson, *Genealogy*, 199.

24. Ibid., 46–47.

25. Wilson, "Old Testament Genealogies in Recent Research," 181.

26. Wilson, "Geneaologies," *ABD*, 2:930–931.

27. Wilson, *Genealogy*, 158–163.

28. Wilson, *Genealogy*, 166.

29. Of particular interest within these lists is the segmentation that takes place in the J account at the seventh generation from Adam, where the contemporary children of Lamech are sorted into clearly defined sociological positions defined by their crafts.

30. Wilson, *Genealogy*, 32.

31. Wilson vaguely notes to this point that "filiated individuals are never completely assimilated by the group, and this fact is usually expressed in the genealogy in some way" (p. 32).

32. Hutton, "Levitical Diaspora (I)," 228.

33. Hutton points to the studies of Gellner and Hamoudi on this point.

34. Wilson, *Genealogy*, 200.

35. Wilson, "Geneaolgies," *ABD* 2:931

36. Wilson, *Genealogy*, 201.

37. Möhlenbrink, "Die levitischen Überlieferungen," 197.

38. Leroy Waterman, "Some Determining Factors," 378.

39. Roland De Vaux, *Ancient Israel*, 370.

40. Merlin Rehm, "Studies." See further details below.

41. Exod 6:19; Num 3:20, 33; 1 Chr 6:4, 32; 23:21, 23; 24:26, 30.

42. Rehm, "Studies," 22.

43. Exod 6:18–20 and Num 26:58b.

44. Martin Noth, *Die israelitischen Personennamen in Rahmen der gemeinsemi-tischen Namengbung* (Hildesheim, Germany: Georg Olms, 1966), 56–57.

45. Rehm, "Studies," 233.

46. Numbers 16.

47. Wilson, *Genealogy*, 32–36. For another example see the genealogy of Adaiah in 1 Chr 9:12 and Neh 11:12. In this case, three generations are collapsed or "tele-scoped." For more further discussion see Sparks, *The Chronicler's Genealogies*, 20ff.

48. 1 Chronicles 6:3 in English.

49. In the narrative of Exod 2, the sister of Moses is unnamed.

50. Wellhausen argued that the character of Aaron was originally completely absent in J, and was only introduced with the combination of J and E. See Wellhausen, *Prolegomena*, 142–143.

51. See Tobolowsky, *The Sons of Jacob*, 80–84 for other compelling examples of P's creativity and use of fluid genealogical imagination.

52. Consider the following clusters of names, etymologically similar names, similar sounding names, and priestly affiliations to be considered in a forthcoming monograph.

Gershonite:
- Mushi, Moses
- Gershon, Gershom (Shamgar?),
- Jonathan, Eli, Abiathar

Kohathite:
- Aaron, Hebron,
- Nadab and Elihu,
- Eleazar = Eliezer,
- Phineas (Num), (Phineas & Hophni, 1 Sam?)
- Zadok (Chr?)

Kenite:
- Hobab, Jethro, Moses, Gershom (Shamgar?)

Chapter 5

Holy Priests

Moses, Aaron, and Priestly Authority in the Pentateuch

This chapter has three primary aims. First, I will look at those key passages from the Pentateuch describing conflict between Moses and Aaron through the lens of the narratological integrity of the passages. This narratologically driven reading calls into question Cross's analysis on a significant number of cases. Second, I will sketch the contours of the unique perspectives of the Pentateuchal sources on the institutive narratives, activities, and abilities of Moses and Aaron, with particular emphasis on the specific roles and responsibilities attached to each. Finally, I will summarize the unique perspectives of E, P, J, and D as they relate to Moses's and Aaron's priestly duties and authority, as well as the literary dependencies between the sources that emerge in the analysis.

SOME METHODOLOGICAL NOTES

This chapter is, perhaps even more than the previous, the point in this monograph where I might transgress irreparably the suspension of disbelief with which readers doubtful of the source critical study of the Pentateuch have indulged me thus far. The methods and methodologies of Pentateuchal criticism have become highly divisive, leaving fissures the size of an ocean in the scholarly community. Speaking in most general terms, on the one side are those scholars[1] who may loosely be described as "Fragmentarians" or "Supplementarians,"[2] and on the other side are those designated[3] as Documentarians or "Neo-Documentarians."[4]

I acknowledge that positioning this study within a conversation of Documentary analysis, and choosing as my primary interlocutors those scholars working within Documentary analysis, inherently narrows the appeal and scope of this work. Lamentably, this will fall along ideologically and, in many cases, geographically defined lines. Whatever limitations one might discover in my analysis that follows (and there are many, to be sure) within each and every text discussed there are interpretive cruces innumerable that *could* have been discussed, and perspectives that *could* have been treated at great length. My goal is not to exhaust every exegetical and textual possibility, nor is it to catalogue an ideologically diverse collection of scholarly perspectives on each issue, but to sketch a rough picture of the priestly roles occupied by Aaron and Moses and the web of relationships that exist between these two characters.

This investigation positions itself within the Neo-Documentarian camp, all the while recognizing that there is a process of accretion of details and layers within each source, as we have already seen in the discussion of the internal development of P in chapter 4. This analysis also takes as a starting point the rejection of the historical schemas of classical source criticism, the dates Wellhausen and those after him associated with each of the sources, and the so-called identifying features and vocabulary lists used to define the sources. *Narrative continuity* forms the sole basis for a productive understanding of the source divisions and provides the only reliable criterion for delimiting the voices.

For Cross and the scholarly climate in which he wrote, the source divisions of the Pentateuch had been well established in the preceding century. Likewise, the historical and social origins associated with these sources were often accepted *de rigueur*. This is no longer the case, and Cross's analysis of the stories of priestly conflict warrants a thoroughgoing revision. Moreover, his assumptions about the proximity of the Pentateuchal sources to the Davidic monarchy are no longer assumed, and if the Mushite Hypothesis in any form is to have any currency to speak in the present environment, these historical dependencies must be thoroughly dismantled.

The Neo-Documentarian Perspective

Baruch Schwartz,[5] Joel Baden, and Jeffrey Stackert (the intellectual leaders of the so-called Neo-Documentarians) have made great strides articulating more clearly than ever the boundaries of the constituent documents of the Pentateuch. Their work has emphasized the narrative continuity of the hypothetical documents J, E, D, and P documents and freed them from the complex and tangled historical moorings that have attended Pentateuchal scholarship over the last half-century.

Yet, this study cannot proceed without heeding critique of this Neo-Documentarianism, particularly as voiced by David Carr and many others.[6]

Aside from a methodological difference about the discernibility of an independent "E" document, Carr advocates an awareness of the realities of textual transmission, with concern for the accretion of textual material to create harmony in places where it might have originally been lacking. Such a warning is well heeded and will stay within view at all points, particularly as it pertains to disparities signifying the accretion of textual material within individual sources. What is fundamentally in question here is the narrative integrity of the passages and the affiliations that may be found among them. The goal of this analysis is to understand the independent stories of priestly function and conflict with respect to Moses and Aaron disentangled from the historical-interpretive web on which Cross's analysis depended.

NARRATIVES OF PRIESTLY CONFLICT INVOLVING MOSES, AARON, AND THEIR SUCCESSORS

The following four Pentateuchal narrative complexes describe related conflicts between Moses and Aaron and their Successors:

1. The Golden Calf (Exod 32:1–35);
2. Aaron and Miriam challenge Moses (Num 12:1–16) together with the status Moses's Midianite Heritage (Exod 4:24–28, Exod 18, and Num 10:29–32);
3. Baal Peor (Num 25:1–5, 6–15); and
4. Nadab and Abihu (Lev 10:1–7) and Dathan and Abiram (Num 16:1–50).

I will deal with each in turn.

The Golden Calf

Exodus 32:1–35 describes a conflict between Moses and Aaron over the creation and destruction of a Golden Calf. The contours of this narrative and its constituent parts are essential for understanding the nature of the relationship between Moses and Aaron. After reviewing the perspective of Cross quickly surveyed in the previous chapter, I will describe the internal continuity of the narrative as well as its external continuity with surrounding material.

Cross's Reading of the Golden Calf

The creation and veneration of the golden calf by Aaron is perhaps the most perplexing conflict in the account of the wilderness wanderings. Cross divides this passage into its constituent sources, assigning 32:1–6, 15–20,

and 35 to the Elohistic source, and the remainder either to J or to the editor
who in Cross's view produced a combined JE document. The E text Cross
reconstructs reads as follows:

Exod 32:1–6, 15–20, and 35

1 When the people saw that Moses delayed to come down from the mountain,
the people gathered around Aaron, and said to him, "Come, make gods for us,
who shall go before us; as for this Moses, the man who brought us up out of
the land of Egypt, we do not know what has become of him." 2 Aaron said to
them, "Take off the gold rings that are on the ears of your wives, your sons, and
your daughters, and bring them to me." 3 So all the people took off the gold
rings from their ears, and brought them to Aaron. 4 He took the gold from them,
formed it in a mold, and cast an image of a calf; and they said, "These are your
gods, O Israel, who brought you up out of the land of Egypt!" 5 When Aaron
saw this, he built an altar before it; and Aaron made proclamation and said,
"Tomorrow shall be a festival to the LORD."

15 Then Moses turned and went down from the mountain, carrying the two
tablets of the covenant in his hands, tablets that were written on both sides,
written on the front and on the back. 16 The tablets were the work of God, and
the writing was the writing of God, engraved upon the tablets. 17 When Joshua
heard the noise of the people as they shouted, he said to Moses, "There is a noise
of war in the camp." 18 But he said, "It is not the sound of the song of victors,
or the sound of the song of losers; it is the sound of singing that I hear." 19 As
soon as he came near the camp and saw the calf and the dancing, Moses' anger
burned hot, and he threw the tablets from his hands and broke them at the foot
of the mountain. 20 He took the calf that they had made, burned it with fire,
ground it to powder, scattered it on the water, and made the Israelites drink it.

35 Then the LORD sent a plague on the people, because they made the calf—the
one that Aaron made.[7]

In this E text, as Cross has identified it, blame for the cultic indiscretion
is shared between Aaron and the people. According to Cross such a strong
polemic against Aaron could not originate in Jerusalem or any place associated with the reputation of Aaron. "[T]he polemical form of the tradition
of Aaron's bull must have originated in an old northern priesthood, a rival
priesthood of non-Aaronite lineage, defenders of an alternate iconographic
tradition."[8] Cross associates the Elohist with the northern kingdom of Israel,
and connects this anti-Aaron sentiment specifically with the Mushites serving
at the sanctuary of Shiloh. This polemic originating in Shiloh was directed at
followers of Aaron and the cultic symbols, namely the bull, employed at the
Bethel sanctuary.

In the E narrative, Moses himself addresses the cultic indiscretion of the calf in v. 20 through burning, grinding, and forced ingestion of the remains of the cult symbol. The narrative in canonical form does not stop there. In vv. 26–29, the "Levites rally to Moses' side and slay . . . about three thousand apostates, neighbor and kindred alike. For their single-minded fidelity they are consecrated priests."[9] Cross notes that such an account of the origin of the Levites' priesthood stands in tension with the Priestly writings, which in his opinion understand Aaron to be the patron of priestly devotion. He notes, however, that this account of the ordination of the Levites finds its nearest analogy in the blessing of Levi spoken by Moses in Deut 33:8–10.[10]

Re-Reading the Golden Calf

The bounds of the Golden Calf narrative and the literary seams within it warrant careful consideration. Richard Elliott Friedman, in his now classic articulation of the source divisions of the Pentateuch, understands the entirety of Exod 32:1–33:11 to belong to the E narrative.[11] Expanding on the conceptual framework Cross laid for the interpretation of this passage, Friedman argues that the author of E was a Shilonite Levite likely descended from Moses, and that this story of conflict between Moses and Aaron and antagonism to the cult of the calf is a narrative method of meting out the actual agenda of the author, that is, in protesting "oppressive Judean [Jerusalemite] economic policies, the establishment of an independent kingdom under Jeroboam, and the superior status of Moses."[12] He sees neither fissures nor seams within the text, only a continuous whole, albeit with slight narratival tensions. This nuance notwithstanding, the programmatic aim of the text is a resounding critique of Aaron and those allied with or descended from him and those who embrace the cultic iconography associated with him. Friedman claims:

> The golden calf story reveals more about its author than probably any other story in J or E. In addition to all that it tells us about its author's background and about its author's skill in fashioning a story, it conveys how deep his anger was toward those who had displaced his group in Judah and in Israel. He could picture Aaron, ancestor of the Jerusalem priesthood, as committing heresy and dishonesty. He could picture the national symbols of Israelite religion as objects of idolatry. He could picture the nation who accepted these symbols as deserving a bloody purge. What he pictured Moses doing to the golden calf was what he himself might have liked to do to the calves of Dan and Beth-El: burn them with fire, grind them thin as dust.[13]

Is the episode of the Golden Calf monolithically Elohist, as Friedman claims or are fragments of other documents discernible within its narrative as Cross's analysis implies? Beyond this, what external narratives does the Golden Calf story develop?

The Internal Continuity of the Golden Calf Story

There are two frequently analyzed points of narrative tension within the Golden Calf story: the conversation between Moses and Yahweh in vv. 5–15 (or perhaps, starting in 6 or 9), and the ordination of the Levites in vv. 26–29.[14]

Julius Wellhausen,[15] Martin Noth,[16] S.R. Driver,[17] Alan Jenks,[18] Alan McNeile,[19] and others[20] have argued that the conversation between Moses and Yahweh is material from a separate source placed into the larger narrative about the Golden Calf. Joel Baden has presented the clearest argument for the intrusion of this material in the E source by appeal to a predictable syntactic pattern of command and fulfillment that is a formal and universal feature of biblical Hebrew style.[21] The form of the pattern includes "a command issued in the imperative followed by the remainder of the speech between the two characters, and then the immediate fulfillment of the command, using the same verb, in the same *binyan*, in the waw-consecutive."[22]

Exodus 32:6 proceeds quite naturally from v. 5, which ends with Aaron proclaiming the following day will be a festival to the LORD (חג ליהוה מחר). "They rose early the next day (ממחרת) and offered burnt offerings and brought sacrifices of well-being; and the people sat down to eat and drink, and rose up to revel." While Moses is still up on the mountain, v. 7 narrates Yahweh communicating to Moses what has taken place down in the Israelite camp in his absence. Yahweh opens with the command for Moses to descend the mountain immediately.

Exod 32:7

וידבר יהוה אל משה לך רד כי שחת עמך

The LORD said to Moses, "Go down at once! Your people have acted perversely . . .

This initial command is fulfilled by Moses in v. 15: "then Moses turned and went down from the mountain . . . (ויפן וירד משה מן ההר)." However, before its fulfillment, the conversation between Moses and Yahweh is interrupted by speech formulae in the waw-consecutive in vv. 9 and 11, and by further action by Yahweh in v. 14.

9 ויאמר יהוה אל משה, The LORD said to Moses . . .

11 ויחל משה את פני יהוה אלהיו, Moses implored the LORD, his God . . .

14 וינחם יהוה על הרעה, Yahweh changed his mind about the destruction

All three of these narrative actions interrupt the standard command-fulfillment pattern, betraying the awkward appendage of vv. 9–14 onto the conversation between Yahweh and Moses that concluded in v. 8 and the proper continuation of the narrative in v. 15 of Moses descending the mountain.[23]

Baden stops short of affiliating this intrusion into the Golden Calf narrative with another Pentateuchal source because the parallel passage in Deut 9:12–14 also includes the same two interruptions in speech found in the Exodus passage. He determines that the passage of E available to the compiler of D must have already included this interruption, that this particular violation of the command-fulfillment pattern is a matter of the internal development of E. Baden goes on to state that this textual interruption "is not relevant to the Documentary Hypothesis in its strictest sense" because for him the reader must focus solely on "uncovering the text of the documents which make up the Pentateuch in their final form before combination."[24] His position on this matters toes the Neo-Documentarian line, as it were. However, the internal development of E must always be of concern in so far as it can be determined. In this particular case, the narratival interruption presented by this seam within E is minimal. Choosing to interrupt the comprehensible narrative at this point is unnecessary, and any choice to do so would be motivated by a commitment other than narrative consistency. As it is, this section of the narrative stands as a whole.

Moses's response to the Golden Calf is quick and decisive. In vv. 19–20, he breaks the tablets of the law at the foot of the mountain, burns the calf statue, grinds it into powder, and forces the Israelites to drink the powder mixed with water. Aaron explains to Moses what happened in vv. 21–24, and how the calf came to be:

v. 24

וָאֹמַר להם למי זהב התפרקו ויתנו לי ואשלכהו באש ויצא העגל הזה

I said to them, 'Whoever has gold, take it off'; so they gave it to me, and I threw it into the fire, and this calf came out.

The events described after Aaron's explanation create a problem of sequence. In vv. 26–29, Moses enlists the help of the Levites (בני לוי) to exact punishment on the people. Moses tells them in v. 27b:

שימו איש חרבו על ירכו עברו ושובו משער לשער במחנה
והרגו איש את אחיו ואיש את רעהו ואיש את קרבו

Put your sword on your side, each of you! Go back and forth from gate to gate in the camp, and each of you kill your brother, your friend, and your neighbor.

In all, the Levites kill about three thousand men (v. 28) at Moses's command. It would appear this punishment is not enough to expiate the guilt incurred. In v. 29 Moses informs the assembly that their great sin is still an offense to Yahweh, but Moses will attempt to intercede for them and to make atonement (אכפרה, v. 30) for their sin. This attempt at intercession fails, and Yahweh strikes down (ויגף v. 35) the guilty parties. The repetition of the punishment for this single indiscretion—punishment at the hand of the Levites and punishment at the hand of Yahweh himself—poses a significant problem for the narrative.

This problem is resolved when the narrative about the Levites vv. 26–29 is isolated from the rest of the text. In this new sequence, immediately after Aaron offers Moses his version of how the calf came to be (vv. 22–24), Moses observes the Israelites running wild (וירא משה את העם כי פרע הוא כי פרעה אהרן, v. 25), and then the next day Moses addresses the assembly and offers to make atonement on their behalf (v. 30), an offer which Yahweh rejects (v. 33–34).

How then shall one understand the material in vv. 26–29, the violent activity of the Levites and the special honor of ordination/initiation into a special role of divine service (מלאו ידכם היום ליהוה, v. 29)? In this episode the Levites do not speak or interact with Moses, they simply carry out his command. Further, there is no explicit mention in vv. 26–29 of the reason for the purge or mention of the Golden Calf. Their obedience to Moses has won their special blessing, and the blessing has come at the price of their sons and brothers: "each one at the cost of a son or a brother, and so have brought a blessing on yourselves this day (כי איש בבנו ובאחיו ולתת עליכם היום ברכה, v. 29). This interruption is out of place in the Elohist narrative. Baden has argued that the episode is equally out of place in the P narrative, which describes the investiture of the Levites in Num 1–4; it is also out of place in the D narrative, which describes the Levites receiving their special status in Deut 10:8–9, after the receipt of the second tablets of the law.[25] The preceding J material in Exod 24:1–2, 9–11b describes the ascent of Sinai by Moses and others. The following J material in Exod 33:1–5 describes Moses's conversation with Yahweh in which Yahweh tells the Israelites to leave the vicinity of the mountain into the promised land, but to go without Yahweh, because the people are too stiff-necked (כי עם קשה ערף אתה, v. 3). Baden argues that the story of the investiture of the Levites makes little sense interrupting the smooth and logical sequence of both of these narratives where there is no occasion for such drastic punishment; rather this pericope is more naturally positioned after J's version of the events at Massah and Meribah.[26] The sequence of the J narrative is better understood as follows:

Exod 17:1bβ–7, 32:26–29

17:1bβ–7 There was no water for the people to drink. 2 The people quarreled with Moses, and said, "Give us water to drink." Moses said to them, "Why do you quarrel with me? Why do you test the LORD?" 3 But the people thirsted there for water; and the people complained against Moses and said, "Why did you bring us out of Egypt, to kill us and our children and livestock with thirst?" 4 So Moses cried out to the LORD, "What shall I do with this people? They are almost ready to stone me." 5 The LORD said to Moses, "Go on ahead of the people, and take some of the elders of Israel with you; take in your hand the staff with which you struck the Nile, and go. 6 I will be standing there in front of you on the rock at Horeb. Strike the rock, and water will come out of it, so that the people may drink." Moses did so, in the sight of the elders of Israel. 7 He called the place Massah and Meribah, because the Israelites quarreled and tested the LORD, saying, "Is the LORD among us or not?"

32:26–29 Then Moses stood in the gate of the camp, and said, "Who is on the LORD'S side? Come to me!" And all the sons of Levi gathered around him. 27 He said to them, "Thus says the LORD, the God of Israel, 'Put your sword on your side, each of you! Go back and forth from gate to gate throughout the camp, and each of you kill your brother, your friend, and your neighbor.'" 28 The sons of Levi did as Moses commanded, and about three thousand of the people fell on that day. 29 Moses said, "Today you have ordained yourselves for the service of the LORD, each one at the cost of a son or a brother, and so have brought a blessing on yourselves this day."

This re-arranged sequence in J provides the narrative with a clear punishment for the quarrelling at Massah and Meribah. Further, the question at the heart of Israelite quarrelling was the question: "is Yahweh with us or not? (היש יהוה בקרבנו אם אין, 17:7)." This question is resumed by Moses's own question/call to action in 32:26, "whoever is for Yahweh, [come] to me! (מי ליהוה אלי). The Levites who rallied to answer this call demonstrated their exceptionality over and above the rest of the Israelites. In J the Levites are not simply the ones willing and faithful to act as agents of divine justice; their ready answer to Moses's question perhaps even intimates they did not engage in the quarrelsome rebellion at Massah and Meribah in the first place. Baden provides further evidence for the re-arranging of the J narrative by appealing to Moses's blessing of the Levites in Deut 33:8–11, which also brings together the themes of Massah and Meribah and the special status of the Levites.[27] The larger implications of this connection for the unique perspective of the Yahwist on Moses, Levites, and the priesthood will be spelled out in 5.3.1 below.

The External Continuity of the Golden Calf Story

The majority of scholars engaged in Pentateuchal source division associate the episode of the Golden Calf in whole or on part with E[28] or with the even more hypothetically rarified JE[29] text. A small minority have understood the text to consist primarily of Jahwistic material, most notably Martin Noth,[30] Brevard Childs,[31] and John van Seters.[32] The primary issue at stake in the affiliation of this and any Pentateuchal text is narrative continuity. The episode of the Golden Calf takes place within the larger literary complex of the Sinai story, beginning in Exod 19. Immediately preceding Exod 32 is a block of instruction and legislation concerning the construction of the Tabernacle in 25:1–31:11 with a brief excursus on Sabbath observance in 31:12–17. This legislative/instructive material unequivocally belongs to P, and the P narrative clearly transitions to introduce another episode in 31:18,[33] but it in no way anticipates the conflict posed by the creation of the Golden Calf, in terms of either salient themes or characters engaged in the action.

The final section of J material preceding the Golden Calf episode is found back in Exod 19:20–25. An enticing element of this text that might seem to anticipate the institution of the Levites in 32:26–29 is Yahweh's warning to Moses about priests in 19:22.

וגם הכהנים הנגשים אל יהוה יתקדשו פן יפרץ בהם יהוה

Even the priests who approach the LORD must consecrate themselves or the LORD will break out against them.

However, as alluring as speculating a connection here to the special institution of the Levites might be, Yahweh also instructs Moses to descend the mountain and to bring Aaron back up with him while leaving the remainder of the priests and other Israelites at the foot of the mountain (v. 24). At this point the J narrative envisions a special, elevated role for the character of Aaron, leaving out other ranks of priests. The episode of the Golden Calf subverts both of these trajectories, denigrating Aaron, and, at least in its canonical form, elevating the Levites above Aaron. Considering all of these factors, it seems quite unlikely in this case that the broader narrative of Exod 32 resumes the Yahwistic narrative left off in Exod 19:20–25.

The last phrase uttered by E prior to the lengthy legislation about the Tabernacle that dominates Exodus 25–31 is a reference to Moses remaining on Mt. Sinai for forty days and forty nights (24:18). Exodus 32:1 opens with the people growing anxious about Moses's delay on the mountain. The earlier portion of Exodus 24 describes the covenant making ceremony that took place after Moses wrote down the words Yahweh spoke on the mountain (v. 4). The ceremony included Moses manipulating sacrificial blood acquired

by the young men of Israel (נערי בני ישׂראל), whom Moses charged with offi-
ciating the sacrifices to Yahweh. After reading the words of the Book of the
Covenant (ספר הברית) to the people, Moses dashed the people with half of the
reserved blood from the sacrifices. This cultic ceremony of covenant renewal
should have inspired the Israelites and prepared them to face new challenges
ahead. However, Moses tarried on the mountain for too long, and they turned
to Aaron for cultic guidance. The trajectory and development of the E narrative between Exodus 24 and 32 is quite clear—a covenant is established, the
covenant is compromised, and the people are punished. This narrative continues through the theophany to Moses ending in Exod 33:23, and it resumes
with the narrative in Numbers 11 and 12, which begins with complaining
(11:1), proceeds through the miraculous provision of food in the wilderness,
continues with Moses appointing elders to officiate in his stead (11:16–30),
and ends with another story of conflict between Moses and Aaron, this time
including Miriam (12:1–16).[34]

Aaron and Miriam against Moses

In Cross's reading of the story of conflict between Aaron and Miriam, on
the one side, and Moses, on the other, he identifies two key objectives in the
narrative. He understands the story, first, to establish Moses's superiority to
Aaron, and second, to affirm the legitimacy of the Mosaic/Mushite priesthood despite its "mixed blood."[35] The story describes Aaron and Miriam's
joining forces to critique Moses for marrying a Cushite woman (אשׁה כשׁית,
12:1) Building on work by Albright, Cross addressed the possibility that
this Cushite wife might be someone other than Zipporah, who features more
prominently in J material, namely in Exod 2:21 and 4:25. Relying on references to a term *kūš* that is a biform of the more frequent *kūšān*—a known
district in the Midianite League—it seems likely, however, that the reference
here is to none other than Zipporah, the daughter of the Midianite priest.[36] The
narrative jumps immediately to question the nature of Moses's authority as
the mediator of divine oracles. They ask in Numbers 12:2:

הרק אך במשה דבר יהוה הלא גם בנו דבר

Has the LORD only spoken by Moses? Does he not also speak by us?

Yahweh harshly chastises Aaron and Miriam for the insubordination, and
Miriam is stricken with snow-white scales (מצרעת כשׁלג, v. 10). In an ironic
turn, Aaron must now turn desperately and penitently to Moses, whom he
had just criticized. Moses entreats Yahweh with the prayer: O God, pray,
heal her! (אל נא רפא נא לה, v. 13), and Yahweh answers Moses's mediation by

prescribing that Miriam must be shut out of the camp (ותסגר מרים מחוץ למחנה)
for seven days (v. 14).

That this episode explores a conflict between Aaron and Moses is beyond
question. Less clear, however, are Cross's claims that the purpose of the narrative is to address specifically Moses's *priestly* superiority to Aaron and to
address potential questions about the mixed blood of Moses's progeny. What,
then, is/are the conflict/s described?

This passage opens by identifying the source of the tension between
Moses and his siblings as his Cushite wife, and the narrative seems quickly
to transition to a discussion about the unparalleled authority Moses wields.
Are these two separate matters? Friedman claims it is "psychologically
interesting that their actual complaint never refers to the wife,"[37] implying
that the wife and the authority are separate matters. Cross's analysis attaches
greater significance to the mention of the Cushite/Zipporah, but leaves it as
a peripheral issue.

Chapter 12 continues the E narrative found in 11:11–12, 14–17, 24–30,[38]
which describes the divinely initiated sharing of Moses's judicial, charismatic, and oracular authority with seventy appointed elders (11:16). In ch.
11, Yahweh inaugurates this scheme of elder administration in response to
Moses' complaint about the immense burden of his work (vv. 11–12, 14–15).
Yahweh himself makes this sharing of authority possible.

Numbers 11:25

The LORD came down in the cloud and spoke to him, and took some of the
spirit that was on him and put it on the seventy elders; and when the spirit rested
upon them, they prophesied. But they did not do so again.

Significantly, this is not the first time the theme of Moses sharing his
authority has been raised in the E document. However, this time Yahweh
explicitly aided in the sharing of the authority. In Exod 18 earlier in E,
Jethro—Moses's father-in-law, the Midianite priest, and father of Zipporah—
supplies Moses with a plan for sharing his administrative and magisterial
authority with certain capable people (אנשי חיל, Exod 18:25) of his choosing.

There is no specific mention of Aaron or Miriam among either of these
groups of leaders sharing in the delegated authority of Moses. Indeed,
the only elders named are Eldad and Medad, who were among the elect
(המה בכתבים), but who happened not to be with the others at the Tent of
Meeting (Num 11:26). In E, Moses's authority is incomparable, and yet it
is delegated to certain officials for administrative purposes. In light of this,
Aaron and Miriam are complaining about being left out of the administration
scheme of rule by elders. In E this scheme of sharing Moses's incomparable
spirit was inaugurated by Jethro in Exod 18 and instituted by Yahweh in Num

11.[39] It is on the heels of this institution that we find Aaron and Miriam's objection to it. The complaint against Moses's wife and against Moses himself are one and the same. Moses is not sharing authority with them, and he is not sharing it with them because of the influence of his wife and father-in-law. Yahweh's implied answer to their question הלא גם בנו דבר? would seem to be a resounding "No!" In E, Yahweh speaks to those he or Moses has chosen, and that choice coincides with the elders appointed to administrative and oracular offices. Aaron and Miriam are not part of this group of appointed leaders.

Baal Peor

For Cross, the P account of the Affair at Peor (דבר פער, Num 25:18) is the most significant piece of pro-Aaronite and anti-Mushite propaganda preserved in the biblical text. An Israelite, later identified as Zimri (v. 14), brought into his family (ויקרב אל אחיו) a Midianite noblewoman, identified later as Cozbi (v. 18). This indiscretion happened while Moses and the rest of the Israelites were weeping at the entrance of the Tabernacle (v. 6). The nature of their "drawing near" was such that the execution of the couple *in flagrante delicto* was accomplished with a single strike of the spear piercing through both abdomens. Verse 6 specifies that the event took place in the sight of Moses and the Assembly of the Israelites (לעיני משה ולעיני כל עדת בני ישראל). Cross argues that the beginning of the P narrative "suggests a form of the story in which Moses viewed the sacrilege but *failed* to act, at least until Phinehas took initiative."[40] For Cross, the aim of this pro-Aaronite polemic against the Midianites (and by association, the Mushites) is to show that "the priesthood passed to the Aaronites precisely for their service in cleansing Israel from the taint of Midianite rites!"[41] He also identifies parallels to the rejection of Moses's priestly authority in this text in the rejection of the Mushite sons of Eli in 1 Sam 2:22–25, who are also denounced for their sexual indiscretions in proximity to a holy shrine. The gist of the critique is that what Moses merely permitted to occur in Num 25 those descended from Moses did themselves at Shiloh in 1 Sam 2:22–25.

There are three issues at stake in Cross's reading of Num 25:1–18: (1) the role of Moses in what unfolds, (2) the nature of the condemnation of the Midianites, and (3) the extent to which the text is conscious of Moses's relationship to Midian. I will discuss each in turn.

First, Cross recognized that Num 25 contains a story from P (vv. 6–18) appended to an Epic story, which he understood as JE (vv. 1–5). It will be argued below that the Epic story is more precisely understood within the J narrative.[42] These events are set at Shittim, and the offense is described in the opening verses:

Num 25:1–2

While Israel was staying at Shittim, the people began to have sexual relations
with the women of Moab. These invited the people to the sacrifices of their
gods, and the people ate and bowed down to their gods. So Israel yoked itself to
the Baal of Peor, and the LORD'S anger was kindled against Israel.

The Israelites are condemned for entering into sexual relationships with
Moabite women and for subsequent apostasy. Yahweh offers Moses the
prescribed punishment for this offence: the, leaders of the people (ראשי העם)
must be piked in the sun (והוקע אותם ליהוה נגד השמש, v. 4). Moses communicates these instructions to the Judges: "each of you kill his people who have
bound themselves to Baal Peor" (הרגו איש אנשיו הנצמדים לבעל פעור, v. 5). At
this point the story drops off, and this is the last discernible narrative in the
entire Yawhist account.

This account comes on the heels of the poem (21:27–30) preserved in J
recounting the victory of Sihon the Amorite over the king of Moab, a victory
characterized in terms of the Moabite women taken captive.

Numbers 21:29

אוי לך מואב אבדת עם כמוש
נתן בניו פליטם ובנתיו בשבית למלך אמרי סיחון

Woe to you, O Moab! You are undone, O people of Chemosh!
He has made his sons fugitives, and his daughters captives, to an Amorite
king, Sihon.

The Israelites take possession of this land of the Amorites filled with captive
Moabite women in v. 31. It is unsurprising that in the very next J narrative
(placed in canonical form after the Balaam oracles) the Israelite men are
inclined to the range of activities glossed by the phrase in לזנות אל בנות מואב
in 25:1. In this J narrative, the sin is explicitly with Moabite women and fault
is not assigned to Moses in any way. Moses acts immediately in conformity
with the instructions of Yahweh. He communicates at least part of the divine
command to the people, and one might imagine that in its original form, there
follows a narrative of fulfillment. The canonical form, however, appends a
story taken from P in the place of a hypothetical J fulfillment narrative.

That a different story begins in v. 6 is obviated by a subtle but important
shift in the details of the Israelite sexual indiscretion. No longer are Israelite
men involved with Moabite women (בנות מואב); rather, a single Israelite has
brought a forward a Midianite woman (המדינית). Within the description that
this event took place in front of Moses (לעיני משה, v. 6), Cross finds hints
of Moses's complicity. Verse 6 also describes collective weeping, but it is

unclear how the collective weeping (והמה בכים פתח אהל מועד) relates temporally to Moses witnessing the Israelite and the Midianitess. Is this weeping
in response to the profane relationship? Or was some manner of communal
mourning already taking place at the entrance of the Tabernacle when the
two offenders came forward? The notice of weeping is not placed within
the consecution of action in the *wayyiqtol*; rather, it is offered as a notice
outside of the clear progression of time. The very next action after ויקרב in
v. 6 is Phinehas' seeing the events and taking up arms in v. 7 (וירא . . . then . . .
ויקם . . . then . . . ויקח). The narrative provides no time for Moses to express
objection, support, or complicity.

Within the larger P narrative this episode plays an important role in the
story of priestly succession and authority. The last episode related by the
Priestly writer is that of the death of Aaron in Num 20:22–29. There at
Mount Hor, Moses strips Aaron of his vestments, places them on Eleazar,
and Aaron dies at the summit (v. 28). When the two descend from the mountain the following notice is given in v. 29: "When all the congregation saw
that Aaron had died, all the house of Israel mourned (ויבכו) for Aaron thirty
days." The temporally ambiguous weeping in 25:6 is clarified by the P passage that immediately follows it. The action in 25:6–19 takes place during
the period of mourning the death of Aaron. The actions of Phinehas—the son
of Eleazar who now wears Aaron's vestments—is an essential public display
of power, vigor, and priestly authority. Phinehas's actions secure for him and
for his descendants the eternal priestly covenant (ברית כהנת עולם, v. 13). For
P, the priestly line of Phinehas (and perhaps even of all Aaronites, but that
is unclear) is established permanently before the entire assembly of Israel by
Phinehas' enactment of the divine judgement, and it is established precisely at
the time in the narrative when there is a transition in leadership. If any delay,
hesitation, or acquiescence may be perceived on the part of Moses (which
neither grammar nor context warrant), then its sole function would be for the
upcoming heir of the Aaronic line to establish his ascendancy. Beyond this,
the specific conflict presented here with Midianites, sets the stage for P's
account of the Midianite War (31:1–54), as we see in Numbers 31:1–2: The
LORD spoke to Moses, saying, "Avenge the Israelites against the Midianites;
afterward you shall be gathered to your people."

Second, this theme of avenging the Midianites is found in the Pentateuch
only in P. The first reference to Midian and/or the Midianites in P appears
in the event at Peor, and there is not within the narrative a longstanding or
deep-seeded antagonism to Midian.[43] The creation of the Midianite antagonism develops only at the end of the P story. The defeat of the Midianites is
so important because Midian is the last obstacle in the Priestly account of
the conquest of the Transjordan.[44] Enacting vengeance against Midian is to

be the final achievement of Moses's life, after which he may die and transfer leadership to Joshua (Deut 34).

Cross argues that some of the antagonism against Israelite and Midianite sexual relations in Num 25 springs in part in response to traditions understanding Moses to have Midianite connections. According to both J and E, Moses's marital relationship connected him to an ancient line of Midianite and Kenite priests. Cross remarks that "[t]he survival of such traditions in the face of rival traditions of utter hostility to the Midianites is remarkable and suggests that Moses's interconnections with the priestly house of Midian were too old and well established to be suppressed quietly or forgotten."[45] Expanding the work of Aharoni[46] and Mazar,[47] Cross envisions an intertwined Midianite-Kenite-Mushite priesthood operative in Israel initially in the far south at Arad. The family of Heber the Kenite—a scion of this Midianite-Kenite-Mushite priesthood—migrated northward and continued there through the rise of the Monarchy.[48]

Third, it is unclear that P has any knowledge whatsoever of the Midianite connections Moses shares in J and in E. However, it should be observed that D seems to have excised a reference to Jethro in Deut 1:13–18, which, it would appear, is largely dependent on Exod 18:13–27 (E).[49] That the final achievement of Moses's life in P involves defeating Midianites is not in any obvious way founded in reaction to the J and E versions of Moses's life. Rather, it is rooted in the fact that for the Priestly narrative entrance to the Promise Land must be secured through Midian, making it the final foe.

Nadab and Abihu and Dathan and Abiram

For Cross, the stories of Nadab and Abihu (Lev 10:1–7) and the Priestly strata of the Dathan and Abiram story reflect "old rivalries between priestly families" in a web of pro-Aaronite and anti-Aaronite sentiment.[50] About these entangled critiques, Cross observes:

> In Leviticus 10, two Aaronic clans are repudiated, in Numbers 16, a Levitic clan. The ritual of bringing incense burners to the sanctuary appears in both; in both, fire from Yahweh consumes the sinners. In Leviticus 10, Aaron appears to be rebuked; in Numbers 16 it is the Levites who are rebuked, Aaron who is upheld, and both from the mouth of Moses! In short, a similar theme is used in two contexts, one anti-Aaronite, the other pro-Aaronite in bias.
>
> In Numbers 16–17, however, the tradition of ancient conflicts between Levitic or Mushite priests and the priestly house of Aaron stands far in the background. In the present form of the Priestly polemic the hierodule status of the Levite is assumed by the Priestly tradent . . .[51]

It is fitting here to consider each of these texts in turn to determine the nature, extent, and documentary affiliations of the critique Cross finds woven into these stories.

The story of Nadab and Abihu (Lev 10:1–7) is firmly enmeshed in a block of Priestly material extending from Exod 34 to Num 10. The text identifies Nadab and Abihu as sons of Aaron (בני אהרן). In their particular case this designation carries double significance. Earlier in P, Nadab and Abihu along with Eleazar and Ithamar are literally the progeny of Aaron and Elisheba (Exod 6:23). In Exod 28:1, God commands Moses to install the בני אהרן as priests who will serve before Yahweh at the Tabernacle: "Bring near to you your brother Aaron, and his sons with him, from among the Israelites, to serve me as priests—Aaron and Aaron's sons, Nadab and Abihu, Eleazar and Ithamar." The Yahwist also envisions a special role for Aaron, Nadab and Abihu in Exod 24:1 and 9, where they are allowed to see an unmediated vision of the God.[52] Evidently, Eleazar and Ithamar are left out of this experience in J.

Leviticus 10 is the first appearance of Nadab and Abihu in P after their commissioning as priests along with Eleazar and Ithamar in Exod 28. In the Leviticus passage, Nadab and Abihu offer the cryptic and often debated foreign fire (אש זרה, v. 1), and in response fire comes out from the presence of Yahweh, "consumes them" (ותאכל אותם, v. 2) though their clothed bodies still remain, and after Moses cites an otherwise unknown saying about the holiness and glorification of Yahweh, Aaron remains silent (וידם אהרן, v. 3). The silence of Aaron at this juncture has generated much discussion and debate about the place of speech and spoken in sung liturgy in the cult envisioned by P. Exploring all of the intricacies of these arguments is beyond the scope of the present discussion; however, it is essential for our purposes here to understand whether there is a decidedly negative implication to Aaron's silence.[53] Cross claims: "[i]t is obvious that Aaron does understand that he has been rebuked for sufficient cause and is without words to reply." Within the narrative itself there is a dearth of evidence for understanding Aaron as the object of Moses's rebuke. Moses's speech to Aaron in v. 3 following the outbreak of divine fire is explanatory: "Then Moses said to Aaron, "This is what the LORD meant when he said, 'Through those who are near me I will show myself holy, and before all the people I will be glorified.'"

In contrast, in the E account of the Golden Calf, Moses unabashedly questions Aaron about his actions and his motivation for them (Exod 32:21). In the P narrative of Lev 10, Moses presents no request for explanation, no chastisement, and no direct rebuke for influence Aaron might have had in the offering of foreign fire. Further, Moses provides instructions to Aaron, Ithamar, and Eleazar who will continue to serve at the altar of Yahweh. The particular actions Moses commends to them involve forgoing mourning practices for the sake of maintaining their priestly obligations: do not uncover your heads and do not rend your garments (ראשיכם אל תפרעו ובגדיכם לא תפרמו, v. 6).[54] Aaron's silence in v. 3 seems indeed to be a supererogation of the cautionary instructions Moses offers. Given that this text provides for the continued service of Aaron and his progeny at the altar of Yahweh, albeit through Ithamar and Eleazar not Nadab and Abihu, and given that the text contains no unequivocal condemnation for Aaron, it is quite difficult to maintain Cross's contention that this text offers even a muted critique of Aaron and the Aaronites. Indeed, one would never expect to find such a critique within the P document. That Nadab and Abihu alone (and not Aaron) are the characters condemned in this narrative is borne about by later remembrances of them in P.

Num 3:4

Nadab and Abihu died before the LORD when they offered illicit fire before the LORD in the wilderness of Sinai, and they had no children. Eleazar and Ithamar served as priests in the lifetime of their father Aaron.

Num 26:60–61

To Aaron were born Nadab, Abihu, Eleazar, and Ithamar. But Nadab and Abihu died when they offered illicit fire before the LORD.

What is present, however, is a clear statement from P about the gravity and seriousness with which the Aaronite priests must serve as thurifers at the altar of Yahweh, on threat of their lives and the wellbeing of the whole community.

Cross appeals to a second complex of stories in Num 16 involving divine judgement and the use of incense burners in service before Yahweh. Cross sees within the stories of Dathan and Abiram intermingled with the story of Korah a polemic against Levites jealous of their inferior cultic position *vis-à-vis* the Aaronites—that is, antagonism between the Aaronites and Mushites.

Cross notes rightly that Numbers 16 consists of both P material and "Epic"—or more precisely E—narrative.[55] When analyzing the precise contours of the polemics present within this complex of texts great care must be taken to disentangle the stories such that each can speak on its own terms. The three antagonists of this narrative Korah, Dathan, and Abiram are all mentioned together only three times, in 16:1, 24, and 27a.

1: "Now [took] Korah son of Izhar son of Kohath son of Levi, along with Dathan and Abiram sons of Eliab, and On son of Peleth—descendants of Reuben . . . "

24: "Say to the congregation: Get away from the dwellings of Korah, Dathan, and Abiram."

27a: "So they got away from the dwellings of Korah, Dathan, and Abiram . . . "

The complaint offered by Datan and Abiram—who are Reubenites and not part of a tribe with sacerdotal ambitions or affiliations—is quite different from the complaints offered by Korah, who is a Kohathite Levite, precisely as Moses and Aaron are. Korah and the band of others question who Moses and Aaron are to raise themselves above others of the Assembly of Yahweh (קהל יהוה).

Num 16:3

ויאמרו אלהם רב לכם כי כל העדה כלם קדשים ובתוכם יהוה ומדוע תתנשאו על קהל יהוה

They said to them, "You have gone too far! All the congregation are holy, everyone of them, and the LORD is among them. So why then do you exalt yourselves above the assembly of the LORD?

Of particular note here is the phrase in the complaint: כי כל העדה כלם קדשים, rendered into less fluent English: "for the entire congregation; all of them are holy." Holiness and the partitioning of holiness into specific groups and tasks for divine service are the key issues for Korah and his followers. Their complaint is against Moses *and* Aaron. When Moses responds to the complaint in v. 8, he specifically addresses his interlocutors as Levites: שמעו נא בני לוי. This address cannot include the Reubenites, Dathan and Abiram. The complaint of Dathan and Abiram is different from the complaint of the Levites. Not only were they not addressed by Moses in v. 8, it appears they were not gathered together with the rest of the assembly in the first place. In v. 12, Moses sends for Dathan and Abiram to appear before him, and they refuse to do so. Their complaint against Moses is bookended by their refusal to appear.

vv. 12bb–14

"We will not come! Is it too little that you have brought us up out of a land flowing with milk and honey to kill us in the wilderness, that you must also lord it over us? It is clear you have not brought us into a land flowing with milk and honey, or given us an inheritance of fields and vineyards. Would you put out the eyes of these men? We will not come!"

Dathan and Abiram are angry about living conditions and their prospects for the future, and they have directed their anger at Moses. There is no mention of Aaron or Aaron's involvement.

What emerges from this analysis is a picture of interwoven stories with two distinct objectives and two distinct outcomes. In the P story,[56] Korah and a band of 250 Israelite leaders lodge a cultic complaint against Moses and Aaron, and Moses offers a cultic test to vindicate himself—the test of the incense offerings. Korah and the others attempt to serve as incense bearers before Yahweh and, like Nadab and Abihu before them, a fire from Yahweh consumed them (ואש יצאה מאת יהוה ותאכל את החמשים ומאתים, v. 35). The drama of the conflict is heightened by the fact that Moses, Aaron, and Korah are all from the same Kohathite clan of the Levite tribe. For P, the Kohathites Levites are Aaronites conscribed to the service of moving holy objects and cultic furniture within the Tabernacle on their shoulders (Num 4:1–15, 7:9). The conflict at the core of this P narrative is jealousy between the specialized hierodules of the cult and the more prestigious Aaronites.

In contrast, the Dathan and Abiram episode in E[57] has none of these sacerdotal concerns. The question at stake is the authority of Moses as the absolute earthly leader of the Israelites. The incomparability of Moses as administrative and cultic leader is a well-known theme across all of the Elohist narratives, affirmed just a few chapters earlier in the conflict between Moses and his siblings, Aaron and Miriam. This passage is not anti-Aaronite, but it is enthusiastically and unreservedly pro-Moses, and it is marked against anyone who would impinge on this authority or would challenge it.

Preliminary Conclusions

The above analysis has shown that Cross's analysis of the narratives of priestly conflict does expose certain fissures in the biblical presentation of the institution of the Israelite priesthood. However, Cross has identified collections of details that betray strong anti-Moses and/or anti-Aaron sentiment in texts where there are far simpler and more obvious narratological explanations for the details identified. Furthermore, in certain of these cases the anti-Moses or anti-Aaron sentiments identified stand in fundamental tension with the *Tendenz* of the Pentateuchal source in which they occur. That is, Cross's key pieces of the pro-Mushite and/or pro-Aaronite propaganda are in muddled contexts and/or do not take sufficient account of the broader narratives from which the details are extracted. In the next section, I will summarize those points from the analysis above which reveal the contours of larger themes within the J, E, P, and D sources as they pertain to Moses, Aaron, their respective statuses are priests, and the priesthood in general.

SUMMARY OF VIEWS ABOUT MOSES,
AARON, AND PRIESTS IN THE SOURCES

The analysis of the texts of priestly conflict above has clarified the relationships that exist between Aaron, Moses, and their roles as priests within the sources. These observations will be summarized and integrated with an analysis of other texts pertaining to the visions of Moses, Aaron, and their priesthood in the Pentateuch. The goal of this section is to show how J, E, P, and, to a lesser extent, D have each appropriated the characters of Moses and Aaron and how these characters fit within the unique perspective of each source concerning the institution of Israelite priesthood, particularly related to the roles of priests as mediators of divine beneficence, mediators of the divine judgment, and mediators of divine communication.

The Yahwist (J)

I argued above that the account of the ordination of the Levites recorded in Exod 32:26–29 is best understood as affiliated with the Jahwist source. The compiler(s) of the Pentateuch placed it as a secondary (and, indeed, far more intense) response to the Elohist's narrative about the Golden Calf and the conflict between Aaron and Moses. However, within the J narrative, this account is more properly understood as a response to the events at Massah and Meribah in Exod 17:1bb–7. Wherever one places it, the effect of the narrative is the same: the Levites gain the favor of Moses and win for themselves the exalted status of ordination and blessing in Ex 32:29 by means of their outburst, killing some three thousand of their fellow Israelites including their own brothers and children.

This is not the only passage in the Yahwist connecting the Levites with the use of human force causing pain, death, or bloodshed. Joel Baden has collected a grouping of three additional texts that describe the role of what he terms "violence" in the characterization of the Levites: these are Gen 34, Gen 49, and Deut 33.[58] The account of Dinah in Gen 34 tells of brothers Levi and Simeon compelling a group of outsiders (kinsmen of Shechem) into circumcision and then killing them while they were recovering. This account is widely associated with the J narrative.[59] This account is remembered in the ancient poem on Gen 49:5–7, where Simeon and Levi are left landless for their violence. Baden argues that this ancient poem reflects the perspective of J even though it is not properly "from" J itself, but was an ancient text/tradition held sacred by J. "[W]hile the author of J is not the author of the poem, the poem belongs to the source J, just as in a novel in which a character sings a well-known song: the author of the novel is not the author of the song, but the song belongs to the novel."[60] Thus, there is a complex of three Yahwistic (or Yahwist-related) texts specifically linking Levi and the Levites with the use of force causing pain, death, or bloodshed. Of these four texts, the J section of Exodus 32 makes a specific connection between the Levites' use of force and their status as priests.

For J, Moses has other priestly connections outside the confines of the Israelite clans. He is the son-in-law of Reuel (Exod 2:16–18)/Hobab (Num 10:29) the Priest of Midian, marrying his daughter Zipporah.[61] As will be explored below, in E his father-in-law, Jethro, plays a prominent role in the narrative and in the systems of leadership Moses establishes. In J, Reuel/ Hobab the priest of Midian garners little more than a passing mention; his daughter, however, plays an important role in the manipulation of the blood of circumcision. While circumcision itself might not be a priestly activity, the manipulation of the blood of one being to placate divine wrath against another being has priestly overtones (as well as connections to the Passover rites). In Exod 4:24–26, J recounts Yahweh seeking to kills Moses, and Zipporah jumping into action to circumcise her son, applying the blood of the circumcision to Moses's body, and then proclaiming Moses a "groom of blood" (חתן דמים, 4:25). This manipulation of circumcision blood and pronouncement caused the deity to relent (וירף ממנו, v. 26) from the actions intended. For J, Moses is saved from destruction by Yahweh because of the intervention of his wife, the daughter of a Midianite priest, applying blood from another being in a decidedly sacrificial/priestly manner.[62] Describing the role of what he terms "violence" in priestly identity Yonatan Miller has observed: "the right lineage is *necessary*, but not *sufficient* for installation in the priesthood. Entry into the priestly caste is a function of the willingness to engage in sacred violence—even at the expense of, or perhaps especially at the price of, blood relatives."[63] While the category of "violence" is problematic when applied to biblical texts describing divine interactions, Miller's observations stands. Zipporah's circumcision and blood manipulation describes the ritual warding off a greater death by the officiant performing a controlled inoculation of death. This apotropaic use of force causing pain, death, or bloodshed concurs well with the Levite's use of such force later in J in Exod 32:26–29. There the greater wrath of Yahweh against the people (for the sin of Massah and Meribah) is abated by the sacrifice of the three thousand.[64]

Beyond the role of force in priestly identity in J, priesthood also entails an oracular component whereby the officiant comes into contact with the deity for the sake of communicating a message. In J, Aaron and others are able to see God, to speak with God, and even to eat with God (Exod 24:1–2, 9–11). In this particular text God chooses not to lay his hand on these appointed men coming to meet with him on Sinai. This stands in direct contrast to Aaron's status in E, where he (and Miriam) are among those whose access to the deity is indirect, whereas Moses's access is unobscured (Num 12).

The special status of Aaron and other priests to approach Yahweh in J is described in Exod 19:20–25. In particular, there is a special warning about priests approaching Yahweh on Sinai: "Even the priests who approach the LORD must consecrate themselves or the LORD will break out against them." Even with this general permission for priests granted, Aaron is afforded a special provision in v. 24: "The LORD said to him, "Go down, and come up bringing Aaron with you; but do not let either the priests or the people break through to come up to the LORD; otherwise he will break out against them."

That Aaron's access to the divine is unobstructed is particularly significant given the description of Aaron's commissioning in J in Exod 4:14–17.[65] This commissioning opens with Yahweh angry with Moses, and Yahweh's commendation of Aaron, identified as a Levite.[66] Aaron is to serve as the mouth (פה, v. 16) of Moses, and Yahweh promises specifically to be both with (עם) the mouth of Moses and with the mouth of Aaron. This description of Aaron's having direct access of communication to Yahweh without subverting Moses in any way stands in stark opposition to the relationship between Moses and Aaron in E and P.

The Elohist (E)

I argued above that there is a clear and recurrent antagonism between Aaron and Moses in the Elohist document. Aaron is at fault for the episode of the Golden Calf, but his is not entirely to blame (Exod 32). The narrative doles out the burden of responsibility for the calf both to Aaron and to the people. This is seen most clearly in the grammatical ambiguity of the description of the punishment for the episode:

Exod 32:35

ויגף יהוה את העם על אשר עשו את העגל אשר עשה אהרן

Then the LORD sent a plague on the people, because they made the calf—the one that Aaron made

In E there is no record of the forceful outbreak of the Levites to ameliorate the offence; therefore, it is Moses's intercession alone that can placate Yahweh's anger against Aaron and the people. However, even Moses's intercession is not enough; a plague still follows.

Aaron's inferior position to Moses in E is further described in Num 12, where, ironically, Yahweh communicates directly to Aaron and Miriam to tell them that Yahweh does not communicate directly to anyone except Moses (vv. 6–9). In both of these scenes, Aaron's error is rooted in a failure to defer to Moses's authority and guidance. The ordination of the elders as administrative and oracular stand-ins for Moses in Num 11, shows that E takes no issue with others performing functions Moses delegates to them, provided they have been duly delegated. The Elohist condemns Aaron for going beyond the words of Moses's instruction and taking on a role Moses has not delegated to him.

The Elohist's particular focus on the integrity of Moses's absolute rule over the people is seen clearly in the Dathan and Abiram episode extracted from the P version of Korah's rebellion (Num 16). In E's version we see representatives of the Reubenites questions Moses's authority and offering the well-worn[67] complaint that the purposes of the Exodus was to kill the Israelites and to rule over them (כי תשתרר עלינו גם השתרר, 16:13).

While in J—discussed above—Aaron is designated as Moses's mouth and Yahweh is with Aaron's mouth just as he is with Moses's mouth, Aaron plays no role in the Elohist account of Moses's commissioning narrative: 3:1, 4b, 6a, 9–15, 21–22, 4:17–18, and 20b.[68] In E, it is Moses, not Aaron, who officiates in a priestly capacity at the Blood of the Covenant ceremony in Exod 24:8. Furthermore, in order to gather the blood for manipulation in the ceremony, Moses does not send a rank of priests, but young Israelites to perform the sacrifices.

Exod 24:5

He sent young men (נערי) of the people of Israel, who offered burnt offerings and sacrificed oxen as offerings of well-being to the LORD.

For E, Moses's power to appoint who shall do what seems to be the only significant source of authority in the Israelite cult and society, surpassing even the roles reserved for Aaron in the other sources. In this way, it would seem that for E, the priesthood is Mosaic in its origins at least in so far as it will be filled by whomever Moses designates to be priests.

The other significant priestly character in E is Jethro, the Priest of Midian. While in J, Reuel/Hobab was in the background and only his daughter Zipporah emerged as a quasi-priestly figure, in E Jethro rejoices in the good news of the Exodus, acts as a trusted advisor, and even offers sacrifices to the deity in the presence of both Moses and Aaron (18:12). It is unclear whether Moses's role as a priest relates to or derives from the priesthood of Jethro, yet it is clear that Moses, the Delegator-in-Chief, respects and honors the priesthood of Jethro and stands as a beneficiary of the Midianite cult. In E, we find the least favorable presentation of Aaron among the sources.

The Priestly Source (P)

I argued above that the account of Nadab and Abihu in Lev 10:1–7 possesses none of the anti-Aaronite sentiment Cross associated with this story. Within P there is no hint of critique of Aaron, and indeed remnants of such a critique would be wholly unexpected in a story so deeply invested in preserving the ascendancy of Aaron's rightful successors. J understands Aaron to be Moses's mouth (Exod 4:14–16) and understands Yahweh to be present with Aaron's mouth just as Yahweh is present with Moses's mouth. The Priestly writer conceives of the relationship with different language.

Exod 7:1–2

ויאמר יהוה אל משה ראה נתתיך אלהים לפרעה ואהרן אחיך יהיה נביאך

אתה תדבר את כל אשר אצוך ואהרן אחיך ידבר אל פרעה ושלח את בני ישראל מארצו

The LORD said to Moses, "See, I have made you like God to Pharaoh, and your brother Aaron shall be your prophet. You shall speak all that I command you, and your brother Aaron shall tell Pharaoh to let the Israelites go out of his land.

In P Aaron is Moses's prophet (נביא) and Aaron's role is to transmit Moses's message to Pharaoh. About the relationship between Moses and Aaron, Jeffrey Stackert writes: "In the P account, YHWH gives instructions to Moses for Aaron in some instances *when Moses and Aaron are physically together* (e.g., Exod 7:19; 8:1, 12). Yet Moses still must relay such instructions to his brother."[69] The roles of Moses and Aaron are each clearly defined without traces of ambiguity or challenge.

What can be discerned in P is antagonism between priests descended from Aaron and other Levite clans. As discussed above in 3.2.5, the rebellion of Korah in Num 16 describes the objections of Kohathite Levites against the prominence of the Aaronite Levites. The drama of this objection is heightened by P's understanding of the relationship between these clans—Moses and Aaron themselves are Kohathite Levites. In this scene, the cultic superiority of the Aaronites is demonstrated by their success and the catastrophic failure of their kinsman challengers (16:35).

As in J, P preserves a narrative in which the relevance and potency of a priestly line is confirmed through willingness to function as agents of divine judgement. Phinehas' forceful outbreak just after the death of Aaron solidifies the Aaronites in their elevated position, and it propels the Priestly narrative into its next and final chapter, the Midianite War (ch. 31). That the Aaronites would need to assert their claim to power is anticipated by the rebellion of Korah described above, though there is no explicit link between these stories.

About the role of Moses is P, Stackert observes: "Moses is a means for divine revelation, initiation of the cult, and investiture of the priesthood, but once these tasks are accomplished, he fades into history as both an unrivaled and outmoded ancestor."[70] In P, the priesthood begins because Moses has instituted it, and it endures in the progeny of those Moses (and Yahweh) have chosen it to continue.

The Deuteronomist (D)

Little that is affirmative can be said here about the relationship between Moses, Aaron, and their priesthoods in D because of the paucity of data. Absent from D are traditions about Moses's father-in-law and any mention of Midian. Aaron appears only three times in D. In Deut 9:20, he is mentioned in a remembrance of the Golden Calf episode. In 10:6 and 32:50 notices are made about his death. In D, the prophets, Levites/priests, and elders share the authority as Moses has delegated it to them. In this way, D attempts to weave together the emphases of E and P. Moses institutes the priesthood and delegates roles within it to Priests and to Levites.

CONCLUSION

The discussion above has shown the unique perspectives of J, E, P, and to a much lesser extent, D, regarding the roles of Moses, Aaron, and their ancestors as priests. The textual analysis has shown the existence of three distinct perspectives (and one dependent perspective) on the Moses-Aaron relationship *vis-à-vis* their roles and responsibilities as priests. There are clear nuances among these voices in the presentations of how priests function as mediums of divine beneficence, divine judgement, and divine communication, and each of the sources evinces a clear orientation in a spectrum between Moses and Aaron. E is unequivocally pro-Moses and anti-Aaron. P is pro-Aaron, and evinces this pro-Aaron sentiment because Moses also endorses the activities of Aaron and his descendants. J evinces no preference for Aaron or Moses, but sees their roles as intertwined. D is strongly pro-Moses, and is more-or-less indifferent to or silent about Aaron. The independence of these voices has been established on the basis of their narratival integrity alone, and is not predicated on assumptions about the dating of these sources or of their presumed social locations.

NOTES

1. Many texts could be cited here, but the issue is placed in sharpest focus in: Rolf Rendtorff, *The Problem of the Process of Transmission in the Pentateuch. JSOTSupp* 89 (Sheffield, UK: JSOT Press, 1990).

2. It is, of course, grossly simplistic to describe the difference in such stark terms, though such a description is not without precedent See Joel S. Baden, *J, E, and the Redaction of the Pentateuch*, Forschungen zum Alten Testament 68 (Tübingen, Germany: Mohr Siebeck, 2009). Against this claim, Konrad Schmid has offered an important rejoinder claiming that European scholarship does not abandon the

Documentary Hypothesis *ab initio*, rather it seeks to "understand the composition of the Pentateuch in the most appropriate terms . . . includ[ing] 'documentary elements' as well." Konrad Schmid, "Has European Scholarship Abandoned the Documentary Hypothesis? Some Reminders on Its History and Remarks on Its Current Status." in *The Pentateuch: International Perspectives on Current Research* ed. Thomas B. Dozeman, Konrad Schmid and Baruch J. Schwartz (Tübingen, Germany: Mohr Siebeck, 2011), 17–18.

3. The moniker is claimed to have originated at the 2009 annual meeting of the SBL. Jeffrey Stackert, "Distinguishing Innerbiblical Exegesis from Pentateuchal Redaction: Leviticus 26 as a Test Case," in *The Pentateuch: International Perspectives on Current Research* ed. Thomas B. Dozeman, Konrad Schmid and Baruch J. Schwartz (Tübingen, Germany: Mohr Siebeck, 2011), 369–86, specifically p. 370.

4. The Neo-Documentarian manifesto (as it were) is Joel S. Baden, *J, E, and the Redaction of the Pentateuch*, referenced above.

5. Baruch J. Schwartz, "What Really Happened at Mount Sinai? Four Biblical Answers to One Question," *BR* 13:5 (1997): 20–30; Idem., "Israel's Holiness: The Torah Traditions," in *Purity and Holiness: The Heritage of Leviticus* (ed. Marcel Poorthuis and Joshua Schwartz; Leiden, Netherlands: Brill, 2000), 47–59; Idem., "Does Recent Scholarship's Critique of the Documentary Hypothesis Constitute Grounds for Its Rejection?," in *The Pentateuch: International Perspectives on Current Research* ed. Thomas B. Dozeman, Konrad Schmid, and Baruch J. Schwartz (Tübingen, Germany: Mohr Siebeck, 2011).

6. David McLain Carr, "Scribal Processes of Coordination/Harmonization and the Formation of the First Hexateuch(s)," in *The Pentateuch: International Perspectives on Current Research* ed. Thomas B. Dozeman, Konrad Schmid and Baruch J. Schwartz (Tübingen, Germany: Mohr Siebeck, 2011), 63–83.

7. Lengthy English biblical citations are modified from the NRSV by the author.

8. *CMHE*, 198–199.

9. *CMHE*, 199.

10. Ibid., 200.

11. Friedman, *Who Wrote the Bible*, 251.

12. Friedman, *Who Wrote the Bible*, 72.

13. Ibid., 76.

14. Youn Ho Chung has identified six literary seams discussed within the scholarly literature at various points: 1–6, 15–20, 21–25, 26–29, 30–34, and 35. Not all of these bear repeating in this brief discussion, as not all have garnered equal attention in the literature, nor are they of equal significance. Youn Ho Chung, *The Sin of the Calf and the Rise of the Bible's Negative Attitude Toward the Golden Calf* (New York: T & T Clark, 2010), 30.

15. Julius Wellhausen, *Die Composition des Hexateuchs und der historischen Bücher des Alten Testaments* (Berlin: Riemer, 1889), 194.

16. Martin Noth, *Überlieferungsgeschichte des Pentateuch* (Stuttgart: Kohlhammer, 1948), 33 and 72.

17. S. R. Driver, *The Book of Exodus* (Cambridge: Cambridge University Press, 1953), 347–50.

18. A. W. Jenks, *The Elohist and North Israelite Traditions* (Missoula, MT: Scholars Press, 1977), 50–51 and 151.

19. Alan McNeile, *The Book of Exodus* (New York: Edwin S. Gorham, 1908), 37–38.

20. For an extensive list, see Joel S. Baden, "A Narrative Pattern and Its Role in Source Criticism," *Hebrew Studies* 49:1 (2008): 41–54. Especially pp. 50–51 and notes 20–21.

21. Ibid., 41 and 54.

22. Ibid., 54.

23. In "What Really Happened on Mount Sinai," Baruch Schwartz interestingly argues that 32:15 is a snippet of P that is rightly placed between Exod 31:18 and 34:29. The resulting text is particularly compelling:

31:18 ויתן אל משה ככלתו לדבר אתו בהר סיני *שני לחת* העדת לחת אבן כתבים באצבע אלהים
32:15 ויפן וירד משה מן ההר *ושני לחת* העדת בידו לחת כתבים משני עבריהם מזה ומזה הם כתבים
34:29 ויהי ברדת משה מהר סיני *ושני לחת* העדת ביד משה ברדתו מן ההר ומשה לא ידע
כי קרן עור פניו בדברו אתו

When God finished speaking with Moses on Mount Sinai, he gave him the *two tablets* of the covenant, tablets of stone, written with the finger of God. Then Moses turned and went down from the mountain, carrying the *two tablets* of the covenant in his hands, tablets that were written on both sides, written on the front and on the back. Moses came down from Mount Sinai. As he came down from the mountain with the *two tablets* of the covenant in his hand, Moses did not know that the skin of his face shone because he had been talking with God.

24. Baden, *J, E, and the Redaction*, 162–163, and especially note 156.

25. Joel S. Baden, "The Violent Origins of the Levites: Text and Tradition," in *Levites and Priests in Biblical History and Tradition*, ed. Mark Leuchter and Jeremy Hutton (Atlanta, GA: Society of Biblical Literature, 2011), 103–116; quote from 109.

26. Ibid., p. 110.

27. Ibid., 110.

28. See W. Beyerlin, *Origins and History of the Oldest Sinaitic Traditions* (Oxford: Blackwell, 1965), 18–22; L. Waterman, "Bull Worship in Israel," *AJSL* 31 (1915): 229–55; in addition to the publications of Stackert, Baden, Schwartz, and Cross cited earlier.

29. Wellhausen, *Die Composition*, 194.

30. Martin Noth, *Exodus: A Commentary* (Philadelphia: Westminister, 1959), 246.

31. Brevard Childs, *The Book of Exodus: A Critical Commentary* (Louisville, KY: Westminster John Knox, 1974), 558–559.

32. John van Seters, *The Life of Moses: The Yahwist as Historian in Exodus-Numbers* (Louisville, KY: Westminster/John Knox Press, 1994), 290–318. See also Chung, *The Sin of the Calf*, 31–33 for an even more extensive list.

33. See note 23 above for Baruch Schwartz's reconstruction of this verse as a transition into the episode of Moses's shining countenance in the Priestly source.

34. Friedman, *Who Wrote the Bible*, 252.

35. *CMHE*, 204.

36. William Foxwell Albright, *Archaeology* and *the Religion of Israel*, 205n49.

37. Friedman, *Who Wrote the Bible*, 78.

38. See Joel S. Baden, *The Composition of the Pentateuch* (New Haven, CT: Yale University Press, 2012), 82–102.

39. Jeffrey Stackert, *A Prophet Like Moses* (Oxford: Oxford University Press, 2014), 99.

40. *CMHE*, 203. Cross specifically writes here: "Verse 5 suggests a form of the story in which Moses viewed the sacrilege but *failed* to act, at least until Phinehas took initiative." However, the reference to v. 5 must be a typographical error, as v. 5 is the final verse of the E narrative in which Moses calls the Israelites to violent resistance. Moses does not "fail" to act (if indeed he does indeed *fail*) until v. 6.

41. Ibid., 202.

42. Friedman, *Who Wrote the Bible*, 254.

43. The genesis of Midian itself (himself) in Gen 25:2–4 is found in a block of E material.

44. Baden, *Composition*, 176.

45. *CMHE*, 200.

46. Aharoni and Amiran, "Arad: A Biblical City," 43–53.

47. Benyamin Mazar, "The Sanctuary of Arad," 297–303.

48. *CMHE*, 201.

49. Baden, *Composition*, 136 and 141.

50. *CMHE*, 205.

51. Ibid.

52. Schwartz, Stackert, and Baden identify Exod 24:1–2 and 9–11 as an independent J story placed as a frame around the Elohist's account of the Covenant of Blood ceremony (vv. 3–8).

Exod 24:1–2, 9–11

v.1 ואל משה אמר עלה אל יהוה אתה ואהרן נדב ואביהוא ושבעים מזקני ישראל והשתחויתם מרחק
v.2 ונגש משה לבדו אל יהוה והם לא יגשו והעם לא יעלו עמו
v.9 ויעל משה ואהרן נדב ואביהוא ושבעים מזקני ישראל
v.10 ויראו את אלהי ישראל ותחת רגליו כמעשה לבנת הספיר וכעצם השמים לטהר
v.11 ואל אצילי בני ישראל לא שלח ידו ויחזו את האלהים ויאכלו וישתו

Then he said to Moses, "Come up to the LORD, you and *Aaron, Nadab, and Abihu*, and seventy of the elders of Israel, and worship at a distance. 2 Moses alone shall come near the LORD; but the others shall not come near, and the people shall not come up with him." 9 Then Moses and *Aaron, Nadab, and Abihu*, and seventy of the elders of Israel went up, 10 and they saw the God of Israel. Under his feet there was something like a pavement of sapphire stone, like the very heaven for clearness. 11 God did not lay his hand on the chief men of the people of Israel; also they beheld God, and they ate and drank.

53. A fine summary of survey of scholarly discussion and an important new proposal are found in Israel Knohl, *The Sanctuary of Silence* (Minneapolis, MN: Fortress Press, 1995), particularly on pp. 44, 148–152.

54. For the legal rationale for these instructions see Lev 21:10:

והכהן הגדול מאחיו אשר יוצק על ראשו שמן המשחה ומלא את ידו ללבש את הבגדים את ראשו לא יפרע
ובגדיו לא יפרם

The priest who is exalted above his fellows, on whose head the anointing oil has been poured and who has been consecrated to wear the vestments, shall not dishevel his hair, nor tear his vestments.

55. Baden, *Composition*, 149–168.

56. The P story consists of: 16:1a, 2b–11, 16–24, 26–27, 35. See: Stackert, *A Prophet like Moses*, 171n4 and Baden, *Composition*, 153ff. See also Jeffrey Stackert, *Rewriting the Torah: Literary Revision in Deuteronomy and the Holiness Legislation* (Tübingen, Germany: Mohr Sieback, 2007), 191n58.

57. The E story consists of: 1b–2a, 12–15, 25, 27, 28–34.

58. Baden, "Violent Origins," 103.

59. Friedman, *Who Wrote the Bible*, 248, among others.

60. Baden, "The Violent Origins," 105. Baden argues that, much like Gen 49, Deut 33 was originally an ancient and independent collection of sayings about the Israelite tribes, and also belongs to J in the broader sense defined above. On p. 105–106, Baden writes: "We may begin with a process of elimination. Deuteronomy 33 is assuredly not P, which has no interest in poetry. It is also not E; to E belongs the poem in the preceding chapter, Deut 32, which has been introduced in the E portion of Deut 31 (vv. 16–22, 30). It also makes little sense in D, where it has no place either rhetorically or structurally. That leaves only J."

61. Albright, "Jethro," 4.

62. In E, see Exod 24:3–8. In P, see Lev 1:5, 11; 3:2; 4:5–7, 16–17, 25, 30, 34; 7:14; 14:14, 25; 17:6; and Num 19:4.

63. Yonatan S. Miller, "Sacred Slaughter: The Discourse of Priestly Violence as Refracted Through the Zeal of Phinehas in the Hebrew Bible and in Jewish Literature" (PhD Diss, Harvard University, 2015), 50.

64. Miller's comments quoted above and my expansion of them are predicated on an essentially Girardian view of sacrifice as established in René Girard, *Violence and the Sacred*, trans. Patrick Gregory (Baltimore: Johns Hopkins University Press, 1977). A significant challenge to Girardian perspective of sacrifice is found in Kathryn McClymond, *Beyond Sacred Violence: A Comparative Study of Sacrifice* (Baltimore: Johns Hopkins University Press, 2008). McClymond insists that "violence" alone is an insufficient criterion for an act to be considered sacrifice. An act obtains sacrificial status in the confluence of other related factors including details related to appropriate sacrifier, appropriate sacrifice, appropriate place, appropriate ritual, appropriate time, etc. While it might be the case that a conventional act of circumcision would not meet the criterion for a sacrifice, the manipulation of the circumcismal blood would seem to elevate Zipporah's actions above the conventional practice.

65. For more on this source division contra Friedman and others, see Jeffrey Stackert, *A Prophet Like Moses*, 59.

66. Of the Pentateuchal sources, J comes closest to offering a "critique" of Moses, seen here in Yahweh's anger at Moses's reluctance to take on leadership. Trent Butler has identified five texts that convey "critique" of Moses centering on Moses's

relationship to the Midianites: Exod 2, 4, 18, and Num 12 and 25. However, his analysis assumes that within all of these Midian is an enemy. As my analysis above has shown this seems only to be the case in P, and in P only beginning with the Num 25 episode. See Trent C. Butler, "An Anti-Moses Tradition," *JSOT* 12 (1979): 9–15.

67. Exod 14:11, 16:3, 20:4, 21:5, Num 14:2, Deut 9:28.

68. See Stackert, *A Prophet Like Moses*, 56, and particularly his argument in footnote 77.

69. Jeffrey Stackert, *A Prophet Like Moses*, 64.

70. Ibid., 172.

Chapter 6

Geography, Kinship, and Priesthood

A Synthesis

This project has examined three bodies of information related to Cross's proposal about the bipartite nature of the ancient Israelite priesthood: the descriptions and memories of key cultic sites in ancient Israel and information related to the priesthoods that served them; the genealogical affiliations of various priestly groups and the characters of Moses and Aaron; and the Pentateuchal visions of Moses and Aaron as priests. After a brief survey of the principal findings of this study, I will reflect on how Cross's model of competing priestly houses can continue to provide a useful heuristic in the study of the early priesthood in ancient Israel.

GEOGRAPHY AND GENEALOGY

The investigation in the third chapter into the geographic distribution of significant cultic sites and the web of priestly affiliations present at the sites has revealed two (more or less) contiguous regions of influence—a center and periphery. This center includes the region from the northern edge of Jerusalem (Kiryat Yearim) to Mount Hebron. The bulk of the periphery extends from the southern-most foothills of Benjamin northward, but also may extend around the center encompassing certain sites in southern Judah, such as Arad. These regions demonstrate a division in the cultic orientation of their clergy. The clergy of the center are those that attain and hold on to power, namely, Aaronites/Zadokites. The clergy of the periphery manifest a collection of connections to Moses and the priestly legacy of Moses, the Mushites.

The discussions and analyses of the biblical genealogical material in ch. 4 have shown that genealogical relationships are a powerful and useful tool employed by biblical writers to create affinity. Genealogical information is always contextual (the relationships are listed for a reason) and it is fluid (the information can change as context might demand). The biblical genealogical material is historiographically useful to the extent that one may discern echoes of context and account for the fluidity present.

The genealogical material in P demonstrates significant fluidity. P exploits the malleability of genealogical information in its treatment of the second and third generation of Levitical subtribes in Num 26:58a, and, more significantly, in the invention of the brotherhood of Moses and Aaron. Moses and Aaron are brothers in P and D, which is dependent on P. In J and E there is no reference to their brotherhood, though in J they are both identified as Levites.

PENTATEUCHAL VISIONS OF MOSES, AARON, AND THEIR PRIESTHOODS

The analysis of the texts of priestly conflict in the Pentateuch has clarified the relationships that exist between Moses and Aaron. The Pentateuchal source J, E, P, and D evince important nuances in their presentations of the characters and the priesthood, authority, and independence exercised by them. The differences in each voice are set in greatest contrast with attention to the question of who has access to the deity and who may serve as mediators of divine communication, favor, and punishment.

The vitality of one's priesthood in the Yahwist (J) rests on one's ability to mediate divine communication—through action or oracular performance. J records the account of the ordination of the Levites recorded in Exod 32:26–29. This pericope in canonical form serves as response to the Elohist presentation of the Golden Calf and the conflict between Aaron and Moses; however, within the J narrative, it is more properly understood as a response to the events at Massah and Meribah in Exod 17:1bβ–7. In this J narrative, Moses ordains the Levites because of their vigor and willingness to serve as mediators of the divine judgement. They prove their worth by means of their outburst, killing their fellow Israelites.

In J, priesthood also entails an officiant's coming into contact with the deity for the sake of communicating a message. Priests are able to see God, to speak with God, and even to eat with God so long as God permits it (Exod 24:1–2, 9–11; 19:20–25). Aaron is afforded a special place alongside Moses but elevated above the position of other priests (19:24). Aaron, the Levite, is commissioned in J as the mouth (פה) of Moses, and Yahweh promises specifically to be with (עם) both the mouth of Moses and the mouth of Aaron (Exod 4:14–17). Aaron's has direct access of communication to Yahweh and in exercising this access he does not subvert Moses in any way.

In contrast, for the Elohist (E) there is perpetual antagonism between Moses and Aaron. Aaron is at fault for the episode of the Golden Calf, though the people also own a share in the responsibility (Exod 32:35). In E, lacking an account of the forceful outbreak of the Levites to punish the people, it is Moses' intercession alone that assuages Yahweh's anger, though not completely. Aaron's inferior position to Moses in E is further described in Num 12 where, ironically, Yahweh communicates directly to Aaron and Miriam that Yahweh does not communicate directly to anyone except Moses (vv. 6–9). The ordination of the elders as administrative and oracular stand-ins for Moses in Numbers 11 shows that E provides for Moses to delegate his authority, but authority is only legitimate in so far as Moses delegates it, which never happens for either Aaron or the Levites.

In the Priestly Source (P) there is no hint of critique of Aaron. The Priestly writer conceives of the relationship between Moses and Aaron to be that of the deity to a prophet. Moses is to be Pharaoh's god, and Aaron is to be Moses's prophet (Exod 7:1–2). Aaron's role is to be the public mouthpiece of Moses's message.

P also describes priests descended from Aaron in an antagonistic relationship with priests from other Levite clans, particularly so in the Rebellion of Korah in Numbers 16. The Korahites are a Levitical order charged with a minor role in the cult. The narrative asserts the cultic superiority of the Aaronites and the catastrophic failure of their challengers (16: 35). In P, the priesthood begins because Moses has instituted it, and it endures in the progeny of those Moses (and Yahweh) have chosen.

The Deuteronomist (D) provides little information about the relationship between Moses and Aaron. Aaron appears only three times in D. In Deut 9:20 there is a memory of the Golden Calf episode, and in 10:6 and 32:50 notice is made about his death. In D, the prophets, Levites/priests, and elders share the authority as Moses has delegated it to them. It would appear that D attempts to weave together the emphases of E and P. Moses institutes the priesthood and delegates roles within it to priests and to Levites.

SYNTHESIS

What emerges from this analysis is a set of two spectra within which the biblical voices may be situated. The first spectrum is defined by a polarity between Moses and Aaron regarding their priestly capacities. The second spectrum is defined by the attitude and perspective of the biblical voices in their orientation toward the geographical center. The Priestly source occupies a middle position between the poles of Moses and Aaron, but is oriented markedly toward the "center" and away from the "periphery" in its vision of the cult. The Elohist is fixed firmly in preference for Moses over Aaron, and appears to be indifferent to the geographical center. The Deuteronomist evinces the same affinity for Moses and disdain for Aaron found in E, but like P is oriented favorably to the geographic center and "the place that Yahweh will choose." Like P, the Yahwist (J) occupies a middle position between Moses and Aaron, showing no preference between them, and is, unlike P, indifferent to the geographical center. If we may presume that indifference to the geographical center equates to an affinity for the geographical periphery, then we find commonality in geographical perspective between, on the one hand, J and E oriented toward the periphery, and, on the other hand, P and D oriented toward the center.

Furthermore, if position on the spectrum between Aaron and Moses might be translated into terms of Aaronite and Mushite, then we find in P's preference for the center and equal embrace of Moses and Aaron a perspective of a cultically unified monarchy centered in Jerusalem. In contrast, we find in E a perspective harshly critical of Aaronite influences in a unified cult and seemingly indifferent to the geographical center. In J, we find a perspective amenable to the cultic unification and yet apparently indifferent to the geographical center.[1] Finally, in D we see a perspective marrying the pro-Moses affinity of E with the pro-center geographical orientation of P. An orientation espousing Moses and Aaron as brothers and favorable to the center—like that found in P—is completely in line with the cultic and political vision of David, unifying monarchy and cult in Jerusalem. While I will refrain in this brief conclusion from the fraught enterprise of situating the sources within a possible historical framework, the points of commonality and divergence within these polarities point to the primary place of a perspective like that found in P to the aims of a unified monarchy centered in Jerusalem. E establishes itself as a vehement peripheral reaction to the commitments express in P. D would seem to hold both polarities in view and to explicitly establish a place between them.[2]

EARLIEST DIVISIONS IN THE ISRAELITE PRIESTHOOD

The work of Hutton and Leuchter on the sociological, political, and geographical functions of the Israelite priesthood has advanced scholarly understanding of its early history beyond what Cross ever anticipated. However, there is great concord between his model and theirs when the competing priestly factions are situated in ecologically and topologically discrete regions. We see functioning within the Judahite center—the mountainous spine defined in the south by Mount Hebron and bounded in the north by Kiryat Yearim as the topography of this region gives way to the punctuated Ephraimite hills—one house of priest-saints eventually coming to derive their authority from Aaron. We find in the peripheral regions other priest-saints who, either in response to the political prominence of the center or out of an internally construed history, have coalesced into a different house (or collection of houses) eventually deriving authority from Moses. The independent sacerdotal groups might well have pre-dated their associations with the characters of Moses and Aaron, and, indeed, the associations with these characters might well be a very late development.

In order to establish a new pan-Israelite political and cultic center in Jerusalem, David attempted to merge the cults of center and periphery with the installation of a co-high-priesthood of Abiathar and Zadok—Mushite and Aaronite. The administrative complexities of a centralized polity and the clerical realities of an integrated cult proved too volatile to endure. However, seeing the political expediency of a unified religious system, Jeroboam I sought to mimic David's integrated Aaronite-Mushite cult in the Mushite periphery.[3] For his political ambition he won the enduring disdain of the center. For his embrace and/or co-mingling of the iconography of a different cultic region, he eventually attracted the religious condemnation of the periphery.

The findings of this study diverge from the presentation of the Mushite Hypothesis by Cross in a variety of details, but most significantly in: (1) the geographical distribution of the Aaronite and Mushite sites; (2) the genealogical nature of priestly affiliation; and (3) the nature of the orientation of the Pentateuchal sources to the characters of Moses and Aaron and their priesthood. These divergences shed new light on description of the rebellion and cultic reforms attributed to Jeroboam I, all the while retaining Cross's understanding of the political and cultic necessity of priestly engagement in the unification of the Monarchy. What remains of the Mushite Hypothesis is far greater than what has been lost. With these divergences accounted for, Cross's Mushite Hypothesis continues to stand as a "landmark" of biblical criticism and provides a powerful tool for discerning the broadest contours of the Israelite priesthood in the early first millennium.

NOTES

1. A perspective that would be been useful in an cultic-political enterprise like that attributed to Jeroboam I.

2. See Stackert, *A Prophet Like Moses*, 195–99. Compare to Avi Hurvitz, "The Language of the Priestly Source and Its Historical Setting—The Case for an Early Date," *Proceedings of the World Congress of Jewish Studies* (1981), 83–94.

3. For a fascinating exploration of the role of "mimicry" in the description of the revolt of Jeroboam I, see Koon P. Hong, "The Golden Calf of Bethel and Judah's Mimetic Desire of Israel," *JSOT* 47:4 (2023): 359–371.

Bibliography

Ackerman, Susan. "Who is Sacrificing at Shiloh?" Pages 25–43 in *Levites and Priests in Biblical History and Tradition*. Edited by Mark A. Leuchter and Jeremy M. Hutton. Atlanta, GA: SBL, 2011.

Aharoni, Yohanan. "Arad: Its Inscriptions and Temple," *Biblical Archaeology* 31 (1968): 2–32.

———. "Excavations at Tel Arad: Preliminary Report of the Second Season." *Israel Exploration Journal* 17 (1967): 233–249.

Aharoni, Yohanan and Ruth Amiran. "Arad: A Biblical City in Southern Palestine," *Archaeology* 17 (1964): 43–53.

———. "Excavations at Tel Arad: Preliminary Report of the First Season," *Israel Exploration Journal* 14 (1964): 131–147.

Albright, William F. *Archaeology and the Religion of Israel*. 3rd ed.; Baltimore: Johns Hopkins, 1956.

———. *From Stone Age to Christianity*. 2nd ed. Garden City, NJ: Doubleday/Anchor, 1957.

———. "Jethro, Hobab and Reuel in Early Hebrew Tradition." *Catholic Biblical Quarterly* 25 (1963): 1–11.

Avigad, Nahman and Benjamin Sass *Corpus of West Semitic Stamp Seals*. Jerusalem: Israel Academy of Sciences and Humanities, 1997.

———. "The Priest of Dor." *Israel Exploration Journal* 25 (1975), 101–105.

Baden, Joel S. "A Narrative Pattern and Its Role in Source Criticism." *Hebrew Studies* 49:1 (2008): 41–54.

———. *J, E, and the Redaction of the Pentateuch*. Forschungen zum alten Testament. Tübingen 68. Tübingen, Germany: Mohr Siebeck, 2009.

———. *The Composition of the Pentateuch: Renewing the Documentary Hypothesis*. Anchor Yale Bible Reference Library. New Haven, CT: Yale University Press, 2012.

———. "The Violent Origins of the Levites: Text and Tradition." Pages 103–16 in *Levites and Priests in Biblical History and Tradition*, edited by Mark Leuchter and Jeremy Michael Hutton. Atlanta, GA: Society of Biblical Literature, 2011.

Beyerlin, W. *Origins and History of the Oldest Sinaitic Traditions*. Oxford: Blackwell, 1965.

Blum, Erhard. "Der historische Mose und die Frühgeschichte Israels." *Hebrew Bible and Ancient Israel* 1 (2012): 37–63.

———. *Die Komposition der Vätergeschichte*. Neukirchen-Vluyn: Neukirchener Verlag, 1984.

———. *Studien zur Komposition des Pentateuch*. Berlin: Walter de Gruyter, 1990.

Boling, Robert G. "Levitical Cities: Archaeology and Texts." Pages 23–32 in *Biblical and Related Studies Presented to Samuel Iwry*. Edited by Ann Kort and Scott Morschauser. Winona Lake, IN: Eisenbrauns, 1985.

———. "Levitical History and the Role of Joshua." Pages 241–262 in *The Word of the Lord Shall Go Forth: Essays in Honor of David Noel Freedman*. Ed. Carol L. Meyers and Michael P. O'Connor. Philadelphia: *American Schools of Oriental Research*, 1983.

Breytenbach, A.P.B. "Who is Behind the Samuel Narrative." Pages 50–75 in *Past, Present, Future: The Deuteronomistic History and the Prophets*. Ed. Johannes Cornelis de Moor and Harry F. van Rooy. Leiden, Netherlands: Brill, 2000.

Briggs, Charles Augustus and Emilie Grace Briggs. *A Critical and Exegetical Commentary on the Book of Psalms* vol. 2. International Critical Commentary. New York: Charles Scribner's Sons, 1907.

Bright, John. *A History of Israel*. Philadelphia: Westminster, 1959.

———. *A History of Israel*. 4th ed. Louisville, KY: Westminster, 2000.

Brettler, Marc Z. *The Creation of History in Ancient Israel*. London: Routledge, 1995.

Brueggemann, Walter. "Trajectories in Old Testament Literature and the Sociology of Ancient Israel." *Journal of Biblical Literature* 98 (1979): 161–185.

Butler, Trent. "An Anti-Moses Tradition." *Journal for the Study of the Old Testament* 12 (1979): 9–15.

Callaway, James R. "Aspects of Religion and Culture in the Iron II Period: A Biblical and Archaeological Approach to Cult in Relationship to Kinship, Kingship, and Land." Ph.D. diss. Southwestern Baptist Theological Seminary, 1996.

Carr, David McLain. *Reading the Fractures of Genesis*. Louisville, KY: Westminster John Knox, 1996.

———. "Scribal Processes of Coordination/Harmonization and the Formation of the First Hexateuch(s)." Pages 63–83. in *The Pentateuch: International Perspectives on Current Research*. Edited by Thomas B. Dozeman, Konrad Schmid and Baruch J. Schwartz. Tübingen, Germany: Mohr Siebeck, 2011.

Childs, Brevard. *The Book of Exodus: A Critical, Theological Commentary*. Louisville, KY: Westminster John Knox, 1974.

Chung, Youn Ho. *The Sin of the Calf: The Rise of the Bible's Negative Attitude toward the Golden Calf*. Library of the Hebrew Bible/Old Testament Studies 523; New York: T & T Clark, 2010.

Cody, Aelred. *A History of Old Testament Priesthood*. Analecta Biblica 35. Rome: Pontifical Biblical Institute, 1969.

Cohen, Martin. "The Role of the Shilonite Priesthood in the United Monarchy of Ancient Israel." *Hebrew Union College Annual* 36 (1965): 59–98.

Cross, Frank Moore. *Canaanite Myth and Hebrew Epic: Essays in the History of the Religion of Israel*. Cambridge, MA: Harvard University Press, 1973.

―――. *From Epic to Canon: History and Literature in Ancient Israel*. Baltimore: Johns Hopkins University Press, 1998.

―――. *Studies in Ancient Yahwistic Poetry*. Grand Rapids, MI: Eerdmans, 1997.

Deist, F. E. "'By the Way, Hophni and Phinehas Were There': An Investigation into the Literary and Ideological Function of Hophni, Phineas and Shiloh in 1 Samuel 1–4." *Journal of North West Semitic Languages* 18 (1992): 25–35.

Dobbs-Allsopp, F. W. et al., *Hebrew Inscriptions, texts from the Biblical Period of the Monarchy with Concordance*. New Haven, CT: Yale University Press, 2005.

Dozeman, Thomas B., Konrad Schmid, and Baruch J. Schwartz. *The Pentateuch: International Perspectives on Current Research*. Forschungen zum alten Testament 78. Tübingen, Germany: Mohr Siebeck, 2011.

Driver, S. R. *Introduction to the Literature of the Old Testament*. New York: Meridian, 1957.

―――. *The Book of Exodus*. Cambridge: Cambridge University, 1918.

Duke, Rodney K. "Ira." Page 446 in vol. 3 of *Anchor Bible Dictionary.* Edited by David Noel Freedman, 6 vols. New York: Doubleday, 1992.

Emerton, J. A. "Priests and Levites in Deuteronomy: An Examination of Dr. G. E. Wright's Theory." *Vetus Testamentum* 12 (1962): 129–138.

Ewald, Heinrich. *The History of Israel.* vol 1. London: Longmans, Green & Co., 1869.

Faulkner, Raymond O. *A Concise Dictionary of Middle Egyptian*. Oxford: Griffith Institute, 1991.

Freedman, David Noel. "An Appreciation." Pages 3–8 in *Traditions in Transformation: Turning Points in Biblical Faith*. Edited by Baruch Halpern and Jon D. Levenson. Winona Lake, IN: Eisenbrauns, 1981.

Friedman, Richard Elliott. *The Bible with Sources Revealed*. San Francisco: HarperSanFrancisco, 2003.

―――. *The Exodus*. New York: HarperOne, 2017.

―――. *Who Wrote the Bible?* New York: Harper & Row, 1987.

Frolov, Serge. "Judah Comes to Shiloh: Genesis 49:10ab, One More Time," *Journal of Biblical Literature* 131 (2012): 417–22.

Gal, Zvi. "Cabul, Jiphthah-El and the Boundary Between Asher and Zebulun in the Light of Archaeological Evidence." *Zeitschrift des Deutschen Palästina-Vereins* 101 (1985): 114–27.

Gellner, Ernest. *Saints of the Atlas*. London: Weidenfeld and Nicolson, 1969.

Girard, René. *Violence and the Sacred*. Translated by Patrick Gregory. Baltimore: Johns Hopkins University Press, 1977.

Goldziher, Ignaz. *Mythology among the Hebrews and Its Historical Development*. London: Longsman and Greeg, 1877.

Goren, Yuval et al., "A Re-Examination of the Inscribed Ivory Pomegranate from the Israel Museum." *Israel Exploration Journal* 55 (2005): 3–34.

―――. "The Inscribed Pomegranate from the Israel Museum Examined Again," *Israel Exploration Journal* 57 (2007): 87–95.

Gunneweg, Antonius H. J. *Leviten und Priester: Hauptlinien der Traditionsbildung und Geschichte des israelitisch-jüdischen Kultpersonals*. Forschungen zur Religion und Literatur des Alien und Neuen Testaments; Göttingen, Germany: Vandenhoeck & Ruprecht, 1965.

Guthe, Hermann. *Geschichte des Volkes Israel.* Tubingen, Germany: J.C.B. Mohr, 1904.

Halpern, Baruch. "Levitic Participation in the Reform Cult of Jeroboam I." *Journal of Biblical Literature* 95 (1976): 31–42.

———. "Sectionalism and the Schism." *Journal of Biblical Literature* 93 (1974): 519–532.

———. "The Uneasy Compromise: Israel Between League and Monarchy." Pages 59–96 in *Traditions in Transformation.* Edited by Jon D. Levenson and Baruch Halpern. Winona Lake, IN: Eisenbrauns, 1981.

Hanson, Paul D. *The Dawn of Apocalyptic.* Philadelphia: Fortress Press, 1975.

———. *The People Called: The Growth of Community in the Bible.* San Francisco: Harper & Row, 1986.

Haran, Menahem. "Studies in the Account of the Levitical Cities: I. Preliminary Considerations." *Journal of Biblical Literature* 80 (1961): 45–54.

———. "Studies in the Account of the Levitical Cities: II. Utopia and Historical Reality." *Journal of Biblical Literature* 80 (1961): 156–165.

Hauret, Charles. "Moïse était-il prêtre?" *Biblica* 40 (1959): 509–521.

Hong, Koon P. "The golden calf of Bethel and Judah's mimetic desire of Israel," Journal for the Study of the Old Testament 47:4 (2023): 359–371.

Hunt, Alice Wells. "The Zadokites: Finding Their Place in the Hebrew Bible." Ph.D. diss., Vanderbilt University, 2003.

Hurvitz, Avi. "The Language of the Priestly Source and Its Historical Setting." *World Congress of Jewish Studies* 8. Panel Sessions: Bible Studies and Hebrew Language (1981): 83–94.

Hutton, Jeremy M. "All the King's Men: The Families of the Priests in Cross-Cultural Perspective." Pages 121–51 in *Seitenblicke: Literarische und Historische Studien zu Nebenfiguren im Zweiten Samuelbuch,* ed. W. Dietrich. Friborg, Switzerland: Academic Press/Vandenhoeck & Ruprecht, 2010.

———. "Southern, Northern, and Transjordanian Perspectives." Pages 149–174 in *Religious Diversity in Ancient Israel and Judah.* Edited by John Barton and Francesca Stavrakopoulou. London: Continuum, 2010.

———. "The Levitical Diaspora (I): A Sociological Comparison with Morocco's Ahansal." Pages 223–234 in *Exploring the Longue Durée: Essays in Honor of Lawrence E. Stager.* Edited by David Schloen. Winona Lake, IN: Eisenbrauns, 2009.

———. "The Levitical Diaspora (II): Modern Perspectives on the Levitical City Lists (A Review of Opinions)." Pages 45–82 in *Levites and Priests in History and Tradition.* Edited by Jeremy M. Hutton and Mark Leuchter. Atlanta, GA: SBL, 2011.

Jenks, A. W. *The Elohist and North Israelite Traditions.* Missoula, MT: Scholars Press, 1977.

Joseph, Alison Lori. "The Portrait of the Kings and the Historiographical Poetics of the Deuteronomistic Historian." Ph.D. diss. University of California, Berkley, 2012.

Josephus, *The Life; Against Apion*. Translated by Henry St. J. Thackeray. LCL. Cambridge, MA: Harvard University Press, 1926.

Kaufmann, Yeḥezkel. *Ha-Sippur Ha-Miḳra'i 'al Kibbush Ha-Arets.* Jerusalem: Mosad Byaliḳ, 1955.

———. *The Biblical Account of the Conquest of Canaan.* 2nd ed. Jerusalem: Magnes Press, Hebrew University, 1985.

———. *The Religion of Israel: Its Beginnings to the Babylonian Exile.* Translated and abridged by Moshe Greenberg. Chicago: University of Chicago, 1960.

———. *twldwt h'mwnh hyśr'lyt: mymy qdm 'd swp byt šny.* Tel-Aviv: Bialik Institute-Dvir, 1937 [1.1 and 1.2], 1938 [1.3], 1945 [2.2], 1947 [2.1 and 3.1] 1948 [3.2], 1956 [4.1].

Kempinski, Aaron. "Joshua's Altar—An Iron Age I Watchtower." *Biblical Archaeology Review* 12.1 (1986): 42.

Knohl, Israel. *The Sanctuary of Silence: The Priestly Torah and the Holiness School.* Minneapolis, MN: Fortress Press, 1995.

Knoppers, Gary N. "Hierodules, Priests, or Janitors? The Levites in Chronicles and the History of the Israelite Priesthood." *JBL* 118 (1999): 49–72.

Koenigsberg, Zvi. *The Lost Temple of Israel.* Boston: Academic Studies Press, 2015.

Lehmann, Johannes. *Moses, der Mann aus Ägypten: Religionsstifter, Gesetzgeber, Staatsgründer.* Hamburg: Hoffmann und Campe, 1983.

Lemaire, André. "A Re-examination of the Inscribed Pomegranate: A Rejoinder." *Israel Exploration Journal* 56 (2006): 167–177.

———. "Probable Head of Priestly Scepter from Solomon's Temple Surfaces in Jerusalem" *Biblical Archaeology Review* 10:2 (1984): 24–29.

———. "Une inscription paleo-hebraique sur grenade en ivoire" *Revue Biblique* 88 (1981): 236–239.

Leuchter, Mark A. *The Levites and the Boundaries of Israelite Identity.* Oxford: Oxford University Press, 2017.

———. "Jeroboam the Ephrathite." *Journal of Biblical Literature* 125 (2006): 51–72.

———. "The Cult at Kiriath Yearim: Implications from the Biblical Record." *Vetus Testamentum* 58 (2008): 526–43.

———. "The Fightin' Mushites." *Vetus Testamentum* 62 (2012): 479–500.

———. "The Priesthood in Ancient Israel." *Biblical Theology Bulletin: A Journal of Bible and Theology* 40 (2010): 100–110.

Leuchter, Mark and Jeremy Michael Hutton. *Levites and Priests in Biblical History and Tradition.* Society of Biblical Literature Ancient Israel and Its Literature 9. Atlanta, GA: Society of Biblical Literature, 2011.

Levenson, Jon D. "1 Samuel 25 as Literature and as History," *Catholic Biblical Quarterly* 40 (1978): 11–28.

———. *Creation and the Persistence of Evil.* Princeton, NJ: Princeton University Press, 1988.

———. *Sinai and Zion: An Entry into the Jewish Bible.* San Francisco: Harper Collins, 1987.

————. *Theology of the Program of Restoration of Ezekiel 40-48*. Harvard Semitic Monographs 10. Missoula, MT: Published by Scholars Press for Harvard Semitic Museum, 1976.

————. "Who Inserted the Book of the Torah?" *Harvard Theological Review* 68 (1975): 203–33.

Levenson, Jon D. and Baruch Halpern. "The Political Import of David's Marriages." *Journal of Biblical Literature* 99 (1980): 507–18.

Longstreet, C. Shaun. "Native Cultic Leadership in the empire: Foundations for Achaemenid Hegemony in Persian Judah." Ph.D. diss., University of Notre Dame, 2003.

Master, Daniel M. "State Formation Theory and the Kingdom of Ancient Israel." *Journal of Near Eastern Studies* 60 (2001): 117–31.

Mazar, Benjamin. "The Cities of the Priests and Levites." Pages 143–45 in *Biblical Israel: State and People*. Edited by Benjamin Mazar and Shmuel Ahituv. Jerusalem: Magnes Press, 1992.

————. "The Sanctuary of Arad and the Family of Hobab the Kenite." *Journal of Near Eastern Studies* 24 (1965): 297–303.

McClymond, Kathryn. *Beyond Sacred Violence: A Comparative Study of Sacrifice*. Baltimore: Johns Hopkins University Press, 2008.

McNeile, Alan H. *The Book of Exodus*. New York: Edwin S. Gorham, 1908.

Meshel, Ze'ev. "Did Yahweh have a Consort?: The New Religious Inscriptions from the Sinai." *Biblical Archaeology Review* 5:2 (1979): 24–34.

Mettinger, Tryggve N. D. *Solomonic State Officials: A Study of the Civil Government Officials of the Israelite Monarchy*. Vol. 5. Coniectanea Biblica. Old Testament Series. Lund, Sweden: Gleerup, 1971.

Meyers, Carol. *Exodus*. Cambridge: Cambridge University Press, 2005.

Miller, Robert D. *Chieftains of the Highland Clans: A History of Israel in the 12th and 11th Centuries B.C.* Grand Rapids, MI: Eerdmans, 2005.

Miller, Yonatan S. "Sacred Slaughter: The Discourse of Priestly Violence as Refracted Through the Zeal of Phinehas in the Hebrew Bible and in Jewish Literature." PhD Diss., Harvard University, 2015.

Möhlenbrink, Kurt. "Die Levitischen Überlieferungen Des Alten Testaments." *Zeitschrift für die alttestamentliche Wissenschaft* 52 (1934): 184–231.

Mommer, Peter. "Samuel in Ps 99." *Biblische Notizen* 31 (1986): 27–30.

Moran, William L. "Genesis 49.10 and its use in Ezekiel 21.32." *Biblica* 39 (1958): 405–25.

Mowinckel, Sigmund. *Psalm Studies*. vol. 1. Translated by Mark E. Biddle. Atlanta: SBL Press, 2014.

————. *The Psalms in Israel's Worship*. Oxford: Blackwell, 1962.

Myers, Jaime A. "The Wicked 'Sons of Eli' and the Composition of 1 Samuel 1–4," *Vetus Testamentum* 72 (2022): *237–256.*

Noth, Martin. *A History of Pentateuchal Traditions*. Englewood Cliffs, NJ: Prentice-Hall, 1972.

————. *Das System der Zwölf Stämme Israels*. Beiträge zur Wissenschaft vom Alten und Neuen Testament, 4:1. Stuttgart: W. Kohlhammer, 1930.

―――. *Die israelitischen Personennamen in Rahmen der gemeinsemitischen Namengbung.* Hildesheim, Germany: Georg Olms, 1966.

―――. *The History of Israel.* Translated by P. R. Ackroyd. 2nd ed. London: Adam & Charles Black, 1960.

―――. *Überlieferungsgeschichte des Pentateuchs.* Stuttgart: W. Kohlhammer, 1948.

Olyan, Saul M. "Family Religion in Israel and in the Wider Levant of the First Millenium BCE." Pages 113–126 in *Family Religion in Antiquity*, ed. John Bodel and Saul M. Olyan. Malden, MA: Wiley/Blackwell, 2008.

―――. "Zadok's Origins and the Tribal Politics of David." *Journal of Biblical Literature* 101, (1982): 177–193.

Petter, Thomas David. "Diversity and Uniformity on the Frontier: Ethnic Identity in the Central Highlands of Jordan During the Iron I." Ph.D. diss., University of Toronto, 2005.

Pigott, Susan Marie. "'God of Compassion and Mercy': An Analysis of the Background, Use, and Theological Significance of Exodus 34:6–7." Ph.D. diss., Southwestern Baptist Theological Seminary, 1995.

Pioske, Daniel D. *David's Jerusalem: Between Memory and History.* New York: Routledge, 2015.

―――. *Memory in a Time of Prose: Studies in Epistemology, Hebrew Scribalism, and the Biblical Past.* New York: Oxford University Press, 2018.

―――. "Retracing a Remembered Past: Methodological Remarks on Memory, History and the Hebrew Bible." *Biblical Interpretation* 23 (2015): 291–315.

Propp, William Henry. *Exodus 1–18: A New Translation with Introduction and Commentary.* Vol. v. 2. 1st ed. The Anchor Bible. New York: Doubleday, 1999.

―――. *Exodus 19-40: A New Translation with Introduction and Commentary.* New York: Doubleday, 2006.

Rainey, Anson F. "Notes on Two Archaeological Sites," *Eretz-Israel* 29 (2009): 184–187.

Rasure, Matthew R. "Priests Like Moses: Earliest Divisions in the Priesthood of ancient Israel" Ph.D. diss, Harvard University, 2019.

―――. "Zertal's Altar—A Blatant Phony," *Biblical Archaeology Review* 12:4 (1986): 66.

Redford, Donald B. *Egypt, Canaan, and Israel in Ancient Times.* Princeton, NJ: Princeton University Press, 1992.

Rehm, Merlin D. "'Levites and Priests." Pages 297–310 in vol. 4 of *Anchor Bible Dictionary.* Edited by David Noel Freedman, 6 vols. New York: Doubleday, 1992.

―――. "Studies in the History of the Pre-Exilic Levites." ThD diss., Harvard Divinity School, 1967.

Rendtorff, Rolf. *Das überlieferungsgeschichtliche Problem des Pentateuch.* Beiheft zur Zeitschrift für die alttestamentliche Wissenschaft 147. Berlin: de Gruyter, 1977.

―――. *The Problem of the Process of Transmission in the Pentateuch.* Journal for the Study of the Old Testament Supplement Series 89. Sheffield, UK: JSOT Press, 1990.

Roberts, J.J.M. "Genealogy and History in the Biblical World by Robert R. Wilson." *Journal of Biblical Literature* 98 (1979): 115–17.

Rofé, Alexander. "Levites: A Transjordanian Tribe of Priests." TheTorah.com, September 27, 2021. https://www.thetorah.com/article/levites-a-transjordanian-tribe-of-priests.

———. "ברכת משה, מקדש נבו ושאלת מוצא הלויים" pp. 409–424 in‫מחקרים במקרא ובמזרה‬ ‫הקדמון מוגשים לשמואל א׳ ליונשטם במלאת לו שבעים שנה‬, ed. Yitschak Avishur and Joshua Blau. Jerusalem: E. Rubinstein's Pub. House, 1978.

Römer, Thomas. *La construction de la figure de Moïse = The Construction of the Figure of Moses.* Supplément Transeuphratène 13. Paris: Gabalda, 2007.

———. *The So-Called Deuteronomistic History: A Sociological, Historical, and Literary Introduction.* London: Continuum, 2007.

Rosenbaum, Jonathan. "Hezekiah's Reform and the Deuteronomistic Tradition." *The Harvard Theological Review* 72 (1979): 23–43.

Russell, Stephen Christopher. "Images of Egypt in Early Biblical Literature: Cisjordan-Israelite, Transjordan-Israelite, and Judahite Portrayals." Ph.D. diss., New York University, 2008.

Samuelson, Norbert Max. *Jewish Philosophy: An Historical Introduction.* London: Continuum, 2003.

Santis, David Vincent. "The Land of Transjordan Israel in the Israel Age and Its Religious Traditions." Ph.D. diss., New York University, 2004.

Schloen, J. David. "Caravans, Kenites and Casus Belli: Enmity and Alliance in the Song of Deborah." *Catholic Biblical Quarterly* 55 (1993): 18–38.

———. ed. *Exploring the Longue Durée: Essays in Honor of Lawrence E. Stager.* Winona Lake, IN: Eisenbrauns, 2009.

———. *The House of the Father as Symbol and Fact.* Winona Lake, IN: Eisenbrauns, 2001.

Schmid, Konrad. "Has European Scholarship Abandoned the Documentary Hypothesis? Some Reminders on Its History and Remarks on Its Current Status." Pages 17–30 in *The Pentateuch: International Perspectives on Current Research.* Edited by Thomas B. Dozeman, Konrad Schmid, and Baruch J. Schwartz. Tübingen, Germany: Mohr Siebeck, 2011.

———. "Judean Identity and Ecumenicity: The Political Theology of the Priestly Document." Pages 3–26 in *Judah and the Judeans in the Achaemenid Period*, ed. Oded Lipschits et al. Winona Lake, IN: Eisenbrauns, 2011.

———. "The Canon and the Cult: The Emergence of Book Religion in Ancient Israel and the Gradual Sublimation of the Temple Cult." *Journal of Biblical Literature* 131 (2012): 389–405.

Schwartz, Baruch J. "Does Recent Scholarship's Critique of the Documentary Hypothesis Constitute Grounds for Its Rejection?" Pages 3–16 in *The Pentateuch: International Perspectives on Current Research.* Edited by Thomas B. Dozeman, Konrad Schmid and Baruch J. Schwartz. Tübingen, Germany: Mohr Siebeck, 2011.

———. "Introduction: The Strata of the Priestly Writings and the Revised Relative Dating of P and H." Pages 1–12 in *Strata of the Priestly Writings.* Zürich: Theologischer Verlag Zürich, 2009.

———. "Israel's Holiness: The Torah Traditions." Pages 47–59 in *Purity and Holiness.* Leiden, Netherlands: Brill, 2000.

————. "'Profane' Slaughter and the Integrity of the Priestly Code." *Hebrew Union College Annual* 67 (January 1, 1996): 15–42.

————. "Reexamining the Fate of the 'Canaanites' in the Torah Traditions," pp. 151–170 in C. Cohen, A. Hurvitz, S. M. Paul, eds., *Sefer Moshe: The Moshe Weinfeld Jubilee Volume.* Winona Lake, IN: Eisenbrauns, 2004.

————. "The Priestly Account of the Theophany and Lawgiving at Sinai." Pages 103–134 in *Texts, Temples, and Traditions.* Winona Lake, IN: Eisenbrauns, 1996.

————. "What Really Happened at Mount Sinai? Four Biblical Answers to One Question." *Bible Review* 13:5 (October 1, 1997): 20–30.

Seow, C. L. *Myth, Drama, and the Politics of David's Dance.* Harvard Semitic Monographs 46. Atlanta, GA: Scholars Press, 1989.

Shin, Samuel Chong Kyoon. "Centralization and Singularization: Official Cult and royal Politics in Ancient Israel." Ph.D. diss., Union Theological Seminary in Virginia, 1997.

Smend, Rudolf. *Lehrbuch der alttestamentlichen Religionsgeschichte.* Sammlung Theologischer Lehrbücher. Freiburg, Germany: Mohr Siebeck, 1893.

————. *Lehrbuch Der Alttestamentlichen Religionsgeschichte.* 2nd ed. Sammlung Theologischer Lehrbücher. Freiburg, Germany: Mohr Siebeck, 1899.

————. "Mose als geschichtliche Gestalt." *Historische Zeitschrift* 260 (1995): 1–19.

Smith, W. Robertson, *Kingship and Marriage in Early Arabia.* London: A & C Black, 1903.

Sparks, James T. *The Chronicler's Genealogies: Toward an Understanding of 1 Chronicles 1–9.* Atlanta, GA: Society of Biblical Literature Press, 2008.

Spencer, J. R. "Priestly Families (or Factions) in Samuel and Kings." Pages 387–400 in *The Pitcher is Broken: Memorial Essays for Gösta W. Ahlström.* Edited by Steven W. Holloway and Lowell K. Handy. Sheffield, UK: Sheffield Academic Press, 1995.

Stackert, Jeffrey. *A Prophet Like Moses.* Oxford: Oxford University Press, 2014.

————. "Distinguishing Innerbiblical Exegesis from Pentateuchal Redaction: Leviticus 26 as a Test Case." Pages 369–386 in *The Pentateuch: International Perspectives on Current Research.* Edited by Thomas B. Dozeman, Konrad Schmid and Baruch J. Schwartz. Tübingen, Germany: Mohr Siebeck, 2011.

————. *Rewriting the Torah: Literary Revision in Deuteronomy and the Holiness Legislation.* Forschungen zum Alten Testament. Tübingen, Germany: Mohr Siebeck, 2007.

Stager, Lawrence E. "Forging an Identity: The Emergence of Israel in Canaan." Pages 123–175 in *The Oxford History of the Biblical World.* Edited by Michael D. Coogan. New York: Oxford University Press, 1998.

————. "The Archaeology of the Family in Ancient Israel." *Bulletin of the American Schools of Oriental Research* 260 (1985): 1–35.

Talmon, Shemaryahu. "Divergences in Calendar Reckoning in Ephraim and Judah." *Vetus Testamentum* 8 (1958): 48–74.

Tengström, Sven. *Die Toledotformel und die literarische Struktur der priestlerlichen Erweiterungsschicht im Pentateuch.* Coniectanea Biblica, Old Testament Series 17.8. Uppsala, Sweden: Seiten 1981.

Tobolowsky, Andrew, *The Sons of Jacob and the Sons of Herakles: The History of the Tribal System and the Organization of Biblical Identity*, Forschungen Zum Alten Testament 2. Tübingen, Germany: Mohr Siebeck, 2017.

Treves, Marco. "Shiloh (Genesis 49:10)." *Journal of Biblical Literature* 85 (1966): 353–56.

Van Seters, John. *The Life of Moses: The Yahwist as Historian in Exodus-Numbers*. 1st ed. Louisville, KY: Westminster/John Knox Press, 1994.

Vaux, Roland de. *Ancient Israel: Its Life and Institutions*. Translated by John McHugh. London: Darton, Longman, and Todd, 1961.

———. *Histoire Ancienne d'Israël*. Études Bibliques. Paris: Lecoffre, 1971.

———. *The Early History of Israel*. Philadelphia: Westminster Press, 1978.

Waterman, Leroy. "Bull Worship in Israel." *American Journal of Semitic Languages and Literatures* 31 (1915): 229–55.

———. "Some Determining Factors in the Northward Progress of Levi." *Journal of the American Oriental Society* 57 (1937): 375–80.

Wellhausen, Julius. *Die Composition des Hexateuchs und der historischen Bücher des Alten Testaments*. Berlin: Riemer, 1889.

———. *Geschichte Israels*. 2 vols. Berlin: G Reimer, 1878.

———. *Prolegomena to the History of Israel*. Translated by J. Sutherland Black and Allan Menzies, with preface by W. Robertson Smith. Edinburgh: Adam & Charles Black, 1885.

———. *Prolegomena zur Geschichte Israels*, 2nd ed; Berlin: G. Reimer, 1883.

Wilson, Robert R. "Between 'Azel' and 'Azel' Interpreting the Biblical Genealogies" *Biblical Archaeology* 42 (1979): 11–22.

———. *Genealogy and History in the Biblical World*. Yale Near Eastern Researches 7. New Haven, CT: Yale University Press, 1977.

———. "Genealogy, Genealogies," Pages 929–32 in vol. 2 of *Anchor Bible Dictionary*. Edited by David Noel Freedman, 6 vols. New York: Doubleday, 1992.

———. "Old Testament Genealogies in Recent Research." *Journal of Biblical Literature* 94 (1975): 169–189.

Wine, Sherwin T. *A Provocative People: A Secular History of the Jews*. Farmington Hills, MI: International Institute for Secular Humanistic Judaism, 2012.

Wright, G. Ernest. "Deuteronomy." Pages 307–537 in *The Interpreter's Bible*. Vol. 2. New York: Abingdon, 1953.

———. "The Levites in Deuteronomy." *Vetus Testamentum* 4 (1954): 325–30.

Yeivin, Revell, and Revell, E. J. *Introduction to the Tiberian Masorah*. Masoretic Studies; No. 5. Missoula, MT: Published by Scholars Press for the Society of Biblical Literature and the International Organization for Masoretic Studies, 1980.

Zertal, Adam, "An Early Iron Age Cultic Site on Mt. Ebal: Excavation Seasons 1982–7: Preliminary Report." *Tel Aviv* 13–14 (1986–87): 105–65.

———. "Has Joshua's Altar Been Found on Mt. Ebal?" *Biblical Archaeology Review* 11:1 (1985): 26–43.

Zevit, Ziony. *The Religions of Ancient Israel: A Synthesis of Parallactic Approaches*. London: Continuum, 2003.

Index

About the Author

Dr. Matthew R. Rasure is a scholar, non-profit leader, and clergy person. He lives in Milton, MA, with his wife, Rachael, and two children, "Jack" and "Maggie." With undergraduate training as a mathematician, Matt is also a graduate of Princeton Theological Seminary (MDiv) and Harvard University (AM & PhD). He is researching his second book exploring the intersections of rationality, violence, mental illness, and priesthood in ancient Israel.